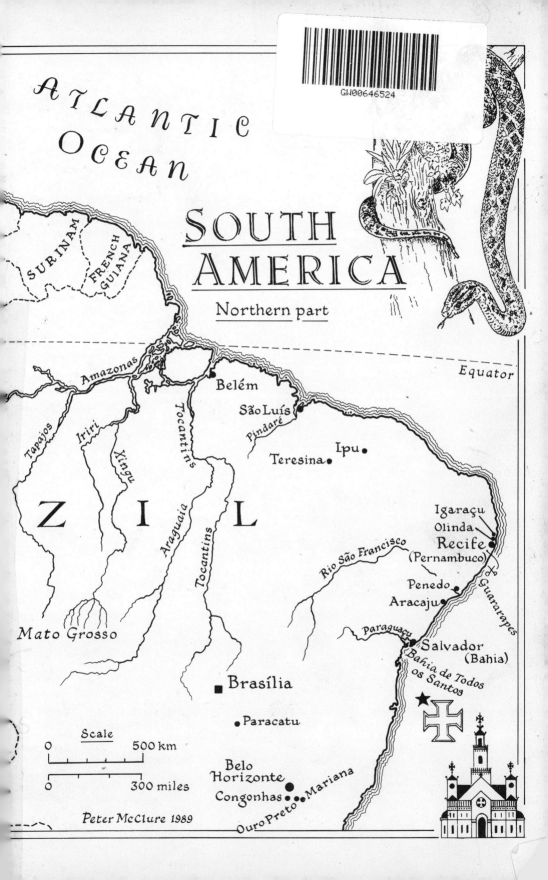

ATLANTIC
OCEAN

SOUTH
AMERICA

Northern part

SURINAM

FRENCH GUIANA

Equator

Amazonas

Belém

São Luís

Pindaré

Tocantins

Tapajos

Iriri

Xingu

Teresina   Ipu

Araguaia

Z   I   L

Igaraçu
Olinda
Recife
(Pernambuco)

Rio São Francisco

Tocantins

Penedo

Aracaju

Guararapes

Mato Grosso

Paraguaçu

Salvador
(Bahia)

Bahia de Todos
os Santos

Brasília

Paracatu

Scale

0 _____ 500 km

0 _____ 300 miles

Belo
Horizonte
Congonhas • • Mariana

Ouro Preto

Peter McClure 1989

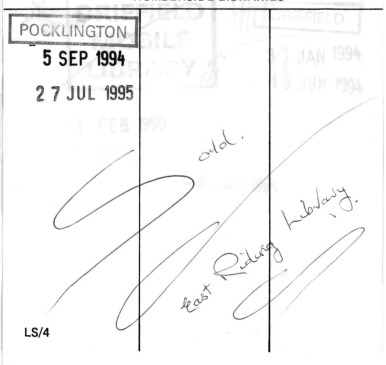

Also by Quentin Crewe

A CURSE OF BLOSSOM
FRONTIERS OF PRIVILEGE
GREAT CHEFS OF FRANCE
INTERNATIONAL POCKET BOOK OF FOOD
IN SEARCH OF THE SAHARA
THE LAST MAHARAJA
TOUCH THE HAPPY ISLES

In the Realms of Gold

TRAVELS THROUGH SOUTH AMERICA

Quentin Crewe

MICHAEL JOSEPH
LONDON

MICHAEL JOSEPH LTD

Published by the Penguin Group
27 Wrights Lane, London W8 5TZ, England
Viking Penguin Inc., 40 West 23rd Street, New York, New York 10010, USA
Penguin Books Australia Ltd, Ringwood, Victoria, Australia
Penguin Books Canada Ltd, 2801 John Street, Markham, Ontario, Canada L3R 1B4
Penguin Books (NZ) Ltd, 182–190 Wairau Road, Auckland 10, New Zealand

Penguin Books Ltd, Registered Offices: Harmondsworth, Middlesex, England

First published in Great Britain 1989
Copyright © Quentin Crewe 1989
Illustrations Copyright © Katinka Kew 1989
Maps by Peter McClure
Symon Robinson kindly supplied photographic references for the illustrations

Made and printed in Great Britain by
Richard Clay (The Chaucer Press) Ltd, Bungay, Suffolk
Typeset in 11 on 13pt Linotron Ehrhardt by Wilmaset, Birkenhead Wirral

A CIP catalogue record for this book is available from the British Library

ISBN 0 7181 2892 3

Contents

To Candida

Acknowledgements

The thanks that authors offer by convention on such a page as this are, in the case of a book of travels, intrinsically inadequate. Those one wishes to thank are themselves the book. Without the kind or interesting people who make up the story, the book would not exist. (It is also true, but should perhaps not be mentioned, that one is grateful to various disagreeable and tiresome people for the addition of a little spice from time to time.) So often I have found myself overwhelmingly grateful to some completely unsuspecting person for providing just that sidelight which illuminates a particular characteristic of a whole nation.

A few, however, do stand out. First, Symon Robinson, who was my companion throughout the journey. He drove twenty-four thousand miles without any mishap. He bore with my impatience without complaint. He pointed out much that I might have missed. He seemed, moreover, to belong to a class of Englishman which, I thought, had disappeared. I felt sure from the first moment that I met him that, if we were held up at gunpoint, he would stand between me and the bandit. I never had a chance to test this belief. I am grateful to him for his courageous cheerfulness, his stamina and his sense of curiosity.

Acknowledgements

I would also like to thank:

In Venezuela: Marcelo Aguirre, Don Cairns, Martin O'Donnell, Kai Rosenberg, Carlos Small, Alberto Urdaneta, Ani Villanueva.

In Brazil: Andrew and Vicky Bell, Tracy Dunlop, Guilherme and Leda Echenique, Patrick and Astrid Hannigan, John and Caroline Ure.

In Paraguay: Anthony and Diane Espinoza, Luis Fernandez.

In Uruguay: Don and Marion Castleton, Nick Langman.

In Argentina: Helios and Gina Caranci, Norberto Narezo Monaco.

In Chile: Patricio Goycoolea, Amina Ricciardi, Lucia Santa Cruz de Ossa.

In Bolivia: Lupita de Krsul, Peter McFarren, Walter Montenegro.

In Peru: Alfredo Fernandini, Joanna Griffiths, Nick Rea, John and Lalage Shakespeare.

In Ecuador: Michael and Veronica Atkinson, Luis and Therese Hernandez, Anthony Salter.

In Colombia: Richard Neilson, Ivan Santos, Felipe Sanchez.

In England: Anne Askwith, Alan Brooke, Bruce Chatwin, Jeremy Fry, Robin Hanbury-Tenison, Kate Hubbard, Selby McCreery, Bobbi Mitchell, Sally Westminster.

1

Venezuela

A MURMURATION OF BUREAUCRATS

The start of a long journey is always dreadful. Cyril Connolly wrote of the angst of arrival, but the insecurity of departure is for me far stronger. It is not a fear of the unfamiliar, nor the wrench of upheaval. I relish those. It is largely occasioned by the way people endeavour to alarm one or put one off. I conceive of journeys almost at whim and determine to go. From that moment, I hear nothing but ill of my proposed adventure.

South America evoked the most spirited opposition. You'll hate it, they said. Anyhow it's very dangerous. Everyone knew somebody who had been robbed or worse. Don't wear a ring or a watch, or anything like that. Drive? You are mad. Not only are the roads quite appalling, but there are bandits everywhere. You cannot buy a car there. They are useless. Anyhow it would be stolen. You heard what happened to Amelia on an Amazon cruise ship? Rio is the most dangerous city in the world. The Argentines obviously won't even let you in. You've read about the riots in Chile? You know the food is unspeakable. If, by some improbable chance, I was not murdered, then yellow fever or malaria would finish me off. Perhaps these Cassandras are inspired by envy.

The authors of that excellent guide, the *South American Handbook*, were hardly more reassuring. They listed the countries of the continent in order of hazard. They warned of gangs at stations who would slash one's shoulder-bag with a razor blade. They advised one never to accept a sweet or a cigarette on a bus. It might be drugged and one would wake hours later to find one had no luggage. They counselled drivers to remove everything detachable, even their windscreen wipers, when parked. They virtually forbade one to go down some streets or on to certain beaches.

I never have a plan for a journey. I prefer to set out impromptu, knowing little and so, more wide-eyed, see not just what I expect to see. South America had long been a puzzle to me. I had never met a disagreeable South American and yet they appeared unusually determined to kill one another. Ever since the *conquistadores*, there had been tales of the vast wealth of the continent, yet its people were so poor and every nation sunk in debt. New ages were forever promised, but they never came. I wondered if there were an explanation.

Then there were the Amazon and the Andes, the churches of Bahia and Quito, Machu Picchu, Rio – everything, in my imagination, a little larger than life.

I longed to go but, after all those warnings, I began to wonder if I were insane. It could not be normal to invite, at great expense, the certainty of discomfort, the probability of disease and the chance of death. At these moments, I start worrying as to whether I am driven by some psychological defiance, scurrying to further and remoter places in a wheelchair. I hate all that stuff.

The moment the plane lands angst melts; certainty returns. I look at the immigration man, be he charming or be he grumpy, and I know why I have come. In any new country, new that is to me, his face will hold a mystery. His features may be perfectly familiar, but his expression will be strange, informed by an inheritance and influences unknown to me. It is when I can look into a face and no longer find it inscrutable that I feel I have learned something of a country or a continent.

Caracas, at five in the morning, was still dark, the way from the airport long and steep. Black velvet hills rose on either side. Some conical ones were evidently crowded with houses, for the lights on them looked like decorations on a series of Christmas trees. There was an improbable amount of traffic but, perhaps because of the hour, the drivers behaved as if there were none. They gave no obedience to red lights and made no signal of their intentions.

By daylight, the city took on a quite different appearance. It lay in a long valley with tree-clad hills rising on either side. The houses swarmed over the nearer wolds and grasped their way up the lower slopes, stopping abruptly when the mountains became almost sheer. Clouds feathered the hilltops and, on some days, mists filled the clefts giving them the look of a cotton-wool colonnade. It is one of the delights of so many South American capitals that one can see mountains from the centre of the city.

I puzzled for several days as to what Caracas reminded me of. Then, trying to cross the junction of two highways under an overpass, it came to me. The city was a distortion of those cartoon drawings of my childhood, which guessed at what a city of the future would be like. There were the aeroplanes and helicopters flying between skyscrapers to land in the centre of the city. There were ring-roads and superways and underpasses and tunnels. The lines of a cable-car swayed up the northern ridge to the top of Mount Avila, a height of 6,000 feet. Only the high-speed trains were missing, but an underground system was building.

The reality, however, quite failed to match the hygienically elegant concepts of the futurologists who drew in the *Beano*. They did not have to plan their cities to work. They knew nothing of the problems of urban South America. There was no place in their drawings for the weals of shanty towns, lived in by betrayed people from the countryside, whose hopes were as unreal as those of the *Beano*-men. The artists had no experience of the Latin-American cast of mind which can allow a building five years old to lapse into near dereliction.

The newer examples of architecture in Caracas vary from pedestrian rectangles of black glass and tubes of concrete to contrived trapezoidal shapes, with little of any real quality, except in the University. The older buildings of importance have mostly been torn down, so that the few that remain look small and inappropriate, having the air of children in fancy dress sitting between faceless directors at a boardroom table. Indeed, little of the city bears any real relation to anything else. There is no coherent pattern. The bureaucratic offices, which Symon, my companion, and I were to get to know well, could be literally miles apart. Areas of intense poverty merged without foretaste into luxurious districts with spreading lawns and high spiked railings.

The long valley had tributaries, each with a character of its own – a residential part and its supporting trade. Only chance seemed to dictate which gully should have brick and tin shanties, piled in precarious despair one above the other on crumbling slopes, while its neighbour had smooth roads and a vast shopping centre on three floors, made up of boutiques, bulging with goods with European names like Gucci and Cardin. While children in the first gully had swollen bellies of hunger, in the shopping precinct there would be several restaurants – some quite expensive, others cheap, sometimes in a cluster with different sections serving Chinese food, Japanese food, Italian food, pizzas, hamburgers or just ices. We sat in one and watched four youths flirting with some girls, who were sitting at a table eating a huge pizza. The girls giggled. The boys snatched their pizza and stood eating it a little way down the arcade. The girls did not seem much put out. After a while, a security guard, armed with a machine-gun, told the boys to move.

Two other boys came and sat at our table. They did not eat, but only smoked. They talked little, sitting aloof from each other and especially from us. I wondered if they were hungry, perhaps from the next gully, and whether I should offer them something to eat, but they looked too proud. They walked and somehow even managed to sit with a swagger, which was comical in its harmony with one's preconception of *machismo*. Later, I would have known that swagger is never affronted by a gift horse. *Machismo* is perfectly real, but it is an arrogance not a pride, and one which can well encompass charity. Its ultimate issue is violence, not dignity.

Those cartoons looked so clean. Their authors knew nothing of the filth that accumulates. The Venezuelan streets are among the dirtiest in the world, full of rubbish scattered like farmers scatter seed. The cartoonists knew nothing of the damp of the tropics which scars paint and stone alike with grey-black drab; nothing of population explosions, which drive youths to risk their lives on superways, trying to sell multi-coloured dusters like candy floss, a newspaper twist of peanuts, a handful of limes or an evening paper; nothing of the traffic jams on those grand highways which often mean half an hour to go a mile.

Against that, there were other things that were missing from their drawings. Vitality, where I had expected lethargy. More than half the population of Venezuela is under twenty; youth somehow charges the air with unlooked-for energy.

It was hard to judge much from the appearance of all these young people. The young men wore jeans and shirts or T-shirts, but their clothes were tidier than those of their European equivalents, cleaner and more neatly ironed. Their faces were innocent of designer stubble. The girls and the older women gave more to ponder. Many of them wore quite fashionable clothes, loose-fitting dresses or baggy trousers. Others wore dreadful trousers, their plump thighs and bottoms bulging like inflatable furniture, always with high-heeled shoes. Nearly all of them wore thick make-up. It was as if they had not yet quite decided.

4

A lawyer, one night at a dinner party, told me that his parents' generation all spoke French as easily as Spanish. They used to look to Paris as the centre of the world and wanted to copy the French.

'I suppose my generation looked to New York when we were young and we all speak English. But my children are different. They all want to be Venezuelan and to assert their own identity.'

He was the first to mention the Falkland Islands to me.

'I consider myself usually as a world citizen, but at that time I felt very Venezuelan, very South American. What I minded most was that the United States supported Britain.'

Hardly anyone was to speak of the Falklands again until I reached Argentina, but from that moment, however familiarly European or old-fashioned a place might seem, I always remembered that I was in the New World.

But still not the new world of the *Beano*. The prophets of the earlier half of this century foresaw a scientific solution to all problems, they dehumanised their imagined descendants who were to live in a state of sterile automation, whereas the happy actuality is that technology, despite its dangers and aberrations, has enlarged our compassion. A bubbling humanity inspired the frolicsome graffiti scribbled and sometimes elaborately drawn by lovers on the walls of their girlfriends' houses. A side effect of futurology was their spurning of nature. There were no trees in those drawings. The greatest delight of Caracas was the abundance of flowering trees – yellow poui, the national flower, showering the earth with its pool of gold, orchid trees, African tulip trees, jacarandas, flamboyant, frangipani.

*   *   *

Our first objective was to buy a car. The Venezuelan Embassy in London had told me that this would be easy. What they did not tell me was that the complications and formalities of registering it in my name and then getting permission to take it out of the country could take many months.

Every embassy in South America has its local Mr Fixit. The British Embassy staff in Caracas were, with one exception, the most helpful, courteous and hospitable of people. (The exception, alas, was the Ambassador, a man of polished, languid appearance called Newington, who used to waft through his waiting-room, nose in air, never deigning to give or acknowledge a greeting. Perhaps he was shy.) As soon as they heard of my problems, they produced Alberto.

'Ah, Mister Quintin, can I help you, boss? May I call you boss? I would like to help you. No problem. Two days, maybe three. We fix everything.'

Alberto had a fine line of patter which I was to come to know well, in all its variations and subtleties. He was a short man, with carefully brushed hair, the silver of it threading through neatly arranged waves – what the Japanese call 'romance grey'. He wore thick, heavy lenses and, on some days, appeared dazed with short sight. Nothing, however, was constant about Alberto. Mostly, he would walk very slowly grumbling, 'Symon, why you walk so fast?' But when something fired him, he would swerve nimbly through a crowd. That would not necessarily be on a day when we had only minutes to reach an office before it shut.

On occasions he would look small and somewhat pitiable, like a Dickensian clerk. On others, he would appear stylish, distinguished – certainly worthy of his surname Urdaneta, shared with an heroic general after whom many streets and an enormous bridge are named, and with whom Alberto never positively denied a family connection. On a couple of occasions, he even looked racy. It was not for two weeks that I realised that he had quite a substantial paunch like a beer-drinker. In fact Alberto drank no alcohol or coffee; nor did he smoke, but he had no disapproval of those who did.

It was fascinating going from office to office with Alberto. His bleary eyes would swivel round the room, assessing the exact status of each person in it. Just the right smile suggested itself on his lips. Suddenly one noticed that he had a beautiful mouth. When he had worked out who he had to deal with, he would modulate his approach accordingly, at the same time orchestrating it so it had the right effect on the other people in the room.

If a man of comparatively modest importance sat alone, Alberto would say, 'Good morning, sir. How pleasant your office is, *pavo*. May I call you *pavo*?'

Pavo was a term I never heard anyone else use. Strictly it means turkey, but I took it to be a slightly humorous equivalent of, say, pal. Sometimes Alberto used it to a very junior official in a crowded office, when it elicited a laugh from the young man's superiors. Everyone always squirmed a little when he employed it, but it always worked.

With senior officials Alberto was comradely, but somehow managed without any condescension to convey that his position in the British Embasssy was at least equal, but probably superior, to theirs. It was certainly not beneath him to come to ask for this favour; rather, it was a measure of his respect for them and of the importance of the request that he, Alberto Urdaneta, had come.

Only once did I see his masterly transformation to a humble, but justified, supplicant. He was endeavouring to extract the impossible from a woman of great importance and power. He stood to attention, his head a little bowed. His voice assumed a *gravitas* I had not heard before and he spoke in polished Castillian rather than his usual colloquial Venezuelan. She succumbed.

We came to know Alberto well although, for some time, we were uncertain which Alberto it was. He was, at first, anxious to find us a good car. There was a German he knew of, who had a Toyota for sale. He would bring it at ten o'clock one morning. All through the day, Alberto rang to postpone the appointment for a couple of hours. The German never came. There were many days like that. Then Alberto's brother had a Range Rover. He came with it one Sunday and we took a drive.

'Low range? What is that?' asked the brother.

'You move that lever down,' I said.

'Ah, I have never done that. I did not know what that lever was for, so I thought it better not to move it.'

We tried. Of course, it would not go into low range.

'You can have it very cheap,' said Alberto. 'Then you do it up and, when you come back from the journey, you can sell it to me.' He paused. 'On hire purchase,' he added.

That day Alberto had promised to take his family for a trip on the cable-car to the top of Mount Avila. We decided to abandon car-dealing and go with them.

Señora Urdaneta was a quiet woman, quite plump and largely unsmiling. Her quietude, I felt, shrouded a forceful character. They had two sons, Denis, who was twelve, was a boy of exceptional beauty and sweet nature. He must have been conceived on one of his father's good-looking days. His eyes, shaped like large tears, glowed with innocent trust and lively enquiry. His impeccable manners seemed instinctive rather than learned. The other child, Christian, was a monster. He was aged four, pudgy and plain and spoilt. His conception must have been on a day when his father felt sorry for himself. Even Alberto referred to him as the '*terremoto*'.

When we reached the cable-car station, it was deserted. The cable-car had not been working for months. We decided to go to the beach instead. Filling up and checking Alberto's enormous American car took, by the time that he had made friends with every one of the attendants and had a gossip with the manager, more than half an hour. For a moment or two he sat with eyes closed, murmuring softly. Then he crossed himself and I realised he was praying. As well he might, as it was one of his shortest days and he could scarcely peer, with his dimmed sight, over the steering wheel. Every so often some unexpected circumstance, someone changing lane or a child sprinting across the highway, would catch his attention. 'Jesus Christ,' he would say, in tones rather less pious than those with which he had recently addressed the Virgin. It was an alarming drive.

The road to start with was the same as that we had travelled on from the airport. This time there was no illusion of Christmas-tree decorations. The knolls were piled-up shanties. A few of the clusters, those nearer to the road, more likely to be seen by foreigners perhaps, were painted in pastel colours which lent a cubist look to them, until one got closer when no cosmetics could powder over their misery.

The coast was dull, much like any Mediterranean shore built up by tourism. We went to a large, modern hotel, bristling with air-conditioners and buzzing with lifts. There were three swimming pools of different shapes and sizes and a sentried doorway to the beach.

There was a self-service restaurant. Alberto foraged up and down the buffet tables, until he had piled up two huge plates of food. He had a prodigious appetite. Alberto then settled down and started to talk to some Canadians who were sitting at the next table. He asked the price of their ticket from Toronto, how much they were paying for their rooms, about their careers and their family arrangements.

Señora Urdaneta spoke hardly at all, breaking her silence only in order to tell Alberto to leave the Canadians alone, or to voice some feeble reproof to the 'earthquake'. Denis told me about the workings of Venezuelan schools and of his interest in geology. Alberto's wife did, however, play the role of a pliant spouse. When choosing his first few courses, he had made a mental selection of the puddings that he would like. He told her to go to fetch them and resumed his quizzing of the Canadians.

At the end of the afternoon, we went back to the district of Caracas where Alberto lived. It was a poor part of the town, with streets of low, colonial-style houses, spoiled by juxtaposition with newer, tall, but dingy blocks of flats. There was an air of general decay and every road was jammed with traffic. There was nevertheless a lively feeling about the area, with much of life being conducted on the street. Alberto assumed his lofty manner, taking long, slow strides and waving myopic greetings a little to one side of those he wished to salute. He pointed rather vaguely to the first floor of a shabby block of flats. 'That's where we live, boss.' He never invited us in.

The next day, without Alberto, I bought a car. It was a Toyota Landcruiser, assembled in Venezuela. Alberto was shocked. He could not bear one's doing anything without his advice.

'How much did you pay, Mister Quintin?' I told him. 'Oh, too much. What kind of car? Oh no, very hard car. I know a woman, she buy one. After three weeks, she have to sell and spend the money on doctor's treatment for her back spine.' He made another attempt to persuade me to buy his brother's Range Rover.

In fact it was difficult to find a good car. The price of new cars was to go up by seventy per cent in two months' time. No one was selling. What I had paid was about right. Every time I took Alberto in the car and we went over a bump, of which there were many in Caracas, Alberto would say: 'There you see, boss. Very hard, like being on a horse. There again, boss, horses, horses.'

The dealer was not allowed to accept traveller's cheques. We tried his bank. They offered a preposterous rate. Alberto's brother (he had six), of course, worked in another bank and he offered a far better rate. I needed to sign thirty-five traveller's cheques; the bank insisted on taking a photograph of me holding each separate cheque. This simple transaction took an hour.

The following day we had to go, with the car-dealer and two witnesses, to the notary public to sign the contract of sale. Then I had to register the car in my name. At one office, the initial form is issued; at another, half a mile away, the form must be stamped. In quite another district, the Judicial Police must check that the car is as described and that the engine and chassis numbers are correct and that it is not on the list of stolen vehicles. Back then to the second office, where they will arrange to print a Carnet de Circulación. These are printed only at night, on Tuesdays. There was a three-month backlog of people waiting. It was not usually possible to achieve more than one visit in a day, and that might prove fruitless. And once we had the registration we would have to get permission to take the car out of the country.

*   *   *

We had come to know Caracas quite well and had seen most of its attractions – the cathedral, the Pantéon, where Simón Bolívar is buried, Bolívar's birthplace or, to be more precise, the site on which a brick copy of the adobe house sits, the trees by the church of San Francisco under which, Alberto said, Bolívar addressed the people.

I was intrigued by this veneration of Bolívar, the Liberator, when the treatment of this hero of South American independence in his lifetime had been so ungrateful and treacherous. I was to think of him often on our journey, for his character and his history, I came to realise, embodied the essence of the continent.

Of all those who fought for freedom from Spanish colonial rule, the least self-seeking was probably Bolívar. He wanted fame and glory, but he did not want power in the ordinary sense. He genuinely believed in liberty, even if he also believed in firm government. He abhorred slavery and was a keen educationalist. He was a visionary with a hopelessly romantic dream of a united South America.

At the same time, he had to be the chief. He was capable of great generosity to his generals, but only when there was no doubt as to who was the true leader. Despite a rather insignificant appearance, he had an ability to inspire men, but equally he was desperate for the admiration of women. He was the supreme example of *machismo*.

Bolívar, with astounding singleness of purpose, did liberate Venezuela, New Grenada (now Colombia), Ecuador, Bolivia and Peru, and for a brief unreal moment wove the first three into one nation – Gran Colombia.

One by one his comrades, for nearly always selfish reasons, turned against him, even attempting his assassination. 'More and more I conclude,' he wrote, 'that nothing, not liberty, not law, not the finest education, can turn us into decent people, let alone into Republicans or true patriots.'

Gradually his dream and his health were destroyed. He died, spurned and poor, in Colombia.

*   *   *

Now, at least, we had the car and could make expeditions with the friends we had made. With Ani Villaneuva and her two daughters we went to Choroni, some two hundred miles west of Caracas, near the coast. The twisting dual carriageway ran over young mountains, like the backs of crocodiles; the dark green of the forest was splashed with the vivid yellows, serious reds and airy pinks of the flowering trees. We came down into an open plain, spread with the feathery stems of sugar-cane, and then had to climb again to cross the range which separated the dismal industrial town of Maracay from the sea. Now the road was little more than a track, recently tarmacadammed, climbing fifteen steep miles and then dropping for a similar distance.

This range was undisturbed tropical forest, dense with ferns and beribboned with orchids. Little waterfalls showered down at each hairpin turn. There were two scant settlements, then as the land grew less steep Choroní, a colonial village as unspoilt as the forest it sat in. The single-storey houses were mostly painted white, their doorways and windows framed with a dark colour; their shutters were closed, so that there was a slightly forbidding look to the two main streets. But, if a door were left open and one could peer in, there were glimpses of flowery courtyards and pretty verandahs. In the small square there was a plain, ochre and white church but its doors were locked. With the tall trees of the forest as a background, everything seemed to be on a rather tentative scale, as if the builders were unsure of their tenure.

We were to stay in an *hacienda* beyond the village. It was lived in by a couple called Glenda and Chino. The house belonged to her family, who were grand, provincial landowners. The house was built on two sides of a courtyard, twenty yards square, which had originally been used for drying cacao, but none grew now. Glenda was an old-fashioned hippy, thrice married and with a son by each husband. Chino had trained as an electronics engineer, but only liked working on the land. Their life was simple. They cultivated some acres, not many, round the *hacienda*, growing vegetables and fruit. It was a happy place – humming-birds busied round the flowers, oriole blackbirds, so much less skulking than their European equivalents, flashed boldly yellow among the shrubs, parrots yapped overhead and I saw a young iguana lurching its way into the scrub beyond the garden. For $15 they gave us a room for Symon and myself, while Ani and her children slung hammocks on the verandah.

After lunch, we drove on beside the widening river, fed by those falling streams, into Puerto Colombia. There was a police post. The men searched the car in front of us, but waved us on. There appeared to be no purpose to the checkpoint. It was a dull little town, ruined by trippers. There was a ford across the river and, a short distance beyond, a beach which may once have been pleasant. Now it was ghastly – a long row of booths sold junk, hideous clothes and greasy food. Music blared at an insupportable volume. The beach itself and the straggly grove of coconut behind were covered in empty cans and plastic detritus. Even the sea was inimical, with treacherous rollers and a strong undertow. I fled back to the *hacienda*.

Later, we went down to the port again to watch the sunset and to engage a boat for the next day. In the evening light, the little park by the water's edge was pleasant to sit in and, when dark came, the new moon hung a crisp U-shape in the sky, to the surprise of Symon who had never seen any other but crescent rampant.

Ani met a friend in the street, a young man who, like most of the people in the region, was much darker than those in Caracas. He carried us off to his family's large, meandering house. The life of the equally rambling family took place on a huge verandah, filled with rough furniture of all sorts and with hammocks hung on the walls partly as decoration, partly for use. On every flat surface, there were hideous china bibelots – Father Christmas, pink and mauve angels in sickly poses, animals of all kinds.

At one end of the verandah the patriarch, Domingo, sat in an armchair, watching a snowstorm pattern on a small television. The volume was turned up, but I could discern nothing through the blur. Domingo had the look of a peppery old general, but he was very welcoming. I looked at him with interest as I had been told that he and another, much blacker than he was, had fathered practically the whole village between them. His wife, Doña Rosa, a woman of exuberant shape who seemed, with her halo of grey hair, to belong in a rocking-chair, looked at Domingo with tolerant affection.

'What's he watching for? There's nothing to see,' she asked; yet her eyes kept straying to the fluffy screen. 'He doesn't notice because he drinks too much,' she said.

At the other end of the verandah, some of the family were still eating, one of the young men laughing a little louder than the others.

'He drinks too much too,' said his wife, who sat with us. I saw how this could be easy. Doña Rosa produced a bottle of startling, powerful *agua ardiente*, mixed with passion-fruit juice, which she called *guarapita*. After two glasses, I began to feel that this was the most agreeable family I had met for a long time. A bounty of children played all around, of whom not all had two official parents, for there was an insouciance about such things. Indeed, there was an uncritical approach to most things, warmth of spirit being the yardstick, and this extended to regarding us not as objects of curiosity but as new friends. We laughed a lot and, when we left, Doña Rosa pressed on us a bottle of her *guarapita*.

We went to a restaurant in Choroní for dinner. All the customers sat at one table. The owner, a broad man with a face as round and rich as a pumpkin, who wore a yellow T-shirt and a huge necklace, came bringing a fish which I had never seen before, the Spanish name of which faded in the mists of *guarapita*. The dinner became like a large party, the owner singing to his guitar. In the middle the lights went out. They brought candles and the evening became even jollier.

When we had put Ani's children to bed, we went once more back to the port. All the lights were out there as well, but we had a fluorescent torch with us. A drunk shouted: 'That man has taken all the lights of the village.'

A tree had fallen across the power lines and the severed cables had set light to the forest. Great stands of bamboo were burning with ferocity, each fat segment of their stems bursting in a firework explosion, sending plumes of livid coals into the sky and spreading the blaze. The bars had all shut as there was no light, and the whole population came to sit and to watch the display across the river, as if it were entertainment.

One man said: 'My cows are in there.' Not knowing what to do, he did nothing. 'The Guardia should put it out,' he said without rancour. But the Guardia were playing dominoes. It was Saturday night so they were drunk; too drunk, they had decided, to tackle a fire of this magnitude. No one disagreed, nor did anyone seem to mind, except possibly the cowherd.

In the morning, the fire had abated, though it would be a long time before power was restored. Our boatman was ready with quite a large blue fishing boat driven by a powerful outboard motor. On the inner side of the strakes, the boatman had spattered white and red paint on to the blue, so that it looked like a Jackson Pollock painting. The waves were high, but the boatman with the skill of custom rode always on the crest, only rarely whacking down into a trough of flat, hard sea. Once we had left behind the littered beach of the day before, the coast was wild and rocky. Pelicans dived from the promontories, frigate birds planed overhead and two outsize, white herons flapped past like lost sails.

We came to a beach as enchanting as the last had been hideous. It lay in a gentle bay surrounded by palms. A river flowed through the centre of the beach, so that one could swim from the warm, salt shallows into fresh water, cool from the mountains. By the pier there were two or three houses and a bar. This cluster was the port, if you like, for the little village of Chuao, which lay six miles up in the hills. The only way to Chuao was by a rough track, most of which was impassable to all but a tractor.

While the others lazed on the sands, I talked to an old man of his youth. We had drinks from the bar. The whole of this region was once the most prosperous in Venezuela, made rich by the quality of its cacao. Old Jaime, who used to work in the plantations, told me that Chuao was once a name to conjure with among Swiss chocolate-makers. The land here had belonged to the family of the dictator Juan Vicente Gomez, but the discovery of oil to the west put an end to these good times. The cacao industry was forgotten and with it Chuao.

Jaime invited me to stay in his house; his father, who had lived to be ninety, had been many years in a wheelchair. When we parted, he embraced me and we swore eternal friendship as if we were characters in *Forza del Destino*. He started up the stony track, carrying his shopping – two small fish and one electric light bulb – in a transparent plastic bag, like those ones that children carry home from fairs with the goldfish they have won. He was a little unsteady on his feet.

Back in Caracas, the car was at least properly registered in my name. I even had my laminated Carnet de Circulación. We drove proudly and felt no qualms when the police waved us one morning on to the hard shoulder. Papers, Licence, Carnet. All in order. No one in any South American country ever asked for insurance. The curl remained on the policeman's lip; he meant to prolong whatever it was.

'Why are you driving on a Thursday?' he asked with slow pleasure. We looked blank. Fortunately, Alberto was with us.

'It is like this, señor. They are English, *pavo* – may I call you *pavo*? . . .'

It took at least ten minutes and a promise to drive straight to the hotel and leave the car there. By way of reducing the traffic in the city, the Caracas council introduced a law that all cars with numbers ending in a certain figure must not be used on one particular day of the week. Our number ended in nine, for which Thursday was the forbidden day.

Like so many bright ideas in corrupt countries, this regulation was counter-productive. The rich bought another car, two-car families now had four and the streets were more overwhelmed than ever.

The second half of our bureaucratic torture took even more time than the first. When we went to the customs to initiate the process of getting permission to take the car out of the country, the official fixed me with a half-eyed stare and announced that no one was allowed to export a car and that, in any case, they only gave permission on Wednesdays. Venezuelan obsession with days of the week bordered on the astrological.

Our trek from office to office resumed. We would lunch with Alberto on most days and his appetite was a source of much wonder. Often he would finish off anything Symon or I left on our plates. Only once did I see him defeated by the huge helpings that always daunted me in restaurants. He called a waiter and told him to wrap up all that we had not

14

eaten so that he could take it home, not for a dog but for himself. He assured me that this was common practice.

I had to provide a bond to the full value of the car which would be forfeited should I not bring it back into Venezuela. An insurance company called the Royal Caribe provided this for a small fee. It was a branch of the Royal in Britain. A young Scotsman dealt with me. I offered to back this bond with a guarantee from my bank. He said there was no need for this.

'But what if I should not bring the car back?'

'I have your worrrd that you will,' he said with a smile as broad as Ayrshire.

Alberto never gave anyone a bribe. Everything was done, as it were, on the old *pavo* network. Sometimes he would tell me to ask an official and his wife to dine at my hotel. We would sit through stilted evenings and then feel guilty at the evident pleasure it gave to the *petit-fonctionnaire* couple. One of the more senior men at the treasury department was an epicene figure, whose large brown eyes grew even larger when he saw Symon, who, so he told Alberto, he thought was very handsome. He made endless prevarications, in the hope of luring him back for another visit. There were times when I thought I should never emerge from these endless skyscraper offices, but would be found twenty years hence on the thirty-ninth floor in a dusty cabinet, filed under my middle name. After nearly a month, we got the permission.

'I know you are never going to bring the car back,' said Symon's effete admirer.

'Of course, I will.'

'You will sell it in Colombia for four times the price.'

'I will not,' I said, feeling both indignant and foolish. 'I have given my worrrd.' I almost added, I'm British, infected by the Scotsman's trust, so redolent of yesteryear.

*　　*　　*

There was still much to do – further checks with different branches of the police, securing another kind of carnet from the Touring Club and sundry similar details.

Ani proposed another excursion – this time to the *llanos*, the largely treeless plains which lie between the northern coastal ranges of mountains and the southern rain forests. These plains cover nearly a third of Venezuela, that is to say about 120,000 square miles. Ani wanted to take us to a ranch belonging to a philanthropically minded man of many parts, Don Antonio Julio Branger.

Don Antonio has turned his family ranch into a nature reserve and a place of scientific study. It is possible for anyone to stay there and it is of a particular interest to ornithologists and birdwatchers.

Ani instructed us in her brisk, efficient manner. 'We'll fly in the morning. Be ready by seven o'clock.' She appeared at a little before eight, apologising with soft femininity. Her attraction was twofold, first for her bossy energy and secondly for her pliant prettiness – perhaps threefold, for the element of surprise as to which aspect would be uppermost.

The flight itself was an excitement. The airfield lay in the middle of the city, a matter of a few hundred yards from, for instance, the British Embassy. I have never seen an airfield with so astonishing a number of private planes. There were aircraft of all sizes, from trembling things no bigger than a clothes hamper to big jets for whole boardroomsful of executives; not just hundreds of planes but surely thousands. In the mornings and evenings, they leave and arrive at a rate of one every forty-five seconds. We cobbled ourselves into a Cessna 152 and took off.

Caracas from the air confirmed all that we had learned of it on the ground. Long, tin caterpillars of traffic jams were humping their way into the city. The river lay in its litter-strewn, concrete bed, looking little different from the congested highways. Through the mantilla of pollution two colours stood out – the red of the knolls of poverty and the blue of the rich swimming pools. The largest open space by far, in the midst of the grey of concrete, was the Country Club, with its golf course and wooded park of luxury. It is not so big as it used to be, for chunks have been taken to build great mansions for the immensely rich. From the air, the disparity between opulence and want is even more marked. The only real surprise lay in how much bigger the conglomeration was than I had realised. The fingers of slums and shanties reached out into valleys and hollows that I had not known existed and curled round the mountains in search of flatter spaces well beyond what I had supposed were the boundaries.

Soon we rose over the mountains, grey and rumpled and somehow dusty, when compared with the green forests we had driven through on the way to Choroní. In all directions, there were forest fires in the hollows, and we could see flames vaulting up the mountainside. In places there were bowls, black as cooking pots, from earlier fires. Gradually the hills levelled and we flew over flat, equally grey-looking country, freckled with lakes. This landscape stretched without limit in all directions.

We flew for three-quarters of an hour and landed on a strip of ruddy earth, among the only hillocks for miles around. The plane stopped by some of the biggest mango trees I have ever seen. The house was completely hidden by trees and, as we went towards it, I looked up and saw a great horned owl sitting asleep on a branch of a tall, thick *ficus*. Later, I saw its droppings, spiked with a little jaw and other mouse bones.

It was hard to judge the age of the ranch house, perhaps seventeenth century. A broad, enclosed verandah, flagged with stone, ran all around the house giving a feeling of cool space, while the bedrooms which opened off it were small. In one corner of the verandah, there was a little chapel. The furniture was heavy and paintings rather like icons lent a sombre, almost monastic tone.

A large guest house, built by Don Antonio for paying guests and visiting scientists, stood a little apart from the original building. It was done in such good taste that one might have supposed it to have been an intelligent conversion of some old stable or outbuildings rather than an entirely new construction.

When we arrived, a very small man was sweeping the fallen leaves into neat geometrical piles. The skin on his face was strangely smooth and unlined, yet from his movements I assumed that he was about seventy. He looked like a Tibetan elf. A month before, he had come to ask Don Antonio for permission to marry a fifteen-year-old girl. Don Antonio, having in any case no say in the matter, gravely gave it.

A remarkably thin man came across to meet us; he looked cool in the gathering heat, as if the warmth ignored such a slender figure. Eduardo Cartaya was a young biologist; he had not yet reached the age of thirty, but was a rich granary of knowledge from which poured a generous stream of information.

Eduardo was anxious that we should set off at once, before the heat soared and the birds and animals hid away until the cooling of the afternoon. In all the *llanos*, there were few hills and those of Hato Pinero, as the ranch was called, were apparently interesting to scientists, as the rocks which form them date from the Cambrian period, two billion years ago, and are some of the oldest in this geologically restless continent. They also helped to attract a wider variety of creatures of all sorts.

We drove out from the ranch building along a track bordered on both sides by rows of pink, flowering trees, which Eduardo said were a kind of jacaranda. They had not been planted as an avenue, but were merely fence posts, sprung to life like so many staves from Arimathea.

The way led through a spread of pasture dotted with oil trees

17

(*Copaifera officinalis*), which looked as if they were drawn by children – straight trunks with a curious bark, topped by a perfect sphere of branches and leaves. Beneath these parasols, cattle sheltered from the sun. Beyond, we came to rougher land, interspersed with ponds and marsh.

At once, we began on an orgy of birdwatching that was to last for twenty-four hours. Overhead, three kinds of vulture, two of kite, four of hawk and, while on birds of prey, two sorts of caracara from the falcon family, vigilant on posts beside the road. Again above, pairs of scarlet macaw squawking. 'I always think of them as married couples,' said Eduardo. 'On and on she nags and he just says "Yes, dear".' Five kinds of dove, yellow-headed parrots, brown-throated parakeets, green-rumped parrotlets and, as dark and lively as she was, a smooth-billed Ani.

From a tree came a grating noise resembling a moribund baby-alarm, not much like a frog for there was a hiss in the sound, certainly not like a bird. It was a hoatzin, a most singular bird in every way, being the only one of its genus or even family. Eduardo said it was prehistoric, a remnant which had survived from soupy ages. How, that was the question. I have rarely seen so ill-organised a creature. It was the size of a small turkey; its head, with a spiky crest like a punk and patches of bare blue skin round its large staring eyes, made me think of a distracted phoenix. It could fly, but very badly and with little hope of going more than a few yards. Its feathers were all dishevelled like the clothes of senility. It would have seemed impossible for it to escape from any predator; indeed it eyed us with severe distaste, but could apparently think of nothing to do about it, apart from repeating its raucous hiss. It always builds its nest in the high branches of a tree over water. The young, which are even more hopelessly built than the adults, have two claws on their wings so that, if they fall in the water, they can swim to a tree and climb up it. Even so it seems extraordinary that the hoatzin has survived. I could only wonder whether its flesh had a repulsive taste, so that no other animal could eat it.

All the time, there were little birds swooping, flittering, darting, all with enchanting names – crested bobwhite, glittering-throated emerald, tropical kingbird, vermilion flycatcher, rough-winged swallow, red-capped cardinal, tropical mocking-bird, carib grackle, saffron finch.

The sun stripped the sky of colour and we went back to the ranch for lunch. There was only one other visitor, Louise Raymond, a gentle American woman of some age, who spent solitary days wandering on foot around the ranch, happily notching up new discoveries. She tried to coax Eduardo to eat what was the best simple food I had in all South America –

pumpkin and carrot soup and a rich *asado* with sultanas – but he ate almost nothing. It was hard to guess where his energy came from. In the full heat of the day, when nothing on the land moved, he took us to see the working of the estate.

The ranch covered 185,000 acres, on which they ran 80,000 head of cattle. Most of them were of Indian stock, some pure-bred Nelore, Gir, Guzerat and Sachiwal. Don Antonio experiments, crossing these with Holstein and Brown Swiss for milk and Gelvieh and Red Angus for meat. He also has a herd of Criollo, the descendants of cattle brought from Spain by the *conquistadores*, which are virtually the same as Longhorn in the United States. Don Antonio experiments too with grasses, using in the best pastures one which he found in Africa.

There was a small dairy herd of only thirty cows. In surprising contrast to the advanced breeding techniques, we watched milkmaids milking the cows by hand and men searing the young stock with a savage red-hot iron, leaving on each one the pretty brand of a butterfly.

In the haze of the afternoon we drove off again, at first through scrubby country, crossing many streams and one river, where kingfishers sparked. The land became flatter and bare of trees. Four-fifths of the ranch lies under water from June until November. Each year, when the waters recede, they have to rebuild the roads that lead across the low land. Now it was February, the driest season, but there were still many marshy tracts and we stopped on a huge dyke, built up at the end of a *caño*, a long strip of water, many miles long – one of the natural irrigation canals of the savannah.

Already we had seen nine kinds of heron, five sorts of ibis, three of egret, and several groups of glowing, roseate spoonbills. Eduardo never tired of telling us the name of each bird or even of repeating it when I was too dim to recognise one we had seen several times. Only Louise Raymond knew as many birds as he did. One could not have hoped for two more informative but unpatronising companions.

We scrambled down the side of the dyke and into a flat-bottomed boat, driven by an outboard motor. The *caño* was about thirty yards wide and its banks were thronged with birds and animals. Wattled jacana fussed among the reeds, stilts stepped like automata across the mud patches, a white-headed marsh tyrant tripped over the pads of the water hyacinth. Sometimes the hyacinth, with pretty-blue deception, choked the whole waterway, tangling our propeller so that we had to punt.

I hated the weed, but was grateful for the piercing silence in which we could listen to the birdcalls and the soft, muddy gurgle of a cayman slithering into the water. These snouty, scaly Orinoco crocodiles lounged on the flatter spaces, their dozing eyes glared with a mixture of apprehension and resentment. I dared Symon to step ashore near a group of them, but they were more timid than he was and melted away into the ooze. More nervous still were the capybara, lumbering chestnut shapes among the high grasses, the largest rodents in the world, looking like labrador-sized guinea-pigs. There were many families of them, with large numbers of young. Eduardo thought there might be as many capybara on the ranch as there were cattle, despite the difficulties of their coupling. The male capybara is too heavy and maladroit to copulate on land and has to mate in the water, somewhat to the peril of the female which may drown.

We came to a wide lagoon. A group of scarlet ibis sat like a wound on the grey-green of the savannah. On the top of dead and branchless palms stood storks as heraldic as St Mark's lions on their columns. At this dry time the aquatic populations crowd into the small remaining waters. Below, we could see the outlines of turtles scraping their way along the bottom. Herons plucked fish with the ease of a gardener gathering flowers. The lagoons and pools and rivers seemed to be simmering. Twice, a leaping fish fell into the boat and whipped around our feet like an agitated spring.

When we got back to the dyke, the sun was setting and the birds were choosing where to roost for the night. One large bush changed colour from green to white, as more and more cattle egrets perched themselves on it, pushing like schoolchildren for a better place. Louise Raymond sat quietly wondering at the extraordinary multitude of birds; Ani, silhouetted on the dyke, stretched herself in a *t'ai chi* exercise, matched by the last flappings of the settling herons. One indefatigably greedy kingfisher dived again and again until I could no longer see it in the dusk.

We drove back and, every few yards on the road, small, glitter-red pairs of eyes reflected our headlights. As we came close, the eyes would rise up transformed into whirring tops. 'White-tailed nightjar,' said Eduardo. The white on their wings made complete circles as they beat at alarmed speed. I wondered whether their wings flap higher and lower than most birds, but the next day I noticed that jacanas give a similar effect.

We were hoping to see a jaguar of which, Eduardo thought, there were about thirty on the ranch. An animal ran across the road. 'Crab-eating fox,' said Eduardo. Another creature, hard to see, scampered ahead in the verge. 'Fox,' said Eduardo; then it ran across the road in front of us. 'Well, a fox disguised as a rabbit – you know they are very cunning.'

Suddenly, a larger animal stock-still on the road looking at us. It was the epitome of feral beauty – not as it happened a jaguar, but an ocelot, which Eduardo said is perhaps even rarer to see. He was so excited, so pleased for us that we laughed all the way home.

By the time we left this most civilised place, we had seen seventy-eight species of bird, besides the iguanas, agoutis, deer, bats, fish, toads and frogs that Eduardo had illuminated for us, and we had acquired a store of knowledge which we were to draw upon throughout the journey.

The pilot flew over the flat, wet land we had seen the day before. He swooped down scaring up great clouds of ibis, both greeny-black and scarlet, and of egrets. They rose as a mass, wheeled and sank again, as if they were giant red, green and white sheets, lifted and dropped by the wind.

* * *

There was another week of bureaucracy to grind through before we could leave. Alberto had decided that we needed a young man to come with us, to guide us through the hazards of South America. It seemed a good idea; Symon would otherwise have to do all the driving, look after me and perhaps deal with officials without having a word of Spanish. Alberto came with an angular boy of seventeen, called Xavier. Symon and he, having no evident language in common, spent a lot of the time nodding and grinning and repeating Duran Duran, *sí, sí*. More nods and grins, Police, *si, si* and so on through unending names of pop groups. I thought it a slender foundation for a journey of six months, but they appeared well pleased.

When we were nearly ready, Xavier appeared and said that his father had forbidden him to go with us. The boy maintained that his father, a colonel in the army, who had 'a head as hard as a donkey', was doing it out of spite, because he was divorced from Xavier's mother. I thought it possible that the Colonel genuinely might not like the idea of his son's going off for so long with two unknown foreigners.

Xavier, still grumbling about his father and rolling his eyes in exaggerated despair, produced a substitute for himself. Marcelo was twenty-three, a half-Chilean vegetarian, much interested in yoga. He had a cocky look, his chin well up, and a certain sophistication written on his slightly Simian face. His hair was cut short and he moved with an alert step; he gave the impression of efficiency. I liked him at once. Moreover, he spoke some English. He had no job, but made a living selling clothes in a loose partnership with a Trinidadian friend, called Robert de la

Bastide. Robert, making me wonder at the way phraseology survives in strange places, said, 'I can tell you, he's A1.' Neither of them, nor Marcelo's mother, thought it in any way odd that he should set off on a long journey with two people he had met only the day before.

Alberto, not being the discoverer of Marcelo, was mildly put out at my decision to take him. 'You never know with these people, boss,' he said, leaving a vague menace hanging there to worry us.

We arranged to leave at ten in the morning. Marcelo arrived an hour and a half late; he had to get tax clearance. Knowing, I suppose, that everyone is always an hour and a half late, Alberto arrived at the same moment. He brought with him, as a last bid, a handsome youth with unnaturally green eyes. 'You take him, Mister Quintin,' he said with no real conviction or expectation. He just laughed when I refused. And we left.

2
Venezuela
PREHISTORIC BIRDS AND THE LURE OF GOLD

The country to the east of Caracas was a disappointment. At first, dry hills then, at climatic whim, lush vegetation and villages growing cacao, manioc and plantain, Caribbean in feeling but, when we rejoined the coast, the landscape reverted to dry scrub. We went through the dowdy resort of Puerto La Cruz, past Cumaná until we reached Carúpano where we had planned to stay. It was such a drab town that we forsook the sea and headed south. Nevertheless, nothing could really douse our good spirits at being at last on the road.

Inland, at once everything became interesting. The mountains rose high and we had fine views over valleys patterned with crops. I had seen prints of paintings by Bellerman, a German who worked in Venezuela in the last century, of the cave in the state of Monagas, known as La Cueva del Guácharo. For a century and a half, the Chaima Indians had told missionaries about this mysterious, mountain home of an uncommon bird. In 1799, Alexander von Humboldt, in the course of his voyage round South America, found the cave near Caripe.

It lies at the foot of a jagged cliff about two hundred feet high; its entrance is lofty, like that of a gothic abbey round which , when we arrived in the dusk, twisted trees sprouting from the irregular rock stood substitute for statues. As the cave is the only object of interest in the whole state, the local authorities have built a small amphitheatre from which, in season, a hundred or more people can watch the flight of the birds. There was only one family of six people besides ourselves, but the guide went through his timeworn recital with all the grandiloquence designed for a large audience, boring himself as much as us with his threadbare jokes.

I longed for him to be quiet, so that we could listen to the eerie noise which started to come from the throat of the cave. It began as a low growling, punctuated occasionally by a sharp, high note. It built in a crescendo to a cacophony which, in fancy, might have been the falling out of a choir of hysterical singers – furious, grumbling deep basses yelled at by termagant sopranos. Then the birds came out; at first, singly – dark outlines like huge bats with large fantails. Then in pairs and threes, until they thickened into scores and hundreds and, at the zenith, a broad, black stream of beating wings flared out of the cave, screaming. They wheeled above the cliff and headed south. We watched until it was quite dark.

The birds are *guácharos* or oil birds. The Spanish name means wailers and the English one derives from the fact that, when cooked, they leave in the pan a heavy, rich oil. Though we could not see it, they are red-brown in colour and about twelve inches long. They are purely nocturnal, leaving the cave at seven in the evening and coming back at four or five in the morning, never resting, for they hover when they eat. They navigate like bats emitting, apart from the screech, 250 echo-sounding clicks from their beaks every second. They eat oil-nuts, and some authorities maintain that they may fly three hundred miles or more in a night in search of food. The guide thought that they only travelled to a distance of about fifty miles and said that they ate *Coba longa*, a kind of nut, which is also the word for a Venetian gondola. The young stay in the nest for four months, fed so liberally by the parents, regurgitating for them the food they have gathered in the night, that they often weigh twice as much as the adults.

Such inconvenient lives made me wonder, as I had wondered about the hoatzin, what conceivable Darwinian advantage these creatures could have. I felt lured by Lamarckian heresies.

*   *   *

24

We pushed south, crossing the Orinoco on an ancient yellow ferry. Beside us on the deck was a speedy pick-up truck. Two sturdy horses stood in the back of it, wearing goggles to protect them as they peered, unconcerned, over the cab roof. An old man was selling oranges, carefully peeled, three for four cents. The brown water of the river was choppy, with flocculent crests to the waves; two little boys stood in the spray, chewing the oranges we had bought for them, so that the juice and brown water striped their faces like tiger fish. Ciudad Guyana lay on the other bank, green with trees – a desert oasis in the blank land.

Whenever we felt really free, we were tweaked back, like Juliet's sparrow, by bureaucracy. Three days we had to stay, while papers shuffled from customs office, to *guardia nacional*, to export agent and back to customs. As always it was for the car. We whiled away the time, taking two girls we chanced to meet to the Guri dam, three hundred feet high on the Caroni river; to an iron mine; to a pretty fort on a hill overlooking the river, where Symon and Marcelo hoped to romance the girls in the still evening. They soon came back to the car where I was reading, the girls unblushing, the boys buttoned with mosquito bites. My sympathies lay more with Sir Walter Raleigh's son, also Walter, who, it is thought, was killed here on his father's last expedition in search of El Dorado, in 1617.

The string loosened once more and we managed to escape as far as Upata, a town of single-storey houses, founded in 1762 by Catalan Capucins, its economy based on cattle raising. Although it lies only a matter of forty miles away from the new-found commercialisation of Ciudad Guyana, this colonial town, with some sleepily pretty streets, seemed decades apart. The hotel, with shabby, stygian bedrooms off a peeling courtyard, was run by an Italian woman from the Abruzzi. Her husband had a bad heart and could do little but sit in a wicker chair. The woman who ran the restaurant down the road was from the same region, but when I suggested that it must be pleasant, in so remote a place, to have a compatriot, they showed no concern for each other, but no animosity either.

In the morning, I asked the hotelier what she had here that she would not have had in the Abruzzi. Her long, Appenine face puckered. 'Niente,' she said, but struggled on to find something which might have made it worthwhile leaving home. Grasping two of her children close to her with both arms, she said at last, with an effort at defiance: 'I would not have had air-conditioning in the Abruzzi.' I wondered what hope had been the spur that had prompted her and her husband, fifteen years ago, to take such a decision, but did not like to ask, so lightly are people's whole lives contorted.

*   *   *

If Upata felt removed, El Callao was almost a ghost town. We had gone through dry, rolling countryside. I missed the flowering trees and the birds – an occasional mocking-bird, some kestrel, and bold or lazy turkey vultures that did not trouble to move off the road, were all that we saw. There was an abrupt dip into a valley, where dense thickets of trees grew beside a rocky river. A silvery span-bridge led off the main road towards the town. As soon as we reached it, the tarmac stopped and we rocked over broken roads, red with mud. The houses, lacking all colonial charm, were nonetheless peeling and forlorn.

A friend in Caracas had given us an introduction to Señor Carlos Small. We went to his house but, finding him out, we left our letter of introduction and wandered off to have a drink. When we got back, a large, round, black man was standing outside the house. A moustache and whiskers befuzzed his jowly features. His greeting was gruff.

'Why don't you wait at my house?' he asked. I mentioned something about a hotel.

'Who say hotel? You say. I say this house. Kai would not send you unless you mean something to him.' We went in, feeling nervous.

The design of the house was peculiar. To get to any room, it seemed that you had to go through two others. We sat in the formal living-room – it had a plastic-tile floor, with alternate squares of imitation wood and imitation crazy-paving. Six austere chairs and a settee, which had once had wicker seats, were arranged round a high, small table on which stood a vase of artificial flowers. There was a brass trolley, with oversized bottles of drinks; on another table a very small television set sat on the top of a much larger set. More artificial flowers, some of them furry, hung in baskets from the ceiling. A screen divided this room from the dining-room; on it hung a wicker sunburst, covered in flowers and ribbons, and above it a portrait of Simón Bolívar. On the walls, there were pictures of rose garlands and half-naked, sylvan nymphs, and a framed bottle of Cointreau, labelled 'In case of emergency', which hung beside a mock diploma to Carlos' late wife – 'for her love and solicitude'.

Carlos sat with us for a few moments. His father, he said, had come from Grenada, his mother from Martinique and he was born in 1909. After almost every piece of information he would add, 'Sí Señor,' in orotund tones, as if to forestall doubt. We had hardly settled down to talk when two girls arrived at the door. Carlos disappeared with them into some other part of the building. Soon a strong smell of incense filled the house. It turned out that Carlos was, among other things, a witch doctor. The girls had come for a consultation.

He did not appear for an hour, by which time a neighbour had arrived, who made some lunch. Evidently she now came every day to help, since Carlos' wife had died four months ago. He treated this neighbour with some curtness, accepting her benevolence as a right. He did not talk much during lunch, but every so often would say apropos of nothing: 'Sí, Señor,' pronounced with incontrovertible emphasis.

After lunch, he took us for a drive through the countryside. El Callao, before the Second World War, had a population of thirty-six thousand, all working in the gold mines with which the region was dotted – 'Sí, Señor.' The mines, which were started by the English, were later run by the Americans. The group was one of the most important mining concerns in South America and its shares were quoted on the London and New York stock exchanges. There were some parts still working, under the control of the Venezuelan government, but mostly we drove past ill-shapen mounds, the old spoil-heaps, now overgrown, from shafts once fifteen hundred feet deep.

The whole area was divided into sections. 'Now this is Chile and next is Finlandia.' The names of the districts and the shafts rolled with solemn grandeur from Carlos' deep-sounding lungs. Laguno, St George, St Georgito, Panama and Buenos Aires all lay hugger-mugger in Chile. In Finlandia were El Mamon, Sasamende, Bolívar, Austin, Hansa, Mocupia, Minerven. Carlos' eyes curved like scythes when I got muddled by the multiplicity of allusions and associations. He wanted me to learn all there was to know.

We passed the old English quarters, half-eaten by the jungle, their Caribbean verandahs at intoxicated angles, their corrugated roofs shouldered up by nonchalant young trees; notices still murmured in the faintest lettering of long-forgotten rules.

At the mills, piles of pinkish dust, left after the extraction of gold from the ore, were still growing, but I got no sense of excitement to compare with the lively days that Carlos spoke of, when all was haphazard and there was no scientific exploration and no money, just adventure tinged with greed – and yet they survived, sometimes in fortune, sometimes by a prayer's breadth.

When we got back to the house, we sat on chairs in the street. There was about it a mixture of decay and optimism. Some of the houses were tumbling, abandoned; others were newly built. Carlos, for example, had built his own. The street represented so much of what informs the character and circumstance of the Venezuelans. The past is of little importance. Conservation is foreign to their nature, as is orderliness or tidiness. Reminiscence is rare. The things that matter are youth and what is going to happen next.

The youth and children of the street were preparing for carnival the following week; hanging bunting from the trees and telegraph poles, and painting designs on the road. Symon and Marcelo joined them, touching up the pictures of caterpillars, clowns, butterflies and animals.

Carlos had not much faith in the carnival, though he kindly asked us to stay on. Kai was coming from Caracas, as he does each year, bringing any number of friends and a storehouse of food and drink. He had asked me to order twenty cases of beer against his arrival. 'He never fumbles to spend money,' said Carlos in happy anticipation. 'Sí, Señor.' Nevertheless, Carlos thought the carnival was debased and he was shocked that the young went on playing carnival music long after Shrove Tuesday, as if it were a month-long party. Two people came to ask him for some paint. He sent them away. 'They know I do have some. They think they can ask for anything' – manners were a particular concern of his.

'We were taught in school. There were many workers from the Caribbean, from St Lucia and St Vincent and the teaching was in English. Even now, it pass more than three hundred in El Callao who do speak English. They call the children Veronica, Joshua, Norman, such names as these. Sí, Señor.'

Carlos married his second wife, Esther, in 1949; they had no children of their own. 'But we brought up forty-five people in this house. We taught them manners. We were domestically educated – never ventured into a house with a hat on; held that hat until it was taken and hung-up; never sat down until asked.'

Over the years, Carlos had been a blacksmith, a wheelwright and a carpenter. The most important moment in his life was a visit from Prince Charles. He brought photographs of the Prince talking to Esther.

'He came to my house . . . he was here fifteen minutes. Sí, Sénor.' Bedtime. Although Carlos had said that he read through much of the night, I wanted to make an early start.

'I am always afoot by five o'clock. It was the time I get ready to go to work, until two years ago. Even if I drink and am fusticated the night before, I am afoot by the same time.'

He woke us at five and we left in the dark.

* * *

The vegetation grew thicker and more exotic and the air richer to breathe. Superb, tall trees with no low branches flowered, leafless, in a tracery dome of purple. We arrived in Tumeremo, a small town of no great interest, at the moment when everyone was having breakfast out of doors. We stood with them at the street stall which sold fresh juices – orange, papaya, passion-fruit – scalding coffee and *empanadas*, which Symon insisted on calling cornish pasties. An aeroplane flew overhead, an event evidently so rare that everyone looked up into the sky. These upturned faces were all white – a surprise after El Callao, where they were nearly all black. At the same time, they were a wild mixture, woven into unfamiliar patterns, so that one had no instinct as to whether the owner of a particular face was likeable or grumpy, honest or malign. American films have conditioned us to see the South American cast of features as a sign of shiftiness. The people of Tumeremo were, in the event, most agreeable, chatting to us with pastry-filled mouths.

We drove on to El Dorado, a pretty town on the banks of a river. The church bell tolled a lugubrious, cracked clang as the villagers gathered for a funeral. Cars rushed past the mourners with no deference to grief. It was here that Papillon was imprisoned on an island in the river. When I tried to read his book, I did not get far, feeling that it lacked verisimilitude. I would have liked to visit the prison in order to compare his impression with mine, but this was forbidden. It held, I was told, many homosexuals and transvestites incarcerated without trial. They are not, I could only hope, subjected to the barbarities which Papillon claimed to have witnessed.

*   *   *

Jesus Peña ran an ironmongery and repair shop by the road at kilometre 88. There was no apparent reason for the scramble of buildings, mostly made of corrugated iron, that littered the forest edge at this point. It was not even clear from where it was distanced by eighty-eight kilometres. There were stalls selling fruit, cooking utensils, tools, batteries, drink, rough clothes – little that one might ordinarily want, a lot that one might need in an emergency. There was no sign on the road, apart from the kilometre mark, but we knew it to be the place to turn off for Las Claritas.

Jesus was handsome, his face alert with more than ironmongery. He offered to guide us immediately to the mines. Unlike El Callao, Las Claritas is an independent affair, with individual concessions granted by the government to optimistic prospectors. Kai had told me that a rich businessman had been determined that this was the place to find gold. He had spent his whole fortune, garnered over twenty years, on searching in the forest. With mythic flourish, when he was reduced to his last few dollars, he found the gold of his fancy. In no time, the forest rang with the sound of axes clearing the ground for hundreds of little burrowings, in short a gold rush.

Jesus explained that we would have to travel over a rough track to the mines. As we started, a large helicopter pirouetted down to a pad a hundred yards away, paused and surged up again, dangling a heavy motor below it, and chattered off over the forest trees.

The way was little more than a broad track of red, red mud. It twisted among the trees with boles like rocket fins, rose in slippery squirms and fell again to deep puddles that lapped the bottom of the car doors. Butterflies as big as handkerchiefs danced fitful measures in the filtered sunlight. The forest felt solemn and secure. After forty minutes, there was a clearing. Grey trees lay felled at unnatural angles like broken legs. Beside them were pools of stagnant water. A few shanty huts stood around the pools. Two men were walking along the wet, red track; one of them carried a wooden gold-pan, in the shape of a coolie hat.

The clearings became frequent; great acreages of forest had been ripped out and the land scoured for gold and then left desolate. We came to a big working, fenced off with high wire, behind which large machines spurted fountains of mud. Jesus explained that this was one of the larger and most successful enterprises. Symon got down from the car and went to take a photograph. At once, a man on one of the machines raised a gun and shouted to him to fuck off.

We went on through the sodden destruction, until the shanties huddled closer into a town of tin. There can be few places which so well match the conjurings of imagination. There were steep, bumpy streets, lined with dirty restaurants, tacky shops, unisex hairdressers, dentists and, naturally, gold merchants who poured nuggets into our hands like helpings of peanuts. All these establishments were housed in ramshackle huts. Everything was absurdly expensive, except for the gold which was cheap. There were 'rooms to let' in houses where capaciously built whores, with tussocks of orange hair and tinselled clothes, sat stroking their bared thighs. Open drains trickled with noisome sludge. Very occasionally, next to rows of mean hovels, there would be the house of someone who had found a fortune, but was seized still of the gold fever. He would have Doric columns by his door; his mud garden would be lit by large globes of gold-tinted glass and, inside, one could glimpse hideous chandeliers and huge, coloured photographs of the cool of the

Andes. More than thirty thousand people lived in this slough of greed, in degradation, squalor and danger.

Jorge had a concession of 1,250 acres, which he worked with four colleagues. When we came close to his land, a man with a rifle stopped us. He recognised Jesus and, after peering into the car, waved us on, but no smile even hovered.

We stood at the rim of a deep and broad hole that Jorge and his colleagues had gouged over the months. Three of them were working down at the far side. They might have been baby hippopotamuses for they were the same colour all over as the mud they toiled in, and it was hard to make out their shapes. A rickety machine, resembling a large slide in a children's playground, made a squelchy clatter as a mixture of mud and water poured down it, sifting out any gold, by a method which I never fully understood. While they worked, three sentinels stood guard all day with rifles.

When Jesus led Symon and Marcelo down nearer to the workings, one of the guards came to talk to me. He was young and lonely in his vigil. He seemed quite gentle at first, with soft, apologetic eyes in an unmarked face.

'It is hard to get work in the city, so I came here, where I make more money than my mother dreams of. I don't want to dig for gold. These people have no peace, they think only of the yellow gold.'

There was constant trouble. A guard had to watch every minute of the day. There were many shootings and killings, and few questions were asked. Señor Jorge had a lot of gold – many villains were after it. I asked the boy if he would shoot to kill. His yellow eyes sharpened. Suddenly, his pudgy face was taut with muscle.

'I would shoot straight between his eyes,' he said with unnerving satisfaction. I wondered if he had someone in mind.

Even when Jorge came closer, emerging from his gummy mudhole, he was shapeless in the uniformity of his earthen colour. It was difficult to tell where his clothes started and finished. Only his teeth peeked off-white beneath his brimmed hat. But one could sense that he was tough and still not much more than forty.

The life was a hard one. There were no comforts, he said, but the rewards were great. Jorge was certainly not one of those who would build a vulgar villa in this dank hell.

'I make two thousand dollars a week, and my colleagues take a thousand dollars a week each.'

He chose the word colleagues, I thought, because in this place one was never sure who was a friend, although they lived and worked together in easy intimacy. Nor were they partners. He had paid for the equipment which, he said, had cost forty thousand dollars. Jorge had worked before in diamond mines and he had come to Las Claritas five years ago.

Then a roseate, cloud-born look came into Jorge's eyes and a mildly fatuous smile made cracks in his mud-clad cheeks. He would not go on much longer, he said. He had a target. All he needed was one really big strike and he would crawl out of the mud for the last time.

'I know a place that no one else knows,' he intoned, almost as if he were rehearsing the script of *The Treasure of Sierra Madre*. 'Soon, I will go there. And Jesus will come too, won't you Jesus?'

Jesus, with an embarrassed sidelong flash at me, smiled in unconvincing agreement. 'Of course,' he said. 'Cómo no?'

As we went back over the slimy forest road, Jesus explained how much money there was to be made in the frenzied atmosphere of a gold-rush town. The dentists, the unisex hairdressers, the whores, could all earn ten times the normal fees of their callings. The helicopter pilot, ferrying machinery over the forest roof, made more than three thousand dollars a day.

In a few months of each year, Jesus himself made enough money to lead a completely different, cultivated life in Caracas. He was immune from the fever. He would never follow Jorge to his El Dorado.

*   *   *

It would take days, I thought, to purge the dejection induced by the squalor of Las Claritas. Even the surrounding forest was somehow tainted and we drove for miles in silence. We came then to a rapid climb, zigzagging up a staircase road, past an awesome monolith known as La Piedra de la Virgen. At the top, the change was so abrupt that it seemed impossible that it was natural. Our eyes, shut in for days by the curtain of the forest, swerved wildly over an immense plain, innocent of trees, save where rivers ran in valleys or in deep clefts. In the distance, what looked like the strongholds of giants stood full-square, rising dark blue and high in the amber of the evening. It was a new world, airy and immaculate, expunging for us the stains of the mine.

We camped in a hollow by a swift river which broadened there into a pool, burnished bronze by the last of the sun. The boys were excited, slinging their hammocks for the first time. We preened ourselves that we had forgotten nothing. We cooked well and slept early. In the morning, the boys' faces sagged, pinched and tired. They had shivered miserably, having put nothing under themselves, and each complaining that the other had wriggled all night, shaking the bough of the lone tree to which they were both tied. The great plain had the quality of a desert, being rigidly cold at night and drily warm by day. The sun rose, instantly genial; Symon and Marcelo swam in the river, forgetful of their raw night.

The relationship between the two boys was a rather uncertain one at this stage. They shared an enormous enthusiasm for the company of girls and the *lingua franca* of pop music, but otherwise had little in common. They were both charmingly anxious to be helpful to me. Symon mistook Marcelo's eagerness for interference, while Marcelo mistook Symon's for arrogance.

The Gran Sabana, as this immense plain was called has, like the *llanos*, lain undisturbed by geological caprice for unconscionable ages. We wandered in its vastness for some days, puzzled by the strange and lonely feeling of the land, which seemed to belong to another age, but held by its beauty. The plants were unfamiliar: three-petalled, yellow flowers on tall stalks, bushes a little like cistus but not quite right, whole areas of tiny cacti and, in the damp, weird spiky things which could have emerged from a primordial marsh. We forded rocky rivers and, cresting each rise, gazed at a new great sweep of country. Along a bumpy track, we came to Aponguao and the tin huts of some Arecuna Indians – short, stumpy people, with faces as broad as Buddhas. They lived, they said, on fish and cassava.

They wanted us to see their falls, promising that they were only a few minutes away. They ferried us across the river. Symon pushed me in my chair along the path that started by being only mildly stony. Then we had to cross streams, over stepping stones. After that, the bushes pressed close and tangling. Eventually, the path plunged steeply over boulders. Symon and Marcelo struggled, cursing. It took an hour in the full blaze of the sun.

The river smoothed its way to the lip of a six-hundred-foot drop, curled over the edge, seemed to hesitate for a second and then spread into a moirée pattern of feathery froth, falling like folds of rich, fine silk, until it crashed with an unlooked-for roar into the basin below. It made me uneasy, to think of this perpetual falling.

The sense of sempiternity was enhanced by the lack of wildlife. There were no animals of any sort and we would go for hours without seeing a bird. No hawks hovered, for there was nothing to swoop on. No herons waited. There were fish in the rivers, yet the Indians said there was nothing to hunt and they had names for no more than three or four kinds of bird. They themselves kept only chickens but no goats. There were many snakes.

When I learned about these serpents, I decided that it was a kind of Eden, this great spreading land, tumbling with waterfalls fed by rivers from the titan fortresses or *tepuys*. These tall mountains rose sheer out of the plain, so much bigger than the mesas of America, enormous blocks of rock, proud to have withstood the eroding winds of the millennia. To the south-east of us was the greatest of them all, Mount Roraima – the inspiration of Conan Doyle's *The Lost World*. It took really no imagination to people this towering flat-topped range with dinosaurs and pterodactyls and every long-lost creature of the scaly past.

Somewhere to our west, from the summit of Auyantepuy, fell the three-thousand-foot silver thread of Angel Falls, the highest in the world, not named after the image of some Botticelli tress, but after an aviator, Jimmy Angel, who discovered it in 1937, only to die a few years later, his plane plunging into his eponymous cascade.

We visited Kavanayén, a mission with grim, stone buildings. The Indians here lived in strong, stone houses and seemed busy and content. Their traditional life was forgotten. They were now just Venezuelans growing a few crops, working on the new roads; the only difference was that their village was scrupulously tidy, but was that their nature or the influence of the Fathers? I was glad to leave them and drive into the dusk to where we were to camp, passing on the way three or four large patches of land, each perhaps thirty acres in extent, which shimmered with a sea of dancing fireflies. In the morning those patches looked the same as the rest of the land, but they must have held some special plant.

As we headed south, the land fell. Gradually, the vegetation changed and I noticed a new, pink bush like a superb azalea. The further we dropped, the greener the landscape – wide, verdant valleys with palm trees, a patch or two of forest with a shrill flight of parrots, and what appeared to be closely grazed downs, but there were still no animals. It was eerie to see such green country, with abundant water, so deserted by beast and man.

We stopped to look at more waterfalls and, at Quebrada de Jaspe, watched the clear waters of a brook illuminating the flat, red jasper of the stream's bed, scored with lines so regular as to seem to hold some message.

In among all this, there must have been Indians living but, following the road through valleys which were kaleidoscopes of shades of green, there was no cultivation, no sign of cattle.

It was not until a few miles from Santa Elena that we saw a horse and a few cows. This was the border town, where we found people again, people with that roguish, restless look which is common to frontier folk.

The time had come, too, for another bout of officialdom. Here, in Santa Elena, we had to have three more inspections of the engine and chassis numbers. Two branches of police must stamp our documents. First, we must visit the immigration office, go next to the *guardia nacional* and then return to the first office. When we got back to the immigration office, at eleven in the morning, the official had gone home for the day. We went to his house. He was happy to go back to his office if he could ride in our car; he had not been in the new Toyota Landcruiser.

It was comic to watch the boys dealing with these officials. Marcelo, so Latin-American, moved with elastic step, his chin high, his arms swinging across his back so that each hand actually passed the final point of the other arm's sweep, like windscreen wipers. His monkey teeth were uncovered by an eager smile. He prefixed every question with: 'Por favor, una pregunta . . .' Often he said *preguntita*, being fond, as are all South Americans, of diminutives – *horita, momentito, whiskycito*.

Symon, so English, clutching the documents and leaning forward, thrust his head out like a ram, taking long strides, so that it looked as if he would not have time to bring the next leg forward and that he would fall like a collapsed step-ladder.

After half a dozen re-recordings of our names and stampings of our documents, we were at last loosed across the frontier to Brazil.

3

Brazil

A RIDE ON THE AMAZON

The half-built base of a splendid highway petered out into a confusion of mud tracks at the edge of Boa Vista. What was evidently planned appeared exaggerated for this rather uninteresting town, but it was said that the region was booming and was in the vanguard of Brazilian development. We found a new hotel by the wide river, and watched the sun dim feebly into the mists of the flat horizon.

Carlos Small had said that carnival in Boa Vista would be more lively than in El Callao, and that we should not miss it. Now it was Sunday, the first day. We had seen stands as we drove in and, at the hotel, they told us the celebrations would begin at eight. We went a little early but, as we walked, we met a solitary girl, very pretty, nearly naked apart from some silver tinsel. She was meandering home. It was all over for the day.

There was a television set in our room and we watched the parade in Rio de Janeiro which was to go on, both in fact and broadcast to the whole country, continuously for three days – the samba beat throbbing without cease. There seemed, on that first day, to be merely a mesmeric quality about the music. There was much to astound us as we sat, feeling somewhat foolish to be still there, long into the night. We gaped at the meretricious splendour of the costumes, spangled and sequinned and silvered and gilded until they sparkled in Golcondan profusion, feathered and plumed beyond the dreams of a crazed taxidermist. At what point, I wondered, did vulgarity so overreach itself as to become almost majestic? The cameramen were obsessed with bottoms, even more than they were with naked breasts, zooming their lascivious lenses with carnal abandon. The same song, for there were only voices and drums, pulsed over and over and over for the hours that it took one 'school' or group to pass the judges' stand.

The unending repetition had a pagan feeling that I had felt once at Padstow on the First of May, when the 'obby 'oss dances all through the drunken day, to the druidical melody of an endlessly repeated tune, for some reason quite irretrievable the next morning.

On the second day, the beat entered into our whole bodies. We strolled about the shabby streets, stopping sometimes at a bar which thumped out the all-pervading samba. This time, we were not late for the street parade. The music thrummed from hoarse loudspeakers and the people danced with a funny tripping step, using each beat evenly. It was largely a family affair, the costumes rather hopeless and touching. The richer children were dressed in gossamer, fairy costumes. The poorer ones wore everyday clothes, but coloured their faces and threw flour over everyone. One little white girl rubbed her hand thick with white and pressed a neat handprint on the naked back of a black man dancing.

A whole family came in Ku Klux Klan outfits in black. Many of the men wore drag but two, whom I took for brothers, were dressed in bright rags and straw hats, looking like a cross between the Pied Piper and Worzle Gummidge. They danced with springed energy, leaping and vaulting, apparently untiring, for two hours without pause. They gathered enchanted children up in their arms, swirling them in a mad cavorting and setting them down again, laughing.

When we wearied of the scene and went back to the car, we found two girls sitting on the bonnet. Antonia was nineteen, not especially pretty with a formless, round face, but with a beautifully proportioned figure; Belani was smaller, thinner and only sixteen. Symon had muddled the combination lock of the car's handbrake, so we struggled for an hour to release it. Marcelo chatted to the girls. On and on went the boom of the samba.

When the brake was freed, we asked the girls if they would like some dinner. They said that they were a little nervous because, the night before, four Venezuelans had tried to assault them and they had had to be rescued by the police. Their hesitation, considering our number plates, lasted a surprisingly short time, and we found ourselves to be the only diners in what the girls maintained was Boa Vista's best restaurant. They explained that carnival here took place mostly in clubs, rather than in the streets and that we ought to go to one which they liked.

First, they said, they must ask their parents' permission. We drove to the suburbs and waited outside a modest villa while the girls went in. After ten minutes they reappeared, in different clothes, and basking in parental approval. What, I wondered, could they have said to reassure their mothers? That they had met, in the street, two Europeans and a Chilean?

The club occupied the space of a small block. We crushed through a narrow doorway, paying as much as one would for a London discothèque. The dance floor was under a big circle of thatched roof. The music started soon after we arrived, never to stop again – mostly the eternal samba, enlivened occasionally by a slightly faster 'carnival' music. The floor was forever crowded, the people held in thrall by the beat of the music so that, even far from the centre, away in the dusty garden, figures tripped their one-beat step, in endless spasm.

The dancers needed no partners. One grossly fat woman, in a preposterous costume of sequins, her skirt short and one breast bare, danced all night alone, with hideous shaking. Others, gratefully prettier, were topless and I remember a particular girl in a spangly top-hat and fishnet stockings, who had a fig leaf on each nipple. And another who danced alone on a chair for more than an hour. The Ku Klux Klan family were there too, but without their children.

There was an element of unsophistication partly, perhaps, because nearly everyone was under forty. But, as I watched, I grew more and more to feel how far removed the scene was from any European equivalent. As in everything Latin-American, there was an undercurrent of politics – an anti-police song, another about economics, all in the same throbbing pitch.

The sexuality had its own emphasis. The girls in their tinsel were provocative in just that manner abhorred by feminists – their bottoms so plumply postured, their breasts aquiver. The men, on the other hand, with their martial moustaches and studied strut, making frequent, scratching adjustments to their genitals, achieved only a hollow masculinity. They, in the end, were insignificant: the women triumphant.

The music ate into me, so that I began to hate it, but quite as strongly could not bear to think of leaving it. The composer, Jeremy Lubbock, once suggested to me that there is a kind of music that one listens to, not with one's ears as one listens to Mozart, but with one's vitals. He described a day when he sat in his garden and became aware of a sound, a guitar playing the same three chords over and over again. It annoyed him but, as it came closer, he was drawn to it and, when it passed, he got up and followed it down the street. The music became, he thought, one's heartbeat.

The sambas for me had a strange dying cadence that induced a melancholy kind of happiness, a contradictory sensation, like an explosion of vitality on a lazy summer's afternoon – a blend perhaps of Portuguese *fado* and Negro rhythms. At last, the girls said they must go home and we wrenched ourselves from the spell.

On the last day, our energies were nearly spent. We went to the streets for the final parade. The crowds were rougher than on the day before, poorer that is, but it was once more a family affair and the pulse still worked its magic. The floats came by, pathetic, of course, by comparison with the glittering fantasies still shimmering from the television, but poignant in the effort they revealed. They prompted memories of English village fêtes, but would that any village fête were like carnival in Boa Vista.

Carlos Small would have been pleased, at least, that on the next morning no drums trespassed into Lent.

*   *   *

In Venezuela, they had said, one person in six had been born outside the country. Immigrants, refugees, adventurers of all sorts make up a large proportion of the population. I had noticed particularly that the rich often had foreign names. In every country it was the same, in what proportions it would be impossible to guess, but in the loneliest places there were wayworn people who had come to rest for no clear reason. In Caracarai, a lost village in a flat landscape, we stopped for petrol.

A dignified man, rather too well dressed for the heat, approached me after talking to Marcelo. In formal English, invaded occasionally by an unexpected colloquialism, he asked if it were true that I was a writer. I said I was.

'Might I trouble you then, sir, for a gracious memento of your valued presence in this flea-pit?' I blinked, and hoped that a visiting card might do.

'Indeed. And would you, most kindly, further honour us by putting your moniker on it?'

Guillermo Alfaro Garbanzo who, once I became accustomed to his way of speech, was far from either being pretentious or dull, told me that he was Costa Rican and also a writer. He never explained why he was in Caracarai, nor what kind of things he wrote. We discussed Shakespeare and how well or ill he was translated into Spanish. We touched on Victor Hugo, whom Señor Alfaro had read in the French.

'Now,' he said, raising his shoulders in pride, 'I am reading Eric Ambler.' Perhaps I could now account for his phraseology.

A little further down the street, we found a pizzeria. The cheerful, helpful woman who ran it also spoke to us in English. She came from the south of the country, some two and a half thousand miles away, but her husband had worked for twenty years in the Mato Grosso. He had been orphaned as a child and was adopted by a Scottish family, called Clifford. When she married, she joined her husband on their farm, and they were happy.

Three months ago, the whole Clifford family went on a trip to Roraima. On the way home, they were killed – all five of them. A petrol lorry hurtled brakeless into their pick-up. Eleven people died in the crash. There was nothing left for her husband in the Mato Grosso. So they came here and opened the pizzeria. It was said to be a thriving area for development. I felt daunted by their courage.

That afternoon we crossed the Equator.

*　　*　　*

Now we were in the Amazon forest. From here to Colombia, to Ecuador, to Peru over three million square miles, there spread out this enormous expanse of trees, unimaginably large, with wide tracts still unexplored, several tribes as yet unmet. At first, we cudgelled our imagination to encompass the statistics. I had read that each year four per cent of the forest was cut down. That meant that in twenty-five years it would all be gone. It was not possible. No one could, in one year, cut down the infinitesimal fraction of this vast space that we had travelled through in three hours. It was too big, too dense, impregnable.

Then we came, in this virgin place, to a clearing of burnt forest. Then another, and more and more. Where the clearings were, some trees escaped, the proud ones of the canopy looking naked with nothing growing beneath them. In the clearings, too, were lagoons of rank water from which rose a grim miasma. The wastelands of Passchendaele might have been like this.

It was difficult to find anywhere pleasant to camp. Where the trees grew unharmed, the forest was impenetrable. Where the trees were gone, the forest floor was sodden and reeked of wet ash. We found a rare turning off the main road. After a few narrow miles, there was a shed standing a hundred yards down a rough track and, beyond it, a tidy clearing with signs of cultivation.

There was no one about. Pairs of macaws flew overhead in constant dispute and formations of whistling duck piped their way home. We unloaded our equipment and started to attach the boys' hammocks to the hut. An old man appeared. He was small and dark, his cheeks had thinned to lined paper, and he scratched a lot. He said he was Italian and he was pleased to speak his own language, though he stumbled in it after long years of disuse. The land, he told me, belonged to his son-in-law and, of course, we could camp there. 'Cómo no?' he asked, slipping back into Spanish, and we said good-night.

How not was soon apparent. The son-in-law came almost at once. He was tall and powerful, lightly bearded and could, from his looks, have been of German stock. 'Why don't you camp at my house? You will be welcome,' he said, his eyes looking firmly into mine. He was very insistent. Symon went with him to see where the house was and returned with news of shrieking children and a cramped porch. I sent Marcelo to explain, as best he could in Portuguese, the tedium of reloading and then unloading. The son-in-law came again. This time it was clear that the offer of his porch did not stem from hospitality. I asked what he was worried about.

'You may steal my corn from the shed,' he said with embarrassed truculence. I offered to give him the car keys. He snorted his suspicion.

'You will have another set.' His mistrust was dispiriting.

'Take my passport then.'

At last he smiled. I thought of all those warnings about never parting with your passport. Then he asked if we needed anything and went away, as relieved not to have us on his porch as we were not to be there.

In the morning, Vlamir returned punctually at the time he had promised. His reticence had vanished. He had been brought up on a farm in Paraná, in the south. But there was no work. Like all his friends, he had gone to São Paulo where he had had jobs in building. He stayed there twelve years, doubtless losing any trust he may have had.

The government offered people like Vlamir land in the Amazon. They must clear it and work it and it would be theirs. The parcels were usually 175 acres, but Vlamir was exceptionally given three hundred. He grew maize, coffee and cacao, and he had four cows. Marcelo tried to engage him in an ecological discussion about the destruction of the forest, but plainly it was meaningless or, at least, cranky to him. His instincts were those of a farm boy. He cared nothing for useless trees.

It so happened that, before sleeping, I had been reading Patrick Leigh Fermor's *Between the Woods and the Water*. He remembered, as I did now that he reminded me, learning at school that in the time of King John a squirrel could have crossed England from the Severn to the Humber without touching the ground. Who were we to reproach Vlamir?

The old man came to say goodbye. In the secrecy of Italian, he told me that he had a terrible rash in the groin. He thought it was caused by damp heat, but he did not like to ask anyone in case they thought that he had a worse complaint. I gave him half a tube of ointment, and ached when he offered to pay me.

We travelled for miles through that raped forest, over the rutted, shuddering road. I was amazed to see occasional log cabins with television aerials. What could people here make of the carnival in Rio, let alone of an American movie?

Sometimes, there were far older clearings and grass grew on the banks. In one of these more open spaces, a boa constrictor basked on the dry, red mud of the road. It was about five feet long. When we got out to look, it lazed on, torpid and untroubled. On the first two-thirds of its body, the markings were faint and foxed like an old print. On the last third, the pattern was vivid, brightly coloured and sharply marked. Symon would not go near it, but Marcelo picked it up without fear and we put it to safety from the wheels of lorries.

Before Manaus we came to an Indian Reservation. There were barriers across the road and we had to report to a guard post. Fortunately, it was still early in the day, for no one was allowed through after three in the afternoon. Whether this rule was for the sake of peace for the Indians or for fear of attack, no one vouchsafed. The solemn way in which our names were written down, inclined me to suppose the latter.

The abrupt change beyond the barrier, where only Indians might live, gave ghastly emphasis to the extent of the debauchment of the forest. Here it was untouched and a magical peace pervaded the whole air. After a mile or two we felt compelled to stop just to look and to listen. The forest was almost eerily quiet in the middle of the day. Only a muttered squawk or the exhausted sigh of a falling branch cracked the shell of silence. The trees in their right places made a beautiful pattern, piling up their tangled hierarchy. The sun, piercing down where the new, metalled road sliced through the trees, spotlighted the stately dance of iridescent butterflies, sparkling blue in a world of green. I wondered whether, behind the wall of the forest, dark Waimiri-Atroari eyes were fixed on us with hatred.

Further on, there was a monument to those who had built the road two years ago. A special tribute was paid to a missionary Father for his work in the pacification of the Indians – the Church, even now, laying the way for commerce.

*　　*　　*

Outside Manaus, the soldiers of another checkpoint wanted to search the car, growling to us to unload everything. The boys, damp with the heat, gazed miserably at the sweating soldiers. We opened our cool-box and gave them each a bottle of tonic water and they waved us on.

Being in Manaus is harder to believe than it is to imagine from afar. Surmise had built for me a crumbling toytown. Nowhere in the middle of the Amazon jungle could be more than that. It was extraordinary, of course, a stupendous achievement, yet jerry-built. In imagination, the jungle pressed, greedy at the end of paved streets. Roots toppled ancient walls, and lianas dripped from deserted balconies.

We walked, instead, through the most ordinary streets. Skyscrapers pointed up to the bleached sky. Trams groaned past. Traffic raced uncaring of pedestrians. One driver, hitting my usually protective wheelchair, gave a grinning thumbs-up and sped on. Even the older part of the city had such modernisms as pedestrian precincts, and the old buildings stood as stolid as the Mansion House in London. In the new suburbs, we might have been back in Caracas. The normality of the place made it almost inconceivable that a few miles in all directions lay only forest; that until ten years ago no road reached this city of a million people; that every girder, every piece of glass, every car, every saucer, every needle, everything that therein is had travelled here by river, one thousand miles up the Amazon.

I loved Manaus. It had a vitality and an optimism, based as far as I could judge on no very tangible expectation – a trait which I later came to recognise as Brazilian. Its past stirred mixed emotions of pride and guilt. The buildings of the 1890s, put up at the height of the Brazilian rubber boom, owed much to British, in particular Scottish, endeavour.

Charles Macintosh of Glasgow, in 1823, discovered a way of water-proofing cloth with rubber. Charles Goodyear of Massachusetts, in 1839, found a way of hardening rubber. These two inventors precipitated a sudden and immense demand for the latex, milked from the tree *Hevea brasiliensis*, which grew only in the Amazon region.

The wild extravagance of the rubber planters and their great mansions filled with treasures from Europe, have been often described. Most of the mansions have gone but, as we wandered, we found superb relics – each one straining credulity still further.

The Municipal Market was a folly of 1880s art nouveau, designed by Eiffel and vaguely reminiscent of Les Halles. Its complicated ironwork was all shipped from Scotland. The stalls of the market were lavish mounds of unfamiliar colours and shapes – cassava, yams, papaya, plantain, watermelon, cashew, guava, pineapple, coconut, *guananá*, *maracujá, taperebá, bacaba, pupunha, buriti, jenipapo, graviola, açai*. There were weird medicines, strange herbs. One whole section sold little idols, incense, candles of vivid colours – the trappings of *macumba*, the Brazilian version of voodoo. At the far end were fish – long, sharp-toothed creatures with mouths like Japanese fish-kites flown for the birth of a boy; *pirarucu*, the fish-seller said. A deep-bellied bass-like fish, *tambaqui*; a flat, round fish, *pacu*; and a score of others – *tucunaré, cará-acu, jaraqui* . . .

At the waterfront, the Italianate Customs House stood square, ugly and impressive. It grew fussier the higher it became, so that it had a top-heavy look. This lumpy, stone building was prefabricated in Scotland, shipped over in blocks and put up in 1906. Beside it was the floating harbour, built by the English to whom the dock area was leased at the beginning of the century. The T-shaped concrete pier jutted out into the river which, even at its lowest point during the year, is one hundred feet deep. At the end of June it may deepen by as much as forty-five feet, the pier faithfully rising and sinking in unfailing tribute to British engineers. A large cruise ship, SS *Astor*, spilled out hundreds of blue-rinsed tourists who swarmed, braying in the accents of Nebraska, over the city.

Passing a large doorway, I looked in to see a staircase with two curving sweeps of elegance, in metal – the treads and risers and the elaborate balustrade were all cast iron. I went in to marvel at this ferrous fantasy and found that the building was the public library, built in 1910. In 1945, a fire destroyed all but sixty of its seventy thousand books, but gradually they have collected nearly four times as many as the original library contained. Leaving, I noticed an inscription cast at the foot of one of the pillars of the splendid stairway. It read: Walter Macfarlane, Saracen Foundry, Glasgow.

We walked on past lofty offices, with high counters of hardwood and bare walls, which would have served well as locations for Dickensian films. Through the windows of upper floors, we got glimpses of Italian plaster ceilings. That smug Victorian confidence, which one cannot help envying as well as mocking, still smouldered in the dying fabric of these heat-worn buildings.

Lastly, the opera house, the Teatro Amazonas – the symbol of the booming age of rubber. The great dome, tiled with sixty thousand shining pieces from Alsace, set in the pattern of the Brazilian flag, still struggles to dominate the city. The whole framework of the theatre is metal, plastered over to look classical. The exterior has an uncomfortable look, the rather flat, oriental dome not fitting in any sense the Italianate rectangle of the building. The portico, with two sets of columns above the arcade at the base, belongs neither to itself nor to the rest of the building. I attributed this awkwardness to the fact that it was designed not by an architect, but by the school of engineering in Lisbon. Henrique Dazzaloni was employed only to enshroud the school's frame with ornament, with the inevitable consequence that it looks like that.

The theatre has been restored three times since it was finished in 1899, and was now undergoing a fourth repair. It was said to be shut, but it was easy enough to slip in and, in contrary spirit, there was a bar open at which a woman was eager to tell one the names of the different Brazilian fruits and sell their juices. *Guaraná*, I learnt, contained twice as much caffeine as coffee.

Inside, the feeling of the theatre was quite different. The engineers understood the purpose of the building. So it worked and the decorators, mostly Italian painters under the supervision of Crispin de Amaral, could frolic their frescoes and decorative panels all over the walls, perch busts on the marble-framed doorways, dangle Murano chandeliers from plastered ceilings, set down inlaid floors of Amazon wood, hang mirrors in the *piano nobile*, and it still worked as a theatre – the metal frame of the engineers peeping out from time to time in stairways, verandahs, seat frames, and always lurking in the columns and superstructure.

For all the decoration, it had a curiously simple and friendly feeling. The auditorium was not so big as I had expected from the outside of the building. There were some eighty boxes in four tiers and I counted 248 seats in the stalls – beautiful, if austere, separate chairs with wooden seats and thinly upholstered backs. Round the pillars between the boxes were written the names of playwrights and composers – Mozart, Aristophanes, Verdi, Shakespeare, Wagner, Goethe . . . Who the hell, I wondered, was Garret?

The whole is wonderfully unspoilt and the restoration unerring in its sense of period. How ironic to think that this opera house, which had inspired the demented Fitzcarrald to try to build another, even deeper in the jungle, had never held one performance of an opera. Its fading and the withering of all Manaus were settled long before its foundations were laid, before even the cathedral, the first of the city's grand buildings, was started.

In 1873, an Englishman, Henry Wickham, smuggled out of Brazil seven thousand seeds of *Hevea brasiliensis*, lying to the authorities at the mouth of the Amazon, backed in his dishonour by the British Consul at Belém. The seeds were fostered at Kew, the orchid houses being ruthlessly emptied to make room for them.

The seedlings were taken to Ceylon, where they did not prosper. Enough were carried on to Malaya, where they flourished, untroubled by Amazonian pests and ills. Twenty-seven years went by, while the extravaganza of the rubber boom sparkled in Manaus. In 1900, the first four tons of rubber came to London from the Malayan plantations. Easier to grow, to harvest, to ship, Malayan rubber surplanted the wild rubber of Brazil in barely a decade. In 1923, the opera house was boarded up.

*   *   *

The only road out of Manaus was flooded and, so they said at the bus station, would not open for three months. At the tourist office, they had assured us that it was open all the year. We went to the travel agent's, looking for a boat to take us and the car down river to Belém. We must wait ten days unless we were prepared to pay more than double, in which case we could leave tomorrow. With luck, they added.

A stranger walked into the hotel. He had noticed our car outside. Did I, by any chance, want to ship it to Belém? He knew of a boat leaving the next day. The price that he suggested was less than the ordinary rate that the travel agent had quoted. I never learnt why he came. For, when he had guided us to the shipping company, he left, asking no reward from us or from the company. The price was more than he had said, but that was hardly his fault, as the company had doubled their rates that week.

At the bottom of a long slope of churned, red mud, two flat, metal barges, lashed together with straining hawsers, floated on the dark waters of the Rio Negro. The rain needled down on the men loading the barges, and I could not see the far bank of the river. Lorries backed, groping like sleepwalkers, down the mud run, easing their trailers on to the clanging metal. Leaving the containers on iron trestles, they crabbed their way back from the river's edge, sticking often in the gummy mud. We waited for two sodden hours until there was only a single gap at the back of the left barge, too short for a container. Symon coaxed the car through the deep flutes of wet clay and into this strangled space.

We were to sail at five in the afternoon, but nothing happened – only the rain and the wind beat on. Food, they had said, was included so we had put only drinks into our cool-box, packed with ice. There was nothing to eat and, in any case, nowhere to eat it. We were alone on the barges. The boys slung their hammocks under a container, their faces close to the oily base of it, so that their bottoms did not sag to the wet deck. I lay in the back of the car, wondering how it was that mosquitoes were able to fly through the implacable rain. One drop, one would have thought and hoped, must surely have stilled their fragile wings. They came, none the less, in squadrons.

In the early light, we found that the rain had stopped. A low mist smudged the surface of the river, but I could see the forest across the broad water. A small tug came, white with a green funnel and flying the Brazilian flag. It shouldered us out from the shore and we drifted loose on the current. The tug, two huge blocks hewn from a vast log fastened to its bows, fussed round to the stern of the right-hand barge and, like a suckling infant, latched on to the back, the crew securing it with ropes and wires. This small craft, not more than thirty feet long, with a beam hardly ten feet, was to push the two barges measuring nearly two hundred feet by forty feet each, for a thousand miles. We should have been three barges, but the wind was strong against us and, as it was, the journey would take an extra day. The tug-boat was called *Giselle*. Apart from the engine-room there was only a tiny washroom, a galley at the back and a tall conning-tower, high so that the captain could see over the containers. I wondered if our journey would be like *Heart of Darkness*.

We had still not met the captain, nor any of the crew. Conversation was anyhow difficult above the noise of the two diesel motors. The men were busy with their tasks, but would, every so often, give us the thumbs-up, which I had come to recognise as the most important Brazilian gesture. We responded with marked enthusiasm to the one who we supposed was the cook, for we had eaten nothing.

I sat at the stern in the narrow gap behind the car. There was no raised edge to the deck, so the water swirled only two feet below me. We had embarked a few miles upstream from Manaus. As we chugged past in the hazed light before the sun had burnt away the mist, the dome of the opera house was barely discernible; only the cathedral stood proud among the skyscrapers, and I regretted that it had always been shut.

Beyond the grand buildings, there were wooden houses on stilts, poised for the time when the river would rise and lap their verandahs. We came soon to the confluence of the Rio Negro, with the even larger Solimões, the real Amazon. The clear brown waters of the Rio Negro, like rich beef tea, refused to mingle with the yellow soup of the Solimões. For three or four miles they followed side by side, obstinate in their reluctance to mix, then the clear water, whirlpooling and bubbling in furious surrender of its purity, succumbed to the stronger silt and mud.

The cook worked at his pots, scooping up water from the river in a Brascoat paint tin, in which the rest of the crew also washed their clothes. Eventually he produced a form of porridge and then went to swing in his hammock, while we hungered for the next meal.

The captain was a small, nut-brown, ugly man, bow-legged and with a stomach which burst from his grubby vest and rippled down over his shorts. His face was pointed, his nose curving towards his chin, like Punch, and his eye had the same lewd glint.

He told me that the *Giselle* could push us at nine miles an hour and that the river flowed at three miles an hour. It would take five days and six nights to reach Belém; the journey back took ten or eleven days. He had charts of the river, but he never used them. He boasted that he could take us to Peru, to Iquitos up the Solimões, without ever looking at a chart. Lest I should think that was easy, he assured me that every year there were many sinkings. His company, even, had lost a ship last year.

The captain humped away and I stared at the water. How odd that, before the Andes pushed up, however many million years ago, the river flowed the other way and that, as Humboldt found, the rivers in one place may today elect to flow in either direction and to render their tribute sometimes to the Orinoco, sometimes to the Amazon.

There was only one other passenger, a good-natured lorry-driver, Carlos, who was travelling with his load. He came from somewhere in the south and said that, when we arrived in Belém, it would then take him fifteen days to reach his destination, but he knew many girls *en route* who would comfort him. He spent much of the day in the cab of his lorry, which was fitted out in some luxury and decorated with bobbles and swags of ribbon, and a picture of the Virgin.

The afternoon grew calm and hot. I was surprised by the bustle of the river. The wake of large freighters grated the two barges together, testing the hawsers; little launches busied past, everyone giving a thumbs-up. On the banks were more houses than I had expected, some looking like the 'desirable riverside residences' of estate agents' advertisements. There were pastoral scenes – a corral of horses, cows in meadows – often a small church and once a large one, São José Apararei. There was a grand mansion, derelict, roofless, its windows blind holes and, a little later, a shocking-pink and green hotel.

The sunset was Rubensesque, the buxom clouds seeming to be lit from within and churning like the angry gases of the creation. Then there hung for a lurid minute a half-sun, bisected by the thin black line of the forest above the glowing Amazon. Swifts flew low over the evening water. A shower of rain fell, then stopped.

In the dusk we hit something. The metal of the barge rang like a temple gong. A violent, swelling thump ran the length of the flat, iron hull. The prow of the little *Giselle* leapt up. Another crash. The engines stopped; the lights went out. An alarmed silence held the air. I watched the whole trunk of a vast tree fall away, spinning in the dark.

Then the engines started again. Carlos told me that the tugs have a propeller-guard. The cook in his galley gave a thumbs-up, but it was not easy to respond when we got his food.

I slept that night under a container, a few feet from the wind-teased water. I lay and watched the filling moon rise over the dark forest. We passed a town, I think Itacararia. The electric lights, picking out the church and the jetty, people walking, even a car, came almost as a shock and, when we regained the moonlit forest, I wondered whether I had been dreaming and fell at once to sleep.

I woke to see low trees, the forest gone. There were thatched huts and birds calling. A big flight of egrets lilted past, under the wispy sky. The *Giselle*'s horn gave emasculated hoots of enquiry. We were passing a settlement where we might have bought fish, but they had none.

The days on the barge lazed into one another. The boys found a way of wheeling me under the containers to the front of the barges, where Carlos' lorry was. Here there was more space and we were screened from the drumming of the engines. I sat in the shade of a container and read or wrote or watched the life of the river.

The colour of the water darkened, but it still reflected the sun, burning me ferociously so that for the second time I, who am usually impervious to the sun, lost all the skin on my forehead. At least I was impervious to the horrors wrought by the cook. For two days Symon lay wretched in his hammock. As soon as he recovered, Marcelo subsided into his.

The confined space of the barge exacerbated the boys' irritation with one another. Symon decided that Marcelo was lazy, but at the same time his resentment at his attempts to help grew. Marcelo merely became melancholy and sought the company of the crew.

Often large patches of grass, half an acre in size, floated by. Carlos told me that he had sometimes seen moving islands, with tall trees and bushes in flower, roaming loose. They were corners of land eroded away by the river, swept like everything else to the ocean.

Dragonflies often landed on my book, exhausted; one had a small, black, perfect square on each of its four transparent wings. But there were curiously few birds. I supposed that, apart from the occasional heron, the majority of the birds stayed safely in the jungle rather than venture over the ever-widening expanse of water.

In the mornings, it was always an excitement to wake to see where we were on the wide river, whether close to the shore where I could see flowers – a yellow creeper or white orchids – or far out, when the banks were just passe-partout lines framing the immense skies. If we were really near, butterflies might falter by – blue and green, yellow and orange, black with white swallow-tails – and the crickets chirruped as loud as a chainsaw. But I saw no cayman and no signs of fish. The captain, with his taste for the grisly, told us that one would not last long in the river. On a recent journey a drunken helmsman fell in. 'We found no bit of him.'

We played turn and turn about with the SS *Astor*. We passed her one day at anchor near the only hill we had seen for a long time. On her deck, I recognised a masterful woman from Yorkshire who, in the opera house, had with long-drawn vowels ordered Marcelo to sit down while her husband took a photograph. I waved and gave a Brazilian thumbs-up, but she looked down with contempt.

The *Astor* passed us a day or two later. She must have stopped at Santarem, of which I did not even see the lights, as I slept on the port side and I hardly liked to wake the boys at one in the morning. She steamed ahead down the mainstream, while we branched off into a peaceful channel no wider than the Ouse at York.

In the afternoons, I struggled to talk in half-invented Portuguese with Carlos. He was an intelligent man with a great breadth of interests. He pointed out a tree, an *apuiseiro* he said. In mime, he explained that it began life as a number of thin lianas straggling, parasitic, down the trunk of a tree. Slowly the strands thicken, as plump as a man's thigh, and entirely encompass the host tree, eventually strangling it. The lianas then join together to become the bark of a new tree, standing shameless in the exact place of its victim.

The only time I did see a fin cut a narrow seam in the water, Carlos said it might have been a *boto*. There were two kinds of *boto*, a smaller greyish one and a larger red one, measuring about six feet. They were like dolphins. The male ones had the ability to turn into men and did so often, coming into the riverside villages and seducing the girls, for they were handsome despite having a hole in the top of their heads. Whenever an unmarried village girl had a baby, it was naturally assumed that a *boto* was the father.

The stories Carlos told were engaging, wavering between fact and fancy. They bored the captain, who preferred lubricious conversations with Marcelo. On the second day, I watched the captain write in the dust on the back of one container with his little finger:

Pica na buceta
Buceta pentelhuda que é gostosa

I could make no sense of it, but hoped it was a poem as I invested it with a certain elegance of rhythm. I recited it to Carlos, asking what it meant. He blushed and looked strangely at me, until I explained where I had learnt the words. It was an obscenity. And whenever the captain talked to Marcelo his vocabulary appeared to me to be very limited – thighs, clitoris, lesbian, gay, penis, girls, boys.

The sunsets of each day surpassed anything I have seen in the deserts or the mountains of any continent. One evening, a row of identical anvil clouds paraded to the north, over distant, higher lands. They were so huge that one would have filled most skies, but there were five – billowing rubescent towers. The sun sank, a great mandarin disc through a thin cirrus haze. The glowing anvils dimmed and as the last colour left them, to the west, towards Peru, golden beams fanned out in perfect symmetry, like an Inca sunburst.

The nights, too, had their beauty. The moon, new at carnival, was now nearly full. As we went to bed, the Great Bear hung upside-down and, by dawn, it stood on end, its pointers empty of purpose, the north star lost below the horizon. Another night was so rough that the containers rocked and fidgeted on their trestles so that we feared they would fall and crush us.

One morning, after a long stretch of untouched forest, we were close to the bank. There were occasional small houses, a horse, half an acre of maize, the same of bananas. A coracle with a trapezoid sail came by, then a boy in a canoe. Soon we came to a settlement and we pulled into the bank and tied up.

Cusari was a village of about three hundred people. The houses were arranged in no comprehensible pattern. Two might be jammed close together, while others were at odd angles, their position bearing no

51

relation to the compass or the river. Between them grew grass, cropped short by cows. The head man's house was set apart and surrounded by a fence, behind which grew fine mango trees. On his house was one of the two television aerials. The houses were well built of wood, on stilts. One was painted a pale, royal blue, with red stripes on the roof.

The children were apprehensive of Symon and myself. Predominantly, their features were Portuguese, although there were many Indian faces. I noticed a good number of boys with fair hair and when I saw the head man, whose hair was almost blond, I wondered whether he had some kind of *droit de seigneur*.

There were no girls to be seen between the ages of fourteen and twenty and few enough of any age. One very black little girl with longish, curling hair stood apart from the others. All the children looked well fed, but their eyes looked uncertain, and so many of the little ones had wizened faces as if childhood and youth, even manhood, had already passed them by.

Symon and I strolled round the village, followed by a pack of mangy dogs. No one took much notice. I looked into the school, where a class sat. The pupils looked more Indian, but Carlos said that this was chance rather than design, the classes being segregated only by age.

There were many pigs and chickens, and two black ducks of so odd a shape that they looked more like decoys than real ducks. Near the bank, a man was cleaning a six-foot *piracacu*. Its hideous mouth gaped like a shell-wound and its plectrum-sized scales fell in a silver shower. It was to buy this monster that we had stopped.

When we got back to the barge, there was a woman of about thirty with her arm round a pregant girl, standing in the crowd of children.

'That girl's a good fuck,' the captain said, in his salacious way, to Marcelo. Then he looked at me and I heard him ask Marcelo:

'Can he fuck?'

'He has had five children,' said Marcelo.

'Yes, but I mean now?' asked the captain.

Marcelo was about to translate the question. When the man saw my face, he stopped him.

Half a dozen of the boys stayed on the barge as we pushed off. They waited as the gap widened and then leapt for the bank. One left it too late and fell in. The current took us away, the villagers and the crew laughing. That day we saw the first gulls, hovering over the barges.

As we came nearer to Belém, we threaded our way through a scatter of islands, some were undisturbed, others inhabited. Life became busier.

Often in a creek we would see wooden houses on stilts and, perhaps, a mission church. In the morning, there would be children in canoes paddling furiously to school. I wondered whether the children at school age got a dug-out, in the way that European children might get a bicycle. They would paddle feverishly towards the barges and loose at us a high-pitched banshee wailing. I never discovered what they wanted.

Sometimes there were bigger houses with larger boats rocking at their jetties. I remember one elaborate blue and white house with a ginger-bread fringe. Nearer still, we passed a large village dependent on a sawmill. There was a church among the workers' houses. It looked so like a child's cardboard model that it made me laugh out loud.

On the last day a storm came suddenly. The wind was so violent that it wrenched off my tightly tied headkerchief. The raindrops beat on the river so hard that it flattened all the ripples. It took, too, all gleam and pattern from the water until it looked like a grey, tufted carpet, stretching endlessly. Inch-deep puddles covered the warm, red metal of the barge's deck, even under the containers. The waves rose high in the mainstream and the *Astor* passed us for the third time. Then we turned once more into narrower ways and, in the calm, the evening sun returned. Women in canoes drifted by, taking their youngest children for an outing, while their older ones trebled their senseless ululation at us.

It proved a pretty night, with the full moon and the upside-down Bear striping the water with their reflections. But we woke to find wide-open space under a grey sky. We might have been in the ocean, were it not for the colour of the water, which now looked merely murky, deprived of its rich, green background.

At length, through the muslin mist, we discerned skyscrapers – Belém. As we came closer, the city grew into a frantic hotchpotch – a graceful, modern building, the Ministry of Finance, neglected old churches and, at the waterfront, stilted shanties, their squalor somehow deepened by their having roofs of charming Roman tiles.

The noise of the city blustered over the water and I felt a reluctance to rejoin the world. I had not been in the jungle or the forest, but somehow had been of it. The immensity, the opulence, the vitality had enthralled me. We had been living in a soothing isolation.

We docked at low tide. Immediately, everyone vanished, scrambling up the structure of the quay. The captain walked away without a word. The *Giselle*, unhitched, chugged away. Only Carlos said goodbye. There was no possibility of my getting up to the quay, so Symon and Marcelo went to ask for the *Giselle* to come back. The company official refused. I could wait for high tide he said. Imprisoned, I longed to get off, the forest quite forgotten.

Inexplicably, a boat did come for me. But the barges could not be unloaded until midnight. The customs would then not release the car until the following day. Belém was like a madhouse. The taxi-driver, swollen with laughter, drove straight at any girls on the narrow pavements, swerving at the last instant, his tyres squirting a salvo of mud all over them. Outside a vet's dispensary, monkeys and anteaters scampered through the complex of tubular cages which covered the whole front of the house. Mould gathered on even the newest buildings and in the dock area, beautiful old warehouses crumbled. Yet there was frenzied activity, markets everywhere; whores in dozens made little dancing gestures as we walked. Belém had the sleazy vigour and the decay of any tropical port and I was glad to leave it.

A few miles out of the town we overtook a container truck. On the back, in the dust, I read: *Pica na buceta* . . .

4

Brazil

A BAROQUE IMMERSION

The coffin shop in Santa Inês, so the girls said, was only open at night, so that it should not cast a blight over the day's happiness. I doubted this, because Brazilian law insists that all burials take place within twenty-four hours of death. This requirement, however, does mean that an undertaker must have a large stock in order to satisfy the breadth of Brazilian taste in sepulchral furniture. The owner did not resent a frivolous visit to his shop; rather he was pleased by my astonishment at the elaborate variety. There were coffins in dark, sombre-grained woods and light, dappled woods. There were lids with tarsia figures of Christ, and sides inlaid with saints. There was a lot of brass and silver. Some caskets were so heavily carved with trees and fruits, even whole scenes in the Garden of Eden, that they must have needed ten pallbearers to lift them.

We had met the girls in a bar and they wanted us to take them dancing. Santa Inês was a town of forty thousand people, but there were several bars with music, much of it varied and unexpected.

It was bewildering to me that the radio, throughout South America, should play fortissimo the same pop music that was being played in Europe. In every café, Madonna trilled of being like a virgin; Chris de

Burgh moaned of dancing with a lady in red. No one could understand the words but that did not matter.

The live music in Brazil, on the other hand, revealed ingenuity and broad skills. The band in the bar slid from reggae, to samba, even to bebop in smooth succession. The Brazilian ability to play bebob, which is both rhythmically and harmonically complicated, is perplexing to musicians. Its intricacies, so Jeremy Lubbock tells me, have confined its playing in the United States to a small group of musicians, the heirs of Charlie Parker, but in Brazil in the remotest places a lone guitarist will master it, apparently without effort.

There was an appealing exuberance about the dancing, but after a while I went to the hotel and slept – the boys creeping back with unlooked-for anatomical information at breakfast time.

*   *   *

São Luís, the capital of Maranhão, sits on an island at the mouth of the River Pindaré. The new town sprawls across the mainland in long-drawn ugliness, but the old city, founded by the French in 1612, is hunched on a steep hill, its narrow streets rising and falling between elegant, colonial houses.

Sleep and decay filled the air with a heavy calm. There were few people about and tropical rain fell in short-lived, weighty showers. The houses were hung with patterned tiles known as *azulejos*, not just as decoration round windows and doorways, but over the whole building, often to the height of three storeys. They were, indeed, mostly blue, but there were reds and yellows, so that four or five houses in a row might lend a faintly glossy, harlequin look to a street.

The centre was formal, with a dull cathedral and an elaborately restored avenue. Along much of one side of the avenue ran the long grey and white Governor's Palace, the Palácio dos Leões. The cast-iron lions, holding shields, that sat on plinths in front of the palace were, I was pleased to see, made by Walter Macfarlane's foundry in Glasgow.

Staircases appeared to be an important consideration in Brazilian public architecture. The Governor's Palace had a silly one, with two flights running side by side. The Forum opposite, which served as a palace of justice, had an overblown affair more suitable, I thought, for a turn-of-the-century spa casino. The Prefectura, once the seat of the local house of assembly, recently damaged by fire, had a pinched attempt at sweeping grandeur.

But it was the back streets and the old quarter where the warehouses stood that drew us. Near the centre, the crumbling buildings were tall and sombre, for nothing looks so woebegone as a tiled façade from which half the tiles have fallen. Many of these were deserted, somehow making it more possible to imagine their original prosperity than if they had been converted to some more modern use.

The mood of nostalgia having taken hold, it was seductive to wander on through poor streets, of low, eighteenth-century houses. From unglazed, ground-floor windows, girls smiled wordless invitations. People stared in puzzlement at my wheelchair, and at one doorway a furious monkey scolded its agitation at me. We passed a small building which was originally the slave market, said to be the only one still standing in Brazil, and a long police building which was a Jesuit monastery until their expulsion in 1767. We came finally to an extraordinary church with a twisted onion dome. An old man standing on the corner suddenly addressed us. 'Byzantine,' he said and walked away.

Strolling at random through the narrow roads, I kept thinking that Lord Cochrane, landing here in 1823, must have seen streets that did not look so different. Cochrane, a distant connection of my family and thus a childhood hero, is one of Britain's most neglected warriors. In the early years of the nineteenth century, as a young captain in the navy he performed astonishing feats of valour, which won him immense popularity and caused Napoleon to dub him *Loup de Mer*. He was a scientist – the inventor of the smoke-screen, a naval lamp, a rotary engine and a form of poison gas (which he kept secret as being too terrible to use) – and an innovator in naval tactics. His weakness lay in an inability to get on with his superiors and, it may be, an equivocal attitude to money.

Cochrane became a Member of Parliament and much antagonised the Admiralty with his exposures of corruption in the navy. A Stock Exchange fraud, in which Cochrane's uncle was a ringleader and from which Cochrane appeared to benefit, gave the Establishment their chance for revenge.

Cochrane was kicked out of the navy, stripped of his knighthood, expelled from Parliament and jailed. The voters of Westminster promptly re-elected him, but it was to be eighteen years before he could clear his name.

When he came out of prison, the Chilean revolutionaries asked him to head their navy in their struggle against the Spanish. He spent the next seven years in South America fighting for the independence of

Chile, Peru and Brazil. In 1823, he was in the service of Emperor Pedro I, trying to drive the Portuguese from Brazil.

Having lured the Portuguese navy out of Salvador in Bahia, Cochrane attacked, capturing about half of their troopships. The other half, he knew, would head for São Luís, one thousand miles north, going at the pace of their slowest vessel.

Out of sight, he overtook them and sailed into the loyalist harbour of São Luís with only one vessel, flying Portuguese colours. The commandant sent a captain in a brig to welcome what he imagined was the vanguard of the Bahian troops who would reinforce his garrison. Cochrane seized the brig and the captain. He offered to release him if he would take a sealed message to the commandant, Dom Agostinho Antonia de Faria.

The message was a part of one of Cochrane's humorous hoaxes. He told the commandant that the Portuguese navy was destroyed, that his own ships, bringing thousands of bloodthirsty, revolutionary troops would soon arrive. He wrote:

> I am anxious not to let loose the Imperial troops of Bahia upon Maranham, exasperated as they are at the injuries and cruelties exercised towards themselves and their countrymen, as well as by the plunder of the people and churches of Bahia.

He painted a picture of wild insurgents, over whom he had slender control, longing to revenge themselves on their Portuguese oppressors. He besought the commandant to accept his magnanimous terms, so as to avoid what would otherwise be hideous slaughter.

Antonia de Faria fell for it. The next day, the local junta headed by the Bishop of São Luís came aboard Cochrane's ship and swore allegiance to Emperor Pedro. Cochrane sent his British and American marines to occupy the forts, hauling down the Portuguese flags and raising the Brazilian.

He knew he did not have much time. There were more captured Portuguese troops in São Luís than he had with him. When the Portuguese navy arrived, they would realise they had been tricked and would rise up.

Presenting the idea as a gesture of compassion and generosity, Cochrane suggested that the prisoners take the merchant vessels that were in the harbour and sail home to Portugal and safety. Grateful for the kindness of such an honourable conqueror, they left.

When the Portuguese fleet arrived, they saw that São Luís was safely in Imperial hands. They sailed onto Belém. Cochrane had already sent ahead Captain Grenfell, aboard the captured brig. Grenfell repeated the same ruse. In Belém, they had heard of the fall of Bahia and São Luís. Like São Luís, they surrendered.

Without the loss of one life, Cochrane had secured the whole of northeastern Brazil for the Emperor, who gave him the title of the Marques de Maranhão, but whose ministers cheated Cochrane and Grenfell of nearly all reward.

* * *

Professor Mário M. Meireles lived in a suburb of São Luís on the mainland. He sat on his little balcony, grinning amiably. He understood English perfectly, but refused to speak it, leaving me to grasp at Portuguese straws.

'Cochrane,' he said, 'had two aspects. First, the great military commander, then the mercenary. Do you know how much he asked for his services?'

'Eight thousand dollars a year,' I said. 'Exactly what he was supposed to have been paid by the Chileans, from whose service he came to you, at your invitation.'

We struggled on in *pesos duros* and other currencies unknown to me. We could not get far. But it was plain that the *liberador* was not loved here. I wondered why, then, there were Brazilian guards of honour at his funeral.

But we shall meet later those who loved him more.

At night, São Luís had the peace of an old-fashioned provincial city. There was none of the menace which trembled in the back streets of Manaus or Belém. I noticed a police post with a sign written thus: *P♡licia Milit♡r*. On the other hand, in the same square, I saw a plaque on the wall recording the death, at that spot, of a journalist of the *Jornal Pequeno*. Violence is never that far to seek in Brazil.

As we walked in the damp night air, we passed a house which I had noticed for its striking façade. It had been shut up during the day. Now it was dimly lit and a familiar sound rattled out of it. I went in. Fifty-year-old linotype machines, made in the United States, were grunting out copies of a newspaper. This was the office and printing works of *Jornal Pequeno*.

There were three men and a particularly beautiful girl working, but they were pleased to have visitors and gave us coffee. The newspaper was founded in the early 1950s by José Ribamar Bogéa, a liberal of considerable courage. The murder of his journalist by a lawyer was but one of a series of incidents. Senhor Ribamar Bogéa was himself beaten up by government thugs, his machines smashed and his type scattered in the street. He persisted. Now he is sixty-five; and his five sons and his niece run the newspaper.

It was strangely exciting to be in this elegant, eighteenth-century house, now dark and grubby, the black and white diamond wall-tiles echoing the clatter of primitive machinery, with this family dedicated to spreading the truth. They were quite matter-of-fact about the paper, not glorifying their role, only assuming an air of respect when they spoke of their father and his unbending resistance to censorship.

That night's edition, which ran to twelve pages, had as its lead the story of a cattle-breeder from Pernambuco, who had given two cows to a young bank clerk, in exchange for a Fiat. The young clerk refused to hand over the documents. The cattle-breeder followed him, drew a gun and shot him dead. The other front-page stories dealt with the inauguration of the new governor, who was due to be installed the next day, a national bank strike, and a protest by forty thousand people about the cancellation of a bingo festival.

Inside there were serious articles about the future of Brazilian socialism, the position of the Church, and a forceful piece in praise of feminism. There was also advice to the new governor. Apart from that, there was some poetry, several cartoons and what appeared to be comic verse in the rhythm of Longfellow's 'Hiawatha'. From what I could make of it, it appeared to be a most sensible paper and we went happily down the street, the rataplan of the linotype machines fighting with Minnehaha in our ears.

* * *

The size of Brazil gradually impressed itself on our understanding. Recife, where I next intended to go, looked such a short distance on the map, yet it was a thousand miles and we had already travelled nearly two thousand since leaving Venezuela. I decided to avoid Fortaleza and to go inland. We drove through cattle lands that later gave way to vast plantations of Babuçu palms, which produced oil. In Piaui, which is said to be the poorest state in Brazil, we came to the capital, Teresina – one of those huge, uninteresting towns with populations of about half a million people that burgeon all over Brazil. There, a casual acquaintance insisted that I should go to Sete Cidade, a national park with what he claimed were the most extraordinary rock formations in all South America, mysterious and possibly magical.

The country was flat, wet and dull. The park itself had low trees and scrub growing in a drab soil. The rock formations were certainly unusual: some rose high like outsize totem-poles, others were rounded mounds like vast turtles, an effect heightened by there being, on many of the rocks, a geometrical pattern reminiscent of a carapace.

Symon and Marcelo climbed high, in order to see the supposed layout of the streets of seven miniature cities, which gave the place its name. The guardian regaled me with the imaginings of the local goatherds who had given names to the rocks – the Indian's head, the camel, the three wise men, the altar, the elephant, the tortoise.

Marcelo gave a wild howl and I thought he had been bitten by one of the abundant rattlesnakes, but it turned out that a malignant insect had pursued and stung him. He went to sit in the car, nursing a rather small red patch on his neck. Symon looked pleased and pushed me off with renewed vigour to look at two natural arches.

The explanation for the sculptural look of the rocks was quite simple. They were formed of very crumbly sandstone, which surrendered easily to the massaging whims of the wind and rain, leaving the resisting, denser stone in whatever shapes it happened to have gathered.

What had lent a measure of mystery to the place were a few indecipherable inscriptions and some primitive drawings. An Austrian, some sixty years ago, speculated that these marks might have been made by Phoenicians. Naturally, this hazy surmise has acquired the quality of positive fact in some guides, although the even wilder postulations of the lunatic von Daniken are more popular with many back-packers. He maintained that they were the work of visitors from outer space.

I looked at the picture of a caterpillar, a butterfly, a pair of hands and what might have been a ladder. The inscriptions struck me as being more like symbols than writing. As for the drawings, I concluded that anyone who could navigate to this unlikely spot from Carthage, let alone from Venus or Pluto, would surely be capable of finer draughtsmanship.

On our inland route over rough, rain-scratched roads, we climbed through the fertile, higher country of the Serra Ibiapaba until we came to a steep escarpment and looked down over a rich, green plain stretching our eyes for an immeasurable distance. Slim waterfalls spilled ribbons of bright water into a river at the bottom of the cliffs. Ipu, the town at a bend in the river, was a comparatively remote place, perhaps five hours by road from any city. The life of the region was agricultural, the main crop rice. And through the streets goats scavenged.

Gauchos rode through the town. They wore coats and hats made of leather, dark with age and the dust of the red soil. The boys of the town wore T-shirts, as often as not with slogans in English – 'High Action', 'I'm disposable'. Madonna trilled at blasting volume. A sign read: *Gaucho lanche* – the equivalent I supposed of ploughman's lunch.

*   *   *

R equals *H*, I had to keep reminding myself when asking the way to Recife. The scant relationship between spelling and pronunciation in Portuguese was a grave impediment to learning the language. There were about six combinations of letters which sounded like a slushy *J*. In the middle of a word *t* became *ch*. The *R* business was the one I found the hardest. The word for hammock was *rede* – pronounced hedgy. Later in the journey, I spent a long time grappling with Rio de Janeiro – known colloquially as Heeo, though it was hard to get it just right and failure to do so elicited only blank stares.

It was pleasant, amid all this, to hear the accents of Ulster over the telephone. Tracy Dunlop came from Belfast. She had worked in a restaurant in Mayfair and then gone to live in Australia. Now, at the age of twenty-four, she and a partner ran a hostel for the wandering youth of the world in Recife.

Recife was large, the fourth biggest city in Brazil, a mixture of an ancient port and a modern resort, with a beach and promenade five miles long, colonnaded with skyscrapers. At half-mile intervals there were combined digital clocks and thermometers, like large parking-meters. The clocks all told different times and, if one were to believe the thermometers, one would have to believe that the temperature went up and down by three or four degrees every few hundred yards. The smarter areas, I decided, must have the cooler clocks.

Tracy, who found a hotel for us near the beach, had an Irish energy. She was small, her fair hair cut spikily short. Her face was shrewd and lively, with excitable eyes that sprang wide and round with interest and humour. In this unlikely place, she maintained a natural practicality coupled with an amused tolerance. She would spend the morning making marmalade or baking bread and the afternoon sorting out the weird problems of her heterodox clientele.

Tracy called her hostel an *albergue*, a word which used to mean a refuge for the poor but has lately, in Recife, come to have this modern meaning.

62

It had seventy-eight beds, but only five bathrooms. It was always full, mostly with people whose way of thought was represented by the Portuguese poster in the entrance, which read: I am a citizen of no country in particular, I am a citizen of the world.

The Youth Hostel Association did not recognise Tracy's establishment, because they regarded it as too liberal. Yet her rules were clear. There were, for instance, two or three good-natured prostitutes who lived in the hostel, but they were certainly not allowed to bring their customers home, nor were they permitted to sleep, even for affection, with any of the other guests.

Augustine lived entirely by night. He was never seen in the day, but would set off every evening at about eleven and return at dawn. Evidently he did business deals, many of them in forged dollars, but Tracy had dictated that none of his transactions, counterfeit or genuine, was to take place in the *albergue*.

There was a red-bearded German, who spent much of the day on the beach, staring at the sun, because he had once been vouchsafed a glimpse of the god who hides behind it. In any case, even if the god did not appear, mermaids came often to talk to him.

A manic-depressive Argentinian painter had lived for three months in the hostel, his rent taking the form of an unnerving mural in the entrance porch.

Euan Mackenzie was an agreeable New Zealander of about twenty-eight, who was a toolmaker, but presumably one of consequence because, in London, he had bought a Rolls Royce Corniche and shipped it home. Alberto, the hostel odd-job man, wanted to go to New Zealand, where he would be Euan's driver, looking after the Holly Hoish, as he called it. Alberto's ambitions seemed unlikely to be fulfilled for some time. Euan was well content in Recife. He spent his time designing a car visor which could also, in an emergency be used as a splint.

Recife was a haven for people who had decided that both Rio de Janeiro and Salvador were too rough for carefree living. At carnival only twenty-five people had been killed in Recife, as opposed to 187 in Rio.

I was struck by how many of the people we met were first- or second-generation Brazilians. While the overall proportion cannot have been so high as it was in Venezuela where, it may be remembered, one in six people were said to have been born outside the country, nearly all the more educated people mentioned that they had a European parent or grandparent.

An Iranian refugee came to our hotel most evenings, offering to change dollars at an advantageous rate. I never learned his own name though he dropped many famous ones into his conversation. He was beset by the perennially banal grievances of all rich exiles. He was broke, he told me, because his wife had taken all his money. Yet it appeared that he still had a motor-cruiser and a Holly Hoish in Monte Carlo.

He disliked England and the United States because they were quite unconcerned by the fall of the Shah; indeed I gathered there was reason to suppose that they had plotted it. The evidence was that Britain now did far more trade with Iran than it ever did before. Of course Rajid, the former Iranian ambassador to London, was partly responsible – 'a charming rogue, who only got his job because of his charm and his connections'. He assumed that I would, of course, have known Rajid.

He was very anxious that we should not sleep with any girls in Brazil. He knew certainly of ten thousand cases of AIDS.

'Was it not typical of the United States,' he asked, 'to have a three-day symposium on Aids on television and, at the end of it, come up with the conclusion that the only safe methods of sex were mutual masturbation if you had no cuts on your fingers; oral sex with a dental gum-shield; a condom; or prayer?'

He went off to celebrate the Persian New Year with his parents and his sister.

Our days passed in explorations of Recife and expeditions with Tracy and Euan. The old part of the town was run down, but lacked the soothing quality of São Luís's decay. Most of the churches were in a poor state, although they were far more interesting than anything we had yet seen. I soon developed an uneasy dislike for the Baroque. The beautiful exteriors of the Portuguese churches lured me in, only to shatter expectation with swirling-gilded vulgarity and ostentation. But it was later, in Salvador, that my aversion grew violent.

Recife had moved southward over the centuries. The oldest part sat on an island and had worn bare in uninteresting decline. In the nineteenth century, the life of the city centred on the peninsula of São Antonio. This area hovered between dilapidation and restoration. The Teatro de Santa Isabel, originally built in 1850, burned down nineteen years later and reopened in 1876, had been restored seven times since then. It could seat nine hundred people and was in many ways more elegant than the theatre in Manaus.

More curious as a piece of restoration was the old prison. It was an odd building, T-shaped; each of the three wings were of the same length with thirty-six, square, cell windows on each side, making 216 cells in all, on three floors. The ends of the wings had rounded corners and three Palladian windows in the middle. The red, Roman-tiled roofs were low-pitched, and over the central block, where the three wings met, was a hexagonal silver dome. From the outside, all painted white, it looked like the superstructure of a stranded liner. Inside, its sombre origins hit hard. Steep, iron stairways led to balconies with wooden floors and cast-iron rails. A thin light rayed down from skylights. Every footstep sounded final.

This peculiar building had been turned into the Pernambucan Casa de Cultura. Many of the cells were boutiques, selling local handicrafts, carpets, ceramics, antiques, clothes. When I thought about the size of the cells, it struck me that they were spacious for one person, perfectly tolerable for two. Were there more than 432 prisoners in nineteenth-century Recife? On reflection, probably there were.

In this century, while the commerce of the city stayed where it was and tall blocks sprouted among the spilling examples of fallen grandeur, a smart new suburb grew up across the river at Bõa Viagem. It was here that the clocks and thermometers flashed their guesses as one drove by.

It was bewildering to me that so much of South America was falling to pieces and yet building at the same time. I kept on thinking about Sir Fred Hoyle's deposed theory of steady-state creation. There had always been something unsatisfactory about it. I had, aesthetically, long preferred the 'big bang' and was much encouraged when it proved to be more true. Civilisations, empires, nations, almost everything starts or should start with a big bang. South America had never had one. I saw it as an agglomeration of false starts.

I found it difficult to get the measure of this contradictory city. At times it seemed so violent. One morning we drove out along the front. We saw the wreck of a car driven against a palm tree, half a mile further on another knitting-ball of metal, and not much later a dead man abandoned on the road, his bloodied head laid on the kerb as if on a pillow.

And at night, on the street corners one would blink to see transvestites, in long evening dresses, who growled as one went past. Then we would go to a restaurant on the beach and laughing strangers would join us and we would drink gaudy drinks and exchange warm pledges. One evening, in a rather grand restaurant with Tracy, we found we had not enough money for the bill. Never mind, they said. Thumbs-up. 'Tudo bem.' And when we went the next day to pay, they were pleased but not surprised.

The violence had a personal quality about it. It was not the mindless violence of European youth. In the scores of new high-rise blocks, there was no vandalism. I have always been suspicious of the sociologists' patter about living in high-rise buildings. It is some other dissatisfaction that leads people to destroy the place where they live and the things which are useful to them.

I was happiest when we were even a little way out of the town; to the hill of Guararapes, for instance – the site of the last battle, in 1654, in the war against the Dutch, who had occupied Pernambuco for thirty years. The victorious General Francisco Barreto had made a vow to build a church if he should win. The result, Nossa Senhora dos Prazeres, was a very peaceful building hung with blue tiles both inside and out. On the day that I went, they were preparing for a wedding. Tables were set in the courtyard garden. The pews were obscured by cartloads of lilies waiting to be arranged. As I sat before the altar, under the barrel roof of the choir, thinking how glad I was that the scramble-carved pillars were not gilded, the sounds of music reached me. The woman selling postcards in the cloister was listening to Dire Straits on her tranny.

Or to Igaraçu, where the oldest church in Brazil, built in 1535, is dedicated to Saints Cosmas and Damian, those two patron saints of doctors, who grafted the leg of a white man on to the body of a cancerous Negro, which makes for such alarming paintings; and the island of Itamaracá, where we were barred from the old Dutch Fort Oranje and ate oysters on the beach.

Or better to Olinda, the old capital, filled with sixteenth-and seventeenth-century churches and where we dined with Conçepcão. She was an economist and a lecturer in the university – not beautiful, but her intelligence and her wit made her seem so. Furthermore, her voice had a honey timbre, which made me envious of the students that she lectured.

She surprised me by saying that social mobility was very great in Brazil, where I had supposed that there were only rich and poor and perhaps the beginnings of a middle class.

'I come from a poor family. You see, we have the poor and *les misérables*. For *les misérables* there is no hope. But the poor like me can fill the vacuum left by the rich who, until very recently, thought it quite beneath them to do anything. So we could come along and fill the gap and become lawyers and follow other professions.

'Brazil is nearly always the opposite of what it appears. We are said to be very conventional, but we are not. But we must say we are. What we say is very important. Usually we say one thing and do the opposite.'

Did she mean like British hypocrisy, I asked, citing the case of one of those British politicians as ever in trouble because caught out in some trivial sexual affair?

'Oh no, getting caught doesn't matter – but you must never say you did whatever it was.'

I told Conçepcão of a Japanese restaurant where I had stopped for lunch not far out of Belém. The waitress had been Japanese, presumably a daughter of the owners. The food was flawlessly Japanese and the girl explained its intricacies to the lorry drivers who made up most of the custom. I greeted her in Japanese and she responded with a hesitant giggle. It soon became plain that she knew even less Japanese than I did, yet her parents were both immigrants. How had they been absorbed so quickly?

'Foreigners become Brazilians very quickly. There is no tradition in Brazil, so you break in very easily, in a way that is impossible in Europe. The same is true to some extent in the United States. There is another thing about young countries which sounds contrary. They lack the liberal confidence of older countries. They do not like enclaves of people who are different, so they compel them to conform to the ways of Brazil.'

The University of Pernambuco sounded lively. A lecturer in mathematical education described to me a study that they were doing as to why boys selling from street stalls can do such rapid mathematical calculations – twelve oranges at one and a half *cruzeiros*, a paw-paw at three and a half, eleven grapefruit . . . A child of the same age in school could never equal their speed and accuracy. It seemed to me that the answer was obvious, but apparently it was not just a matter of incentive and practice. The route by which they arrived at the answer was quite different. What the route was, they had not discovered.

They were studying illiterate carpenters, too, for their ability to assess what quantities of wood they would need to build something and how much it would cost. To talk of the volume of wood and the price per cubic centimetre had, the lecturer said, no meaning for the carpenters. Neither in the case of the boys nor of the carpenters did their method bear any relation to the purely mathematical approach that schoolboys learn. If the academics could penetrate the mysteries of these intuitive calculations, they might revolutionise the teaching of mathematics.

* * *

As we drove south, we looked with new interest at the motels on the outskirts of the city. I had noticed with some puzzlement that, when rating motels, the tourist guide to Brazil used little red hearts as a symbol in lieu of, say, a star. It was the Iranian refugee who enlightened me. Motels in Brazil are what are called love-hotels. They exist, and there are very many of them, simply as places where couples can go to make love – young couples who would otherwise have nowhere to go, or more often married men with their mistresses.

According to the Iranian, they are the one thing that is really well run in Brazil. They are completely anonymous. You drive in through an arch. A hand gives you a key. You drive on and there is a light flashing over a garage door. As soon as you are inside, the garage door closes, so that no one shall recognise your car. Upstairs it may be simple, or it may be very elaborate with jacuzzis, closed-circuit television, vibrating beds, water beds, winter garden, and other refinements, hair-driers being of prime importance – hence the red-heart ratings.

There is a small door in the wall through which another unseeing hand will pass drinks, in prompt response to a telephone call, and the bill at the end of a two-hour sojourn. Up until midnight, the charge is always for two hours, but after midnight you can stay until the morning for the price of four hours.

The service is impeccable. A friend told me later that he once fell off a circular, vibrating bed in mid-romance and broke his leg. The motel manager drove him to hospital and telephoned to my friend's wife with a lot of circumstantial evidence about how he had been knocked down by a hit-and-run driver, in a street with no other witnesses but himself.

Brazilian women, it was said, are weary of *machismo* and now maintain that if their husbands behave like that, there is no reason why they should not do so too. I was told a story of a practical joker who saw his friend's car parked outside a motel (not a grand one if it had no garage). He let the air out of his friend's tyres. When he next saw his friend, he asked some seemingly innocent question about his car. His friend said: 'The oddest thing happened to my wife last week. She went shopping and when she'd finished, she found she had four flat tyres.'

The signs glowed as we drove south: Casanova, Charm, Pomme d'Amour, Eros, Comodoro. Wherever there was an 'O' the signwriters substituted a red heart.

We came upon wide, billowing stretches of sugar-cane, much of it planted where forest had been newly cut, a double affront when sugar is in glut, but there was a reason for it. When oil prices rose, Brazil turned to alcohol distilled from sugar-cane on which to run cars. It was both an

economy and a new use for a traditional profitless crop. Half the cars on
the road now leave behind them a sickly smell, like the breath of an
alcoholic, although they work well. Alas, the economic benefits disappeared when the oil prices fell again, *alcool* costing the same as petrol. It
was ironic to see among the delicate brushes of cane the shapes of
pecking oil-pumps.

The road to Salvador ran through dull states, Alagoas and Sergipe. We
varied the route, sometimes going by the coast on bumpy, unkept roads
through coconut groves, sometimes on the fast main road. There was
little to hold the attention.

We came to Penedo, a nearly unspoilt colonial town on the banks of the
Rio São Francisco. The houses lining the streets were as sugary as
wedding cakes, in powder blues and ochres and dark reds, picked out in
white. Perhaps it was a mark of Brazilian individual pride that no two
houses side by side were ever the same colour. The hotel had once been a
boy's boarding-school, but it looked over the water and I suppressed my
revulsion. There was an uncomfortable feeling to the town, despite its
cobbled streets and shimmering waterfront, made worse by a knowing
eleven-year-old child who crept in from the street to talk to us as we ate
dinner. She had a husky voice, a somewhat lascivious sharpness in her
eye and no good future.

In the morning, we took the ferry across the river. The town and the
boats looked, in the freshness of the early light, like a nineteenth-century
sketch. Two-masted boats with lateen sails stroked their way over the
spreading water. A smaller craft with only one rich saffron sail, the colour
of an Irish kilt, jigged over our wake. A woman with a parasol sat in the
bow, languorous and gazing; a dark man, in a round straw hat, stood in
the stern, steering with a bright blue oar.

Then we were on the road again. After Aracaju there was a lone,
ruined church on the hill. Behind its early eighteenth-century façade,
trees grew in the nave. I found only one gravestone with any legible
words. It said: *José . . . em Paris 1823*. How could they have brought his
body home to this lonely hill, where no village stood? He must have been
born in France. But there was no room below for any date of death. It
gave me something to worry about on the dull journey.

The sugar and the coconuts gave way to huge acreages of orange trees,
as richly laden as in a Gobelin tapestry. Then the land became hillier.
Brahma cattle grazed moodily over great sweeps of blond grass. And as
we neared Salvador, modernity revived, sharpening the contrasts.
Donkey carts carried away the stones heaved up by yellow brutes of

bulldozers; the smoky flames of oil lamps shone dim from the doors of mud huts, built beside great pylons striding to the lost distance.

*   *   *

The contrasts persisted in Salvador. Slums snivelled at the feet of glassy, indifferent skyscrapers. Baroque churches, fussily rich, stood like islands in a sea of squalor. But it was not just the heartless extremes of wealth and poverty; Salvador had a fragmented quality unmatched by any other city in the world. All large cities have districts with separate characters, well defined in the minds of locals and lightly perceptible even to strangers. But as I moved about this town of perhaps one and a half million people, it felt, when I crossed from one section to another, as if I had moved to an entirely new town. It was a sensation engendered, I think, by the Brazilian lack of concern about the past. There is a view that even the present holds little interest; only the future is of any importance. Each district of the city seemed somehow set in the age when it was built and its purpose thrived, although this was neither possible nor true.

The cathedral square and the old administrative buildings from the time when Salvador was the capital, still in municipal use, gave no impression of being the centre of the city. Rather they appeared forgotten areas, which had been rediscovered when their value as tourist attractions was recognised. The restoration that was going on was inspired not so much by love of the past, as by the prospect of future gain.

This old quarter was an enchantment. The Brazilian delight in colour made dusky rainbows of the streets, each house different – ochre, green, terracotta, blue, brown, yellow, red, all smudged by the grey film of damp. Decoration bubbled on almost every building – swags, garlands, shells, rosettes, stars, putti, caryatids, eagles. The fanlights over doorways were as various and elaborate as those of Dublin.

Guidebooks warned us against walking in these streets, though I did not see how else we were to get from one to another of the churches or monuments that they pressed us to visit. The people stared. Curiously few children begged. And nothing untoward ever happened.

The churches of Salvador were a lecture in the development of architecture in Brazil. The cathedral, built by the Jesuits in 1672, was a perfect example of the plain style of building which they favoured, and which lasted until the middle of the eighteenth century. The stone façade was agreeably severe – two main storeys decorated with Doric pilasters and topped by an attic storey with a pedimented gable. The interior was calm with blue and yellow tiles.

Later, the interiors of so many quite austere-looking churches were covered with the totally incompatible elaborations of the gilded barley sugar of Baroque. At the same time, the exteriors of the new churches burst overripe, with whirligig façade, capped by great whisk-whipped volutes, all confined between plain square towers that looked as if they were policemen arresting a flamboyant drunk.

The most extreme example of over-luxuriant decoration was the church of São Francisco, almost the whole interior of which was gilded. I found it somehow repulsive, doubly so when, in an act of gratuitous unpleasantness, the chapel reserved for slaves was left undecorated. Nonetheless, I could not but admire the skill of the actual carving, the acanthus leaves so cleanly cut, the expressions on the cherubs' faces so distinct (though I enjoyed a fancy that the cherubs' smiles may have been due to the fact that, in the refurbishing that was going on, their genitalia, cut off in some prudish age, were being restored to them). I liked, too, the mermaids supporting the lecterns and the jacaranda screens, with carved, pregnant women. Below them were strange grotesques. Above, a phoenix with fruit in its mouth, for all the world like a hoatzin. The fonts of Brescia marble bound with a mortar of sand and whale oil were beautiful.

But I was glad to escape from the Golcondan oppression to the placid cloister, surrounded by tile landscapes of the seasons and months and of hunting and fishing, mingled with biblical scenes, where the only disturbance was the bickering of two parrots in a cage.

When I went to look again at the statue of São Pedro of Alcántara carrying a cross, which had appealed to me for its fluid, if too tragic, style, I found a service in progress. The scene was like something from a nonconformist tract. The glowing temple of gold was filled with a congregation of raggedly dressed people. Half of them were listening to a sermon with obedient attention. The other half chattered in gossipy groups. A lounging priest in one confessional paid only automatic heed to the penance of a distressed and elderly man. A kneeling nun revealed her probably all-too-innocent doubts to a monk, who affected an expression of bored severity. Outside, an electioneering loudspeaker blasted its empty promises through the main doors of the church, as if in answer to the promises of the sermon.

We walked on and I was saddened by the church of Nossa Senhora do Rosário dos Pretos. This was built by slaves for their own use. There was a pathos about the attempts to imitate, without gold, the lushness of Baroque, emphasised by the results being, for my taste, often more beautiful – the soft patterns of colour far surpassing the gilt.

71

Further, at the end of a steep, cobbled hill was the Carmelite monastery, set in a square. There were only two monks left, one aged eighty, the other eighty-two. These two holy brothers have a lively sense of business. One half of the monastery they have let as a hotel. In their remaining half, they conduct a jewellery business. We lunched in the hotel, where there is now a swimming pool in the old cloister. I noticed that the pewter plates and the coffee-pots were stamped with the Vatican key. As we ate in this once contemplative building, we were deafened by the strains of Lionel Richie, blasting over the loudspeaker system.

Religion was more vividly alive in a completely different area of the city. The white church of Nosso Senhor Jesus do Bomfim, built in 1745, was influenced by a measure of syncretism with *candomblé*, the Bahian religion of African origin. White is the colour of Oxalá, Our Lord of the Good End. The Corinthian altar, piled up white and gold, was far less oppressive than those in the grand churches of the centre.

The large figure of Christ on the cross was thought to be endowed with special powers of protection from disaster. Outside the church, men sold bright-red threads.

'The priest will bless them for you,' the young man said. 'You tie three knots in it and tie it round your wrist. Then you cannot have an accident.'

I told him I was not superstitious.

'Well look inside and see what can happen to you,' he said. His face flickered with a mixture of anger and of pleasurable hope that fate would attend to my meanness.

Inside was a chapel filled with votive offerings – plastic arms, legs, babies' heads, even stomachs hung from the ceiling. Paintings of houses on fire, of cars hurrying over cliffs, of boats subsiding under Hiroshige waves and gloomy photographs of crushed vehicles, children in bed, fallen buildings, covered the walls. In among them, there were photographs of cheerful faces, pinned to solemn attestations that the subjects had been cured of fevers, agues, dropsies, distempers, murrains and all manner of other afflictions.

The bakers were on strike and, more aggravatingly, the banks. We strolled in the lower city, which was devoted to commerce and to the port and naval base. I tried to find papers about Cochrane's blockade of Salvador, but the bored naval authorities said that all records were kept in Rio de Janeiro. (Later, in Rio the weary officials said that anything to do with Salvador was kept in Salvador.)

I had no money. Near the naval headquarters, some youths offered to

72

change dollars or traveller's cheques. They offered a rate well calculated to arouse my greed. By a neat piece of prestidigitation, coupled with the minimum of force, restraining Symon from pursuing the one who had the cheques, they made off with three hundred dollars. I learned then that the gesture for 'I have been robbed' is to put your right thumb at right angles to your left palm and to make a doleful flapping and scooping with the fingers of your right hand.

Our hotel lay in a quiet district from which one could walk half a mile down a sloping street to the ocean. On the right, was a long, white wall which I, at first, imagined hid the private gardens of a rich house. One morning, I crossed over to the rusty entrance gate and found that a cemetery lay behind. The gate was unlocked. The first inscription on the other side of the wall read:

> Sacred to the memory of the English gentlemen, who died of yellow fever during the construction of the Bahia and São Francisco railway and who are buried at Montserrat 1858–60.

It was the Anglican cemetery, a neglected tangle of quiet, hanging above the sea, a forlorn witness to the former extensive commercial involvement with Britain. The soil was rich and red. Creepers writhed through iron Celtic crosses, the roots of acacias humped up great slabs of carved stones, a palm tree burst from a sarcophagus. Flat, black burrs gathered on our clothes as we passed between the close-packed lines of graves. A bird sat on a hand of bananas; its long tail cocked up every time it gave a scratching cry. It was, I thought, a fine place to be buried, looking out over the sea.

The memorials spoke of a grim, capricious fate a hundred years and more ago. There were so many perils. The Wilcox family lost innumerable members. 'My brother Macdonald' died of tetanus, aged 22. S. J. Reynolds Esq., a civil engineer, was the 'victim of a sun stroke. 23rd March 1867'. Nor was grandeur any protection. Capt. John Candlish, 'the Mogul of Liverpool', died 22nd March 1855. Dr Patterson, physician to the British community in the 1880s, was unable to save himself, but he merited a large stone portrait of his head for his tomb.

Oddly, in this Anglican haven, there was a section lower down the hill for Jews. They came from divers places. On one slab was written in French, 'Içi reposent nos regrettés père et mère Raphael Schwab né 19 Juin 1868–1926 et Regina Schwab'. 'F. Cheira Fainstein – nasceu em Moselov Padolsck . . .', the rest was in Hebrew. 'Miriam Aizin born Lugansk, Russia'.

The Jewish section was at one time much larger, but many of the graves were torn away in order to make a road along the shore to the new yacht club. In the middle of what remained, a fine red macaw sat in a cage. I was tempted to let it out.

It is a question how long the graveyard will survive. The English church and its library have gone. They stood in an area irresistible for development – and no one seemed any too clear what became of the money.

There was a small house in the cemetery. The inhabitants were friendly, but vague about the circumstances of their being there. They did nothing towards the upkeep of the place. It later turned out that they were squatters who, by the vagaries of Brazilian law, might be able to claim the whole place as their property.

A philanthropic Briton, Patrick Hannigan, had offered to pay for making the house into a museum and for a gardener to tend to the graves. The offer was refused.

The new Anglican church is a small affair in a distant suburb. The Irish clergyman was on holiday. He was said to be going to retire and to hand over his cure of the souls of the parish of Salvador, to a Brazilian with a spirited sense of commerce. He would doubtless sell all.

I went to Ribeira to look out over the Baía de Todos os Santos, in the hope of working out where the Portuguese fleet were anchored when Cochrane performed one of his feats of humorous daring.

Ribeira was a poor district at the end of a promontory. There were cheap eating-houses where one could sit outside at a cluster of tables, in the middle of a divided road running beside the sea. It was a melancholy place but, despite the poverty, not rough or alarming. At the next table to ours, a group of young men had a cheerful lunch. Some girls sunbathed on the wall by the narrow beach.

A small, emaciated boy, his head on his arms, sat at a table sleeping so deeply as to be almost unconscious. The waiter shook him awake and gave him a plate of scraps. Another boy, who looked better fed, passed by selling peanuts. With grave courtesy, he asked if he might finish the meat on Symon's plate, too tough even for him. The boy took the plate and ate at another table.

A sprightly lunatic came and sat facing me at another nearby table and started to talk to an imaginary interlocutor. He behaved exactly as if it were a conversation, with pauses for his friend to reply – smiles, laughter, frowns, confidential tones. His voice was soft and appealing, but the words made no sense. The timing of his humour, I felt, would have been excellent had the content been sane.

The journey to Ribeira left me a little confused about Cochrane's Bahian exploit. All accounts, including his own, describe his keeping the Portuguese fleet blockaded nine miles from the open sea, up a river. He wanted to lure them out. The basin where the fleet lay could be reached only by a channel which was hard to navigate in daylight.

On a night when he knew that all the Portuguese officers would be at a ball in Salvador, Cochrane sailed up this tricky channel and appeared, a ghostly threat, amongst the moored ships. Consternation in the Portuguese ranks. Consternation, too, for Cochrane. Having achieved his effect, he wanted to sail out again. The wind dropped. He was becalmed. He escaped, by drifting astern on the river current and the ebb tide, steering by dragging the sheet-anchor first on one side of his ship, then on the other. The ruse worked. The Portuguese were so unnerved by Cochrane's seamanship that they decided to make a break, rather than risk being all destroyed at anchor. Cochrane had put it about that he was soon to loose fireships among the fleet. As they left the safety of the harbour, he managed to destroy half their vessels.

Looking across to the island of Itaparica, the entrance to the bay was plainly wide enough for any boat to sail through without difficulty. There were only two rivers of any size flowing into the bay. The mouth of the Paraguaçu was at least twenty miles away on the far side of the bay from Salvador. The Traripe was even further. The place that best fitted the descriptions was Aratu, the present naval base, though my map showed no river there. But Aratu would be quite impossible for anyone to sail to for the first time in the dark. Then again, my hero was the master of the impossible.

A few days later, I crossed to Itaparica on the ferry to go to stay with Patrick Hannigan and his wife Astrid. Patrick was a large, balding man of almost calculated gentleness. He had a British north-country practicality, tinged with Celtic whimsy and a dry humour. His family was Irish, but he was born and brought up in Manchester. Astrid was German, from Hanover, a sympathetic woman of great independence and a marked honesty. She had once taken off to Germany for a spell with her children, without any visible means of support, just in order to prove she could do it.

Patrick had spent many years in some chemical business to do with paint. When travelling in the south of Brazil, they fell in with a dermatologist, whose patients had asked him to devise a make-up foundation to which they were not allergic. When that proved to be a success, they asked for a soap, then for an eau de Cologne. The dermatologist opened a shop in Curitiba called O Boticario. The Hannigans asked for a concession for Salvador and then for the whole north-east of Brazil. They now have seven shops in Salvador and four in Recife. In all there are a thousand shops selling 160 different beauty products. Patrick was hoping to spread to France and to London.

They lived in a flat in Salvador, but had built a simple cottage by the water on Itaparica, looking back towards the city. A forty-minute ferry journey removed us from the kaleidoscope of modernity, superstition, tourism, brutality, swimming pools and slums that compose Salvador, to an island where the excitement at hauling the fishing nets up the beach was as simple as it might be in New Guinea.

It was a strange sensation, not just the difference between rural and urban which one could find in any country, but a feeling that the centres of power belonged to a wholly removed culture.

The first thing that Patrick said to me was that Brazil was quite different from all the Spanish-speaking countries of South America – and so it was. But it was in this intangible dichotomy of cultures, that had nothing immediate to do with black and white, or Indian and European, or riches and poverty, that I felt lay the puzzle of all of South America. The question of why the promise of dawn is never fulfilled, that full morning never comes. It was as if an incubus, in the old nightmare sense, had settled on the soul of the continent.

There was a stimulation about Patrick and Astrid in that they gave one so many things to think about, but of our discussions it is oddly those about the war and war crimes that stick in my memory.

We passed a row of cottages, the tenants of which still pay rent to a man of English descent. His family once had a whaling station on Itaparica. During the war, he sold whale oil to the Germans. He was boycotted by the British community and booted out of the British Club. Only now is he gradually coming accepted again.

Astrid spoke freely of her father's being a Nazi, the first German I have met who did not prevaricate about what must have been true of so many.

'Later he became a socialist,' she said, 'not regretting his past beliefs, but realising that they were wrong. He came to Brazil to visit us, and was horrified to go to a German gathering in São Paulo and to find them still singing the *Horst Wessel* song.'

I lay in bed, listening to the waves on the beach, and wondered what I would do if we were to meet a war criminal. We had talked of Mengele. The Hannigans had heard stories of his living in a remote village, caring for people's health. I had introductions to dubious Germans in Paraguay. A desire for revenge, no matter how great the crime, I decided, was a repulsive emotion, and I went to sleep.

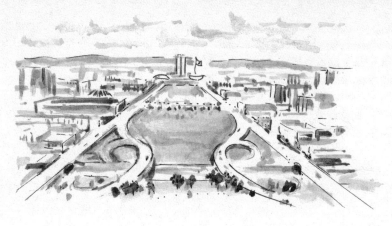

5

Brazil

THE PEOPLE VERSUS THE PLANNERS

Waiting for Symon in Brasília was a large parcel from his mother, sent in the diplomatic bag. It contained an imagination-daunting number of what the South Americans engagingly call *camisas de Venus*. She had heard that the spread of AIDS was alarming in Brazil.

Brasília, at first sight, was not conducive to thoughts of love or sin. The city lies in a hollow with a plain stretching beyond so that, coming as we did from the north-east, the original plan of it is easy to see from the high land. It looks, as it was meant to look, like the outline of an aeroplane, although, as the wings curve back, it is possible to imagine it as a bow and arrow, which could be thought to have an equal relevance.

The original ground-plan of the city was devised by Professor Lúcio Costa. He had not wanted to go in for the competition by which the designer was to be chosen, for he had just lost his wife in a car accident and had himself been injured. His daughter, however, had said to him, 'What would you have drawn had you wanted to enter?' Costa made a rough sketch for her amusement. She sent this off. Most of the entrants had submitted volumes of material to the panel of judges. They chose Costa's simple sketch.

The pattern is plain from the view we had as we arrived or the view from the television tower, but otherwise it is impossible to entertain the idea that this is a cohesive city. It is both too big and too empty. It is something like a thrifty firework display in a large park, in which set pieces are let off at tedious intervals in different places. In between there are a few scattered squibs and children wave sparklers, but it is not a proper show.

The idea of moving the capital from the coast to the interior was mooted long before Brazil won independence. The first suggestion was made by a cartographer in 1750, thirteen years before the seat of government moved from Salvador to Rio de Janeiro. In 1809, a British ambassador to the Portuguese court recommended another move to a more central place. The idea mouldered on. By the end of the nineteenth century it had been written into the first constitution. Under article three, the Union acquired 14,400 square kilometres (5,600 square miles) in the state of Goias for the future federal capital.

A cornerstone was laid in 1922, some thirty miles away from where the capital was eventually built. After a couple of new constitutions, the final site was approved in 1955 and the capital actually moved in 1960.

Being Brazil, there was of course an element of superstition in the story. In 1882, Giovanni Bosco, the founder of the Salesian Order, who was to be canonised in 1934, had one of the visionary dreams for which he was famous. Guidebooks to Brasilia claim to quote from the nineteen volumes of the Saint's *Memorie Biographiche* the prophecy he made as a result of the dream thus:

> Between the fifteenth and twentieth parallels there is a depression . . . where there is a lake . . . here will spring up the Promised Land, flowing with milk and honey . . . There will be inconceivable richness.

This translation leaves out the rather important words: 'When the minerals hidden in these mountains are excavated this place will be revealed as the Promised Land . . .'

Dom Bosco's dream was in many ways curiously prophetic, but it is plain when one reads the whole thing that he was talking of somewhere quite different. Most of the dream is an account of a long train journey, taken with the dead son of one of his benefactors. It starts in Cartagena, in Colombia and goes right down to Patagonia before returning north through Brazil. The relevant passage occurs just before they arrive at La Paz in Bolivia on their way south. It seems to me that Lake Titicaca, which is at roughly the same latitude as Brasilia, would fit the somnambulant description far better. Though, of course, the saint did say rather airily that the train went *qua e là*.

Whatever the case, it was certainly not religious thoughts that primarily moved those regarded as the fathers of Brasilia. The President responsible, Juscelino Kubitschek, was a socialist. Oscar Niemeyer, the architect of most of the major buildings, was a communist. Lúcio Costa was of milder opinion, but the principles which informed the construction of the city were in many ways those of an interfering state, if not positively dictatorial.

About nine miles to the south of Brasília is a curious wooden building known as Catetinho. It was here, in admirable austerity, that the President and the founders of Brasília stayed when they came to watch the progress of the new city which had to be built in three years – that is, within Kubitschek's term of office, otherwise it might never have been finished.

The building is now a museum. As I went from one poky room to another, there did seem to linger an atmosphere of energy, enthusiasm and dedication. Beyond the windows there was an empty wilderness, which must have given them an intense feeling of the carving of a new symbol of nationhood. For, until they came, there was only a rolling land of sparse forest.

The rooms were labelled with the names of those who had used them. Nearly all were now dead with the important exception of Oscar Niemeyer, who is still consulted about any changes to the original plans. One other was still living in Brasília – Doctor Ernesto Silva, a paediatrician whose role had been to watch over the sociological aspects of so vast a new community. We met by arrangement.

He was small and thin, his clothes flapping a little as he hurried with unexpected lightness of step. His face was pointed and alive like a conductor's baton, darting up and down as the rhythms of his speech quickened or slowed. He was sympathetically courteous and smiling, but his eyes were dimmed, I soon recognised, with disappointment.

'The concept has not been fulfilled, there is so much that has not been done.'

The doctor explained how the residential areas had been planned, in blocks known as *quadras*.

'Four *quadras* made up a *superquadra*. A *superquadra* was supposed to house a maximum of three thousand people. Four *superquadras* of twelve thousand people, the population of a small town, were meant to be, as it were, self-sufficient.

'For each two *superquadras* there was to be a primary and secondary school, a clinic, a church and some shops. For every four *superquadras* there was to be a cinema and a supermarket and a club.'

Dr Silva glowed with enthusiasm, his eyes brightening at the recollection of what had been planned and at how splendid he thought it would
have been. Then the light went again.

'So many of these are still not built. Then some people are rich enough
to send their children to private schools. And they join clubs miles away
from their *quadras*.'

There was much to distress this kindly man who had so fervently
hoped that the founders' ideas would work. He really believed that they
would have, if only the plans had been properly executed.

'The city was never meant to be big. It was to be just a capital. But
people flooded in from the north-east and the city grew. The people
squatted and dormitory towns grew up. People call them satellite towns,
but they are not, because they have no independent life. The people come
to Brasília to work. To do so they have to get up at five and don't go home
until eight.'

It was almost painful to watch Dr Silva's heart aching for the people. I
had seen the buses, perhaps four or five hundred identical coaches
waiting to take the workers home in the evening.

'I still fight,' said the doctor. 'I write letters, I protest. It was my dream
and it was not fulfilled.'

It was worse, I believed, than Dr Silva thought. The city had a sterile
feeling to it. This was partly a question of scale, for urban liveliness
depends to a certain extent on huddle. Without it we feel lonely. Nothing
in Brasília was close, except more of whatever it was. The hotels were all
in one sector, several dozen hotels side by side and none elsewhere. The
banks were in another sector, the garages in a third, the embassies in a
fourth. There were north and south commercial sectors and even a
hospital sector. There was no question of walking from the performance
of one errand to another. Dr Silva admitted that this had possibly been a
mistake. But he did not see that the mistake was merely part of the larger
misconception, that of thinking that people are willing to be told how they
should live.

Almost none of the original ideas had succeeded. The friends I visited
in one of the apparently identical blocks of apartments had an extremely
comfortable flat, but it was far removed from the first notions. At the
outset, the planners wanted each block to have a communal kitchen.
Such nonsense was soon forgotten. I noticed that even the communal
garbage chute had been sealed up. In fact, the blocks of apartments were
not identical. The size of the flats varied and some might have had

verandahs while others had an extra bathroom or whatever, but I felt that even the external sameness was depressing.

The private houses in the lakeside developments, which were never part of the original plan, paid no obedience to the founding spirit. For the most part they looked like villas in Marbella, seeking refuge in the cowardice of imitation. Hardly any private individuals have had the courage of their age.

Poor Dr Silva, his eyes losing their last glimmer, said: 'We wanted a modern town not a new town.'

In Catetinho, I had noticed that the founders were fascinated by traffic. Ceramic plaques of the patterns of clover-leaf junctions and elaborate roundabouts, looking like diagrams of nautical knots, hung on the wall. The idea was to have no traffic-lights. In a sense it worked; in no city does the traffic flow more freely. But these exotic, running bowlines of motor roads took no account of pedestrians. No one could cross the roads, so traffic-lights now blink.

Even with a population of nearly two million, the city felt empty. On the long central main road, there were a few joggers and an occasional walker, but not many. Everywhere there was a lack of children. It has been a battle between the people and the planners, who wanted to tell them how to live.

Yet the planners, too, have been betrayed. Their hopes for the people were higher than the people's taste. The national theatre has three auditoriums contained in a building shaped like an Aztec pyramid. When I asked what was on, a bored girl gave me a pencilled list of productions so uninspiring that I abandoned any idea of going to a performance. There was much talk also of the buildings crumbling and the roofs leaking. Brasilia was built in such haste that it is not to be wondered at that it was not built well. But in Brazil, perhaps, the only hope of building it at all was to rush in while the pioneer enthusiasm still burned.

There was a pleasure to be had from the set pieces of architecture, although the question of scale made all Niemeyer's buildings look like models rather than reality. The huge distances of the overall plan dwarfed the structures which were mostly not very big in the first instance.

The eleven ministries beside the road leading to the main square were only ten storeys high, so they had the appearance of dominoes on a table. The Praça of the Three Powers – presidential, congress and senate, and supreme court – was for my taste the most successful part of Brasília, the three palaces sharing a lightness of touch that John dos Passos called Niemeyer's 'paper cut-out style'.

The cathedral, apart from Niemeyer's curious penchant for underground entrances, was impressive, despite the cracked floor and the appalling seats and a ghastly shop to one side of the circular interior. The architect had wanted marble blocks for seating, but these were thought to be too hard.

Fourteen boomerangs of concrete reached up, representing according to some accounts a crown and to others the fingers of hands raised in prayer. From inside, the church was alive with movement; carved angels floated overhead on invisible wires, swaying gently; rippling water outside reflected patterns of bright light onto the clear glass between the high piers; above, beyond the glass, small white clouds fluffed their way across the blue of the high sky. It is an impression which will soon be lost. The cathedral becomes too hot in summer. Dark blue glass is to replace the uncoloured panes upon which these effects depend.*

Outside the army headquarters, a long building like a xylophone on its side, soldiers in grey-green uniforms, with brilliant white helmets and belts, stood guard. Somehow in front of the concrete their faces disappeared. They looked automatic and powerful.

In front of the headquarters was a plinth from which to review parades. Sheltering it was a bow of concrete, shaped like the protector to the hilt of a sword. Under this we played echoes – whispers carrying a hundred feet and louder sounds throbbing back and forth. Then the four soldiers mounted the plinth for a formal changing of the guard with four new arrivals. They performed a comic, dancing manoeuvre and the parting sergeant exchanged his loaded machine-gun clip with the replacement. When this was done, they shed their stiff expressions and joined in our games.

One building was wholly satisfying, both inside and out. The church of Dom Bosco was a cube. The great bronze doors were cast with scenes from Dom Bosco's dream, which evidently included a funambulist. Each wall consisted of twenty high, narrow, gothic windows, nineteen with small irregular panes of blue glass and one with pink. The ceiling had the quality of a geometric puzzle. From it hung an immense chandelier, the only form of artificial light. This simple building had a feeling of peace

*Since writing the above, I have been told that Oscar Neimeyer has designed large patterns of dark and light blue glass, which he hopes will be enough to keep out the heat without ruining the appearance of the building. The effect I liked will nonetheless be lost.

that I certainly did not find in the cathedral. It was designed by a student, who gave his drawings free because nobody wanted to build his church.

On our last morning in Brasília, we drove once more down the long, main road which stretched for more than five miles – past the domino buildings, past the glorious Foreign Office, past the Palace of Justice, spilling water from the giant, gutter-shaped fountains, between its tall, Roman arches, past a building on which the shutters and the sun-blinds made a changeable and satisfying pattern.

I looked back with an unexpected affection, admiring the effort and the inspiration, remembering the dedication of Ernesto Silva. My last glimpse was of the gigantic flag rippling above the city, so big that its titanic flapping on its towering mast means that it has to be renewed each month. It prompted me to think that if the founders had failed in their planning they had achieved one thing. They had made Brazil into one nation.

*　　*　　*

Marcelo flew home to Caracas from Brasilia. He and Symon had come to irritate one another beyond endurance. Symon, spurred by an unconscious jealousy, complained that Marcelo was indolent, not doing his share of the loading and unloading. Marcelo felt that Symon treated him with disdain and did less than ever.

Marcelo's nature was one of great sweetness, yet it was coupled with an indifferent coarseness. He could never understand why Symon and I minded his hawking and spitting and the terrible noises he made in the morning. He barely apologised when one night he got drunk and was sick in the room we all shared. His attitude to girls was the zenith of chauvinism. They were to be used. At the same time, he was kind and affectionate, and the contrary side of his nature never extended to cruelty or violence. Indeed the separation was achieved with infinite tact on Marcelo's part. When it became obvious that they could tolerate each other no longer, Marcelo said that he was afraid of travelling to Chile. As he was Chilean, he was in danger of being called up for military service and no one could wish to serve in Pinochet's army. There was something almost symbolic of South America about Marcelo's dual nature.

As we zigzagged on alone, through the vast spaces of Brazil, the impressions piled up like strata, striped with contradiction, yet forming a compacted whole. We moved in and out of modernity and history, of wealth and poverty, of wilderness and cultivation.

On the way to Belo Horizonte, we drove through eucalyptus forests, where charcoal-burners heaped up mounds of fuel. Lurching lorries carried rhomboid loads, far wider at the top than at the bottom, of this charcoal. Often it was still smoking, once even ablaze. In one, more open, place we saw three gauchos, solemn and silent, two riding and one driving an ox-cart laden with a wicker coffin. Three brothers, I surmised, burying their father.

We went through Paracatú where, behind a hill, a new gold mine was digging. Will Scarlet, of Rio Tinto Zinc, had told me that it will yield six and a half tons of gold a year. Brazil is already the fifth-largest producer of gold in the world and will soon produce one hundred tons each year. Probably it already does so, but much is smuggled out by wildcat miners. To earn foreign currency the government now buys from them at an inflated rate, perhaps twenty-five per cent more than the official dollar rate. Bauxite mines (two million tons of aluminium a year by the end of the century), copper mines, silver mines, diamond mines, mines of emeralds and mines of topaz – the mineral wealth of Brazil is prodigious. But, so far, no zinc for Will Scarlet.

Belo Horizonte was, like Brasília, created out of nothing, in 1897. It was slow to develop, but in the last thirty years has grown to be the third-largest city in Brazil and in many ways is a pleasant place to live, but there was little to detain us.

We wandered instead through the old colonial towns of the eighteenth-century gold rush. Ouro Preto was the most perfectly preserved colonial town we had seen. Its Baroque was theatrical, yet not so vulgar as that of Salvador, and I found the spirit of the churches far more sympathetic. But the town was too geared for tourism. The cobbled streets, lined with rich-hued houses, were too clean. Boys pestered us. In the glittering church of São Francisco, there were sixty-one locked boxes for visitors to leave their cameras.

Mariana was less polished, but again with not one façade spoilt by a modern front. We stayed in a convent, where at breakfast the white-robed Mother Superior gave us the thumbs-up. 'Tudo bem,' she said, her red-scrubbed face assuming the best.

As we strolled round the town, a little boy of thirteen attached himself to me. He was black and his arms and legs were covered with weeping sores. He asked me what I thought of the town. When I said it was extremely pretty, he thanked me with a formal courtesy. He was a descendant in many senses, I supposed, of those slaves who were flogged at the whipping-post in front of the elegant prison – it looked more like a grand mansion than a place of punishment. A white boy on a bicycle tried to tell me that the black boy was a thief. In fact António was scrupulously honest, overseeing a couple of minor transactions with the vigilance of a tax-collector. When, having visited seven churches, I hesitated as to whether to bother with the museum in the old archiepiscopal palace, he became quite insistent. I was grateful as I gaped at the gold and the silver, and the dinner service brought from Goa by the new bishop in 1798.

I went to vespers in the cathedral, its walls bulging not as I liked to fancy with the throng, but with groggy age. The service in Portuguese was moving, having a slurred Latin ring to it. The music had echoes of Arab Africa and *fado*, with the same dying cadence as the sambas of the carnival. The choir and orchestra sat in a gallery above the west door. Unfortunately no one played the enormous, German, Baroque organ, decorated with angels of flourish, and red-lacquer, chinoiserie panels.

Finding back ways between these towns took us through lost country where engines had not yet superseded horses. If we paused for a minute to look at a flowering tree, we would be sure to see a pair of monkeys, a tumble of blue and black butterflies or some parrots. Among the flowing hills, there were the scars of ancient mines, for wherever the soil was touched erosion kept it bare, and the rivers ran red with ferrous silt.

At Congonhas there was the finest work of the sculptor Antonio Francisco Lisboa, known as Aleijadinho. We had seen his carvings and his church façades at Ouro Preto and at Mariana. He was born in the 1730s, the son of an architect, Manoel Francisco Lisboa, who had designed, for instance, the churches of Santa Efigénia and do Carmo in Ouro Preto and installed the organ in the cathedral at Mariana. Aleijadinho's mother was his father's black slave. The twelve soapstone statues of prophets, set symmetrically on the stairway in front of the church of Bom Jesus do Matozinho, were so vigorous and wild of gesture and so ingeniously placed that, far from looking orderly, they appeared to be haphazard and almost on the move.

The passionate determination of this man, whose nickname means little cripple, was impressive and unsettling. Soon after the sculptor's death a lawyer, Rodrigo Ferreira Bretas, gathered material for a biography. The scant notes that he made are the principal source of information about Aleijadinho. According to Bretas he was 'dark brown, had a strong voice, was hasty and irritable, of small stature, fat and misshapen . . . with thick lips and hardly any neck.'

Later in life he fell ill with what we may suppose was a form of leprosy. Bretas wrote: 'He lost all his toes so that he could no longer walk, except on his knees; his fingers atrophied and twisted and eventually fell off, there remained only his thumbs and index fingers, even these almost without movement.'

Aleijadinho had a slave of his own. Mauricio used to tie mallet and chisel to his master's wrists. Finally his affliction became so severe that he could only work lying down. He lived to be over seventy-five, dying in 1814 and leaving, despite all afflictions, a vast collection of some of the world's most beautiful sculpture.

The last of these colonial towns that we visited was Tiradentes, called after a young revolutionary, one of the plotters of a movement in 1788 which came to be called the *Inconfidência Mineira*. It never amounted to much, although many of the conspirators were distinguished people – poets, magistrates and other government officials. They were betrayed and mostly treated with some leniency. One magistrate hanged himself. The poet Tomaz Antonio Gonzaga, famous for one of the finest Portuguese love poems, addressed to Marília, was exiled to Mozambique. He soon forgot the sixteen-year-old original of his impassioned verses and married another girl. Marília, whose real name was Maria Dorotéia de Seixas, never married. Sir Richard Burton, on his travels through South America, reported that she had a child. In fact, the unfortunate girl was forced to adopt her younger sister's illegitimate baby.

Lieutenant Joaquim José da Silva Xavier, known as Tiradentes because of his skill in pulling out teeth, was prouder than his fellow conspirators. To the end, he refused to disavow his part, and his belief, in the plot. Those who did had their death sentences commuted. Tiradentes was executed in Rio de Janeiro. His head was put on a pole in the main square of Ouro Preto. His arms and legs were exhibited in other towns. The other *Inconfidentes* are mostly forgotten. Tiradentes is honoured as the first hero of Brazilian independence.

The town was pretty but again too prinked for tourism; not that I saw much of it for, after a brief tour, I giggled the night away in a fevered attack of malaria and pressed on in the morning toward Rio.

6
Brazil
EMPERORS AND CLOWNS

The rain fell in straight cords, beating on the broad leaves of the tropical trees. The palace lay in a long, winding valley, almost a gorge, running through the Serra dos Orgãos, about fifty miles north of Rio. The main part of the house was two-storeyed, in an awkward, flat neo-classical style. Two long narrower wings, each with twelve debased Palladian windows, stuck out from either side of the square central block. The stucco was a dark terracotta, the columns, windows and pediment picked out in white. Had the rain stopped, it might have been quite attractive. This was Petropolis, the summer house of Emperor Pedro II of Brazil.

Inside, the house reminded me of gloomy, Victorian, ancestral houses in the north of England. The furniture was ponderous and fiercely uncomfortable; the paintings in whirly, gilt frames were sentimental; the jewellery was heavily encrusted. I found it hard to reconcile this grimly tasteless house with the informal, loveable nature of its builder. Perhaps the stuff now gathered here came from the grander palaces of Rio.

The story of the Portuguese House of Bragança in Brazil is strangely sad. In 1807, Napoleon was threatening to occupy Portugal. The regent, Prince João, saw no point in resisting so powerful an army. Moreover, he believed that, if he did fight, Britain would take advantage of the moment and would seize the Portuguese colony of Brazil.

Taking with him his poor, mad mother, Queen Maria, who thought she was being dragged to the guillotine, the whole machinery of government and fifteen thousand people, he set sail for Brazil. Napoleon on Saint Helena said of Prince João: 'He was the only one who ever tricked me.'

Prince João had always been considered rather stupid, hesitant and indecisive. He had a monkish temperament. In Brazil, he came to life. He set about freeing Brazil from the hampering regulations which had been imposed by Portugal. He lifted restrictions on industry and opened the ports to foreign traders. In 1807 ninety ships had called in Rio. The next year, there were 420. Ten years later, two thousand ships called at Salvador. He introduced the printing press. It was for Brazil a new beginning.

The demented Queen died in 1816. The Prince became King João VI. While he loved Brazil, the Brazilians, after an initial display of delight, came not to love the King. His perfectly odious wife, Carlota Joaquina, treated the Brazilians with contempt. Taxes rose to pay for the court and for a long war with what is now Argentina. In Portugal, now free of Napoleon, revolutionaries convened a parliament. João acquiesced in this arrangement in his European kingdom, but continued to rule Brazil autocratically. The Brazilians demanded a similar parliament. Riots broke out. They were suppressed by force. The situation was untenable. João decided to return to Portugal, leaving his eldest son, Pedro, in Brazil as viceroy.

Pedro was very different from his father. He had had little education and had mingled with the roughs of Rio rather than the children of the Portuguese aristocrats who had come over with João. He was a swashbuckler and a womaniser. Perhaps because of his raffish acquaintances, he understood better the independent spirit of Brazilians. He could sympathise with them in their longing for autonomy.

Before his father left, Pedro had persuaded him to agree to a parliament in Rio to match the one in Lisbon. Now, as viceroy, he abolished censorship, did away with many duties, cut state salaries having first halved his own allowance, abolished flogging, dungeons, irons and forced labour. He built an observatory and founded schools and colleges of every kind.

The Portuguese government, who now controlled King João, planned to reduce Brazil to colonial status once again. They ordered Pedro to return to Lisbon. He was also offered the throne of the recently liberated Greece, which the European powers wished to see back in the monarchical fold. Pedro refused both the order and the offer.

He demonstrated immense courage in confrontations with the Portuguese loyalists. Finally, when riding back to Rio from São Paulo, he was met at Ypiranga by messengers who brought him the news that Portugal was mounting a vast expedition to come to reconquer Brazil.

Pedro tore the Portuguese colours from his uniform and drew his sword and shouted: 'I swear to God to free Brazil.' His soldiers drew their swords and yelled, 'We swear it.'

'Independence or death,' shouted the Prince. And the soldiers replied with the same cry.

Always given to the dramatic gesture, Pedro rode back to São Paulo, designed an armband reading Independence or Death, composed an anthem and went to the theatre. There he stood up in the royal box and sang:

> Arise, ye noble citizens
> Cast out all fear for good or ill
> For our brave bosoms and our arms
> Shall be the walls that guard Brazil.

Later in the year, Pedro was crowned the Emperor of Brazil. It was another beginning, but his reign was to be short and uneasy.

Pedro had married the daughter of Francis II of Austria, a short dumpy girl with a small nose and the thick lips of the Habsburgs. Leopoldina was hardly the person Pedro would have chosen, being more given to what his biographers call *modistes* and actresses. The princess was interested in the sciences, especially natural history. She wrote to her father: 'Pohl has brought me a cub, a cross between a lion and a panther, a rare bird from China, a she-mule that has offspring, an ox with a Tartary hump, as well as many other animals and a couple of Botocudo Indians who live near here and I should not care to part with any of them.' Her idea of a good present was to send someone a few animals. However she shared with Pedro a love of music and she bore him seven children.

The Emperor's sensual nature was unlikely to be satisfied by this kind, loving, but homely woman. When he was in São Paulo at the time of his decision to secede from Portugal, he met a woman who was his sexual ideal, Domitila de Castro. She had been married, but had left her husband after he stabbed her in the stomach when she was pregnant with their third child. She was still only twenty-four. Tall and pale, her beauty was enhanced by a tincture of Indian blood mixed with that of her Spanish, Portuguese and English ancestry.

Pedro was usually careful of other people's feelings. He once said to Domitila: 'You can ask anything of me provided it does no harm to anyone else.' Yet, in his infatuation with her, he forgot this precept. He soon made her a viscountess, then a marchioness. She was astonishingly fecund. In her life she had at least thirteen children, four of them by the Emperor.

Leopoldina did not, at first, notice her husband's obsession with his mistress. Unaware of the relationship, she even made Domitila one of her ladies-in-waiting. Pedro on the other hand quite openly acknowledged his illegitimate children, making the first one, born in 1824, the Duchess of Goias.

From 1826, events piled up to destroy Pedro in Brazil. King João died in Portugal. As the wily old man had planned, Pedro became King of Portugal as well as Emperor of Brazil. He did not want to leave Brazil. He therefore renounced the Portuguese throne in favour of his eldest daughter with Leopoldina, Maria da Glória. Before doing so, he gave the Portuguese a liberal constitution and abolished the absolute monarchy. It was a move which horrified Metternich and the other statesmen of Europe. Only the English were pleased.

King João's detestable queen, Carlota, who had never had one liberal thought, at once devoted her large inheritance to promoting her favourite son Miguel. By bribery she paved the way for this weak man, who was supposed to act as regent for his niece during her minority, to seize power. He arrived from Brazil and, supported by reactionary elements, took the throne for himself.

Meanwhile in Brazil, Pedro had other problems. The land known as the Province of Cisplatina, which his father had won in his war with Argentina (or the United Provinces of the River Plate), wanted independence from both Rio and Buenos Aires. The area, now Uruguay, was Spanish-speaking. The Argentinians supported the rebellion against Brazil. Pedro went south, prepared for war.

News came that Leopoldina was dead. Pedro rushed back to Rio. For many months he suffered remorse, for he had grown genuinely fond of his wife. Without him to inspire the troops, the battle with the patriots, supported by the Argentinians, was inconclusive. Finally both Brazil and Argentina abandoned all claims on Cisplatina. Uruguay was born.

Pedro's popularity waned. He had lost the territory his father had won.

He had maltreated the Empress whom the people loved. He was becoming more autocratic. His private life was a scandal.

The last point he remedied. He set about finding a new wife. He asked the Austrian Emperor to help him in finding one. Curiously, Francis seemed inclined to do so despite Pedro's treatment of his daughter. His minister, Metternich, was not. Infuriated by Pedro's bouts of liberalism, he managed to scupper his prospects with almost every available European princess. After several ignominious refusals, it became clear that Metternich was deliberately frustrating any possible match. Finally, he found a Bavarian princess, whose family disliked Metternich.

Princess Amelia Napoleon de Leuchtenberg was a granddaughter of the Empress Josephine by her first husband. Napoleon had adopted her father, Eugene Beauharnais, who had had a distinguished career as a soldier and administrator until Napoleon's defeat, when he retired to his wife's homeland, Bavaria, and bought the Duchy of Leuchtenberg.

Domitila was sent back to São Paulo where she eventually married a brigadier-general by whom she had already had six children. The Duchess of Goias was sent to school in Paris.

Under the new Empress domesticity ruled. But that was not enough. In 1831, the crisis arrived. Pedro was only fitfully democratic. 'I am ready to do anything for the people, but nothing that the people compel me to do.' On no account would he surrender his right to appoint ministers of his choosing. The new Empress had managed to ease out some of the less savoury courtiers for whom, since his youth, Pedro had a liking. But she could not move him from his view that he must defend his rights, 'even if it means sacrificing everything I possess, even my life'.

It came nearly to a riot. The loyal officers of the army suggested that Pedro rouse the militia and fight. In his dramatic style, Pedro declared, 'I will not allow one drop of Brazilian blood to be shed for my sake.' He abdicated with dignity. His five-year-old son became Emperor Pedro II. The older Pedro returned to Europe, there to spend nearly all his last three years fighting his brother Miguel. In May 1834, he won back the throne of Portugal for his daughter Maria de Glória. In September he died.

At the time of his abdication Pedro said: 'Those born in Brazil no longer want me for the reason that I am Portuguese . . . my son has the advantage over me in that he is Brazilian by birth.'

There was some truth in this. The Brazilians always believed that the Portuguese patronised them, even held them in contempt. It seems to me that Pedro I's volatile nature – a mixture of real liberalism and a rather crude autocracy; a somewhat coarse sensuality coupled with a deep familial sentimentality – was extremely Brazilian.

His gentle, almost saintly son, Pedro II, was to appear far more European. As I looked at the Petropolis museum dedicated to this cultivated, unassuming man, I found it hard to reconcile what I knew of his character with what I was learning of Brazil.

Christened Pedro de Alcântara João Carlos Leopoldo Salvador Bibiano Francisco Xavier de Paula Leocadio Miguel Gabriel Rafael Gonzaga, the young prince had a gloomy childhood. His mother died when he was one. His father left when he was five and died within four years.

Pedro's upbringing was almost too serious, because those who looked after him felt a burden of responsibility greater than his parents might have done. His father, perhaps regretting his own lack of education, was determined that the Prince should have a thorough schooling and this idea his guardians enforced with rigour.

The young Pedro's nature agreed well with the arduous courses of study set out for him. The problem, in fact, was often to stop his working too hard. By the time he was thirteen, he could write Latin verses, speak and write English and French and was already embarked on German. When he was fourteen he took up philosophy and rhetoric.

It was as well that his intellect was developed early. The departure of Pedro I had really solved nothing. The different political factions were as much at odds as they had always been. In 1840, many came to believe that the only solution that might hold the country together was that Pedro should be invested with his full authority early. According to the constitution he should not have been crowned until he was eighteen. In the event, a delegation came to him and asked him to end his minority.

'But can you be certain,' he asked, 'that with little more than fourteen years, it is possible to possess wisdom?'

They insisted; he accepted. On the following day, Dom Pedro II took the oath. The proclamation announcing the event ended: 'Brazilians, the hopes of the nation have been made a reality. A new era opens. May it be one of unison and prosperity! May we be worthy of such a great blessing!' He was crowned a year later, wearing his father's cape and carrying the sword he had waved at Ypiranga. Another beginning.

The story of Pedro's reign is depressing to read. As usual, after the first euphoria, the squabbles for political power continued. The Church involved Pedro in a furious quarrel with the masons. The bishops attacked Pedro for imprisoning two of their number and the liberals attacked him for eventually releasing them. Both sides of each dispute always blamed the Emperor. There was a prolonged and expensive war with Paraguay, the ghastly results of which we shall see in the next chapter.

Pedro had decades of trouble with European powers, particularly over the question of slavery. His instincts were always opposed to slavery. He freed all his own slaves in 1840, as soon as he assumed his full powers. His subjects did not. This was particularly galling to the British not only on humanitarian grounds, but also because it meant that Brazilian sugar was far cheaper than Caribbean sugar. Britain seized Brazilian slave-ships. National pride was affronted. The results were horrible. Although an act had been passed in 1831 outlawing the trade in slaves, the import of Africans increased. In 1846, about twenty thousand arrived. The following year, fifty thousand were dragged across.

At this time, the question became embarrassing. The British were sailing into Brazilian harbours and seizing slave-ships. The slave-ships were operating in defiance of Brazilian law. At last the government acted and managed to stamp out the trade by the mid-1850s. Slavery, however, continued. The Benedictines freed their slaves twenty-six years after the Emperor. Final abolition did not come until 1888.

Pedro, throughout his reign, endeavoured to follow liberal principles and fulfil his oath to 'work for the general good of Brazil'. But it was his own life that I found more interesting.

When he was seventeen, he got married. He had approached his uncle, Ferdinand of Austria, with the idea of marrying one of his cousins. This offer was turned down. Metternich however did provide a bride this time. She was Princess Thereza, sister of Ferdinand II of the Two Sicilies. Her father was a Habsburg and her mother a sister of Pedro's dreadful grandmother, Carlota Joaquina.

One cannot help wondering whether Metternich was not still being mischievous. Dona Thereza was nearly four years older than Pedro, bordering on the ugly and decidedly not intellectual. She was also short and lame.

When Pedro went on board the ship which brought her from Naples, he is said to have been so shocked that he turned his back on her, possibly to regain his composure. He wanted to annul the marriage contract; they had already been married by proxy in Naples. His advisers persuaded him that this was unthinkable.

Pedro accepted the inevitable, treated Thereza always with respect and was almost certainly faithful to her, though he was not above being charmed by beautiful women. Their life together was, as it turns out, happy enough. Thereza loved and admired Pedro. He developed a deep affection for her prompted, one biographer suggests, more by her motherly qualities than her wifely ones. They had four children within four years. Two were sons, both of whom died in early childhood.

'Twice already I have died,' wrote Pedro, 'for a father who sees his son die, dies also.'

On both occasions he wrote verses on their deaths. The second time he revealed something of the loneliness of his life.

> Mine has been the most dismal of fates
> In gentle infancy I lived with no father and no mother;
> And my two small sons have died before me.

Apart from Brazil and his family, Pedro had the most diverse interests. In the last twenty years of his life, when Brazilian affairs had become a little calmer and his daughter Isabel was of an age to act as regent, he was able to indulge these a little more.

In 1871, he went to Europe for the first time. He took Thereza with him, but only a small entourage for those days. Typically it included Rafael, his black servant who had been his playmate as a child. He travelled incognito and with the minimum of ceremony. Wherever he went, he protested that he was there as a private citizen. This may not have been entirely artless. In an age of pomp, his modesty naturally won him far greater popularity than any display of grandeur.

Pedro went to Portugal, Spain, France, England, Belgium, Germany, Austria and Italy. He was a tireless sightseer but also made wholly unexpected digressions from any ordinary tourist route. In London, he went to a service in the synagogue in Upper Berkeley Street and went to see the slums. After a visit to Queen Victoria at Osborne, he travelled round the country. In Lancaster he visisted the prison, in Carlisle the lunatic asylum, in Normanton a mine.

On the Continent, apart from his obligatory visits to royal relations and connections, at which he caused immense confusion by always refusing to wear a white tie and tails, he spent most of his time with academics. He paid a visit to Egypt and then returned for some weeks to Paris.

This journey and subsequent ones to the United States, Europe and Africa enlarged Pedro's intellectual life beyond measure. The Emperor was a polymath. He lived at a time when it was possible, if not to know everything there was to know, at least to have an intelligent acquaintance with every subject.

As a child, Pedro had been studious and the habit remained with him. He spoke at least nine languages fluently and could read many more. He translated Shakespeare, Byron, Whittier and Longfellow into Portuguese. He knew Latin and Greek and was particularly interested in Hebrew. He translated parts of the Old Testament into Latin. The last book he wrote, *Poésies hebraïco-provençales du rituel Israélite Comtadin*, was a collection of songs which the Jews of Provence used at family festivals. The Hebrew version appeared on the left-hand pages, with Pedro's translations into both Provençal and French on the opposite page. This extraordinary volume was published in Avignon in 1891. He knew Sanskrit well and had enough Arabic to translate the *Thousand and One Nights* into Portuguese.

His interest in the sciences was as enthusiastic as it was in the humanities. Botany he studied as a boy. When he went to Scotland, he brought back a bush from Sir Walter Scott's garden at Abbotsbury. He was fascinated by physics, in particular electricity. When a youth, he had experimented with daguerreotypes. He read about manufacturing processes. He had his own laboratory and a sizeable telescope to study the heavens.

In Brazil there were few enough people with an equal knowledge on any of these subjects, let alone over so wide a range. His pursuit of knowledge was to some extent solitary. His journeys put him into touch with people famous in every field. To Louis Agassiz in America, the Emperor sent a classified record of the fish in the Rio Grande do Sul, which the Professor said 'would do honour to a professional naturalist'. He corresponded with Pasteur about the possibility of finding a vaccine for yellow fever. He conducted other lengthy correspondences with naturalists, geologists and vulcanologists as well as with authors, philosophers and historians.

He made friends with Heinrich Schliemann, the discoverer of Troy and the excavator of Mycenae. From Alexander Bell, he obtained one of the earliest telephone systems.

He was nearly rebuffed by the devoutly republican Victor Hugo, who, on being invited to meet Pedro, said he did not visit people. Pedro replied that it was he who would visit Hugo, who 'has over me the sad privilege of age and the proud one of genius'. They met in the Senate office in Versailles and got on so well together that Victor Hugo invited Pedro to his house. The first visit was spent mostly in paying each other compliments.

'Luckily, we have no monarch in Europe like Your Majesty.'

'Why, luckily?'
'Because there would then be no republicans.'
After that they became friends.

The Brazilians, ever turbulent, did not agree with Victor Hugo. The South Americans looked always with a mixture of envy and admiration at the North Americans. While they had, like the northerners, thrown off the colonial yoke, they had not prospered equally. In Brazil, the idea that it was the monarchy that impeded them took easy hold. To be the only monarchy in the Americas was in itself unsettling.

Princess Isabel, although admired by many for her intelligence and sense of duty, was disliked by the landowners. It so happened that it was she who had, as regent during her father's travels, signed both of the acts which freed the slaves. The abolition of slavery was probably the principal factor in the rapid rise of republicanism.

More important than Isabel was her husband, the Comte d'Eu, a French prince. In their xenophobic way, the Brazilians disliked him, forgetting that they had thought him a hero in the Paraguayan war. They decided that he was a sinister influence on Isabel. Being rather deaf, he was retiring and did not much enjoy festivals and frivolity. That, of course, was inexcusable in Brazil, where everyone loves a party.

Pedro himself did nothing to interfere with the change of heart of his people. 'Were I not a monarch, I would be a republican,' he said. When his ministers wanted to deny office to known republicans, he refused to listen. His only concern was that the man best fitted for any job should have it. He had none of his father's determination to preserve his rights. He would happily have exchanged his throne for the position of president. Repeatedly Pedro made it plain that if the people wanted to change their system of government, he would put no difficulty in their way.

In the end, it was not the republicans with their talk of democracy and liberty who deposed this exemplary monarch. In November 1889, the army seized power and drove out Pedro and all his family.

The military treated him with a lack of consideration bred probably in shame. They imprisoned him in the palace and then hurried him out under the cover of darkness to the ship which was to carry the family away from Rio.

The Empress could not understand what was happening. 'What have we done wrong to them that they should treat us so?' She had lived forty-six years in Brazil and she loved it. And the Brazilians loved her. She had never meddled in state affairs, and she had done many good works. Before boarding the launch which was to take them to the ship, Dona Thereza, old now and lamer than ever, knelt down and kissed the soil of Brazil. In less than six weeks, she died.

Pedro lived another two years, mostly in Cannes. He never complained of his fate or criticised the revolutionaries. He refused the money they offered him and lived in slightly straitened circumstances as a result.

He died in 1891 and was buried beside Dona Thereza with the Braganças in Lisbon. The pillow under his head was filled with Brazilian soil which he had brought with him for this purpose. Thirty years later, the government in Rio de Janeiro revoked the order of banishment on the royal family. The bodies of Pedro and Dona Thereza were taken back to Brazil and interred in the new Gothic cathedral at Petropolis.

* * *

Rio de Janeiro is both a fantasy and a reality. The reality is unpleasant, at least to a superficial observer. The life of the slums is too hard to be borne. The shacks hang waiting for a disaster, a flood, a fire, a plague. Violence shades the city like smog. There are four murders every week.

There must be another reality, an intellectual and artistic community, but it is the fantasy that most visitors see. For them, the reality hardly trespasses. The industry and the port were far removed. In the hotel, they warned us of muggings and pickpockets and bag-snatchers. They looked alarmed at our leaving the car out at night. That was as close as we came to anything other than invention.

Copacabana, Ipanema. Somehow I had expected beauty from such names. Beaches lined with skyscrapers seem to be oxymoronic. But they were filled with people, eager participants in the unreality. Girls walked from the town to the beach carrying chairs. They lay beside them on the sand, provocative in their *tangas* – no more than a minute triangle in front and only a string behind. The boys struck attitudes and did strange exercises, wearing very little more actual material than the girls, but theirs was so designed as to produce an almost priapic bulge, helped it seemed probable with a fistful of padding.

Nothing was what it appeared or what it was said to be. A man ran past, jogging. Blood was dripping from his navel. Two flirtatious girls proved to be men. Even the sand on Copacabana beach was not natural. Great piles of it were delivered as I watched, heaped up at one end of the beach waiting to be spread. In this city, where amiable vendors on any street corner offer one cocaine, hashish or anything, the chemists would not sell me innocent chloraquine for my malaria without a prescription. In London, one can buy it freely.

Even the stories of danger took on a quality of fable, as we walked the warm streets at night. There were single, respectable women strolling home without fear. The beggars were polite. Other people refused tips. No one threatened us. I could see why Pedro loved these people, but I remembered that an increase in crimes of violence was one of the things he was blamed for.

The Sugar Loaf mountain looked better from a distance. We went up in the cable-car, the passengers howling at each lurch. On the top of the soaring rock, this symbol of Rio became just a lump studded with tourists, though the swooping views were impressive.

In the botanic gardens, on the other hand, I thought of Pedro II and his mother Leopoldina. They must have had a hand in their creation. Here there were no tourists and we roamed almost alone among the superb trees. Unfortunately the gardens were skimpily tended. The labels have rotted and few of the specimens were identifiable. In the Amazon section, I made out some names on trees which looked familiar from our barge journey. A rocket-tailed trunk soaring high with feather leaves said *Parkia multijuga*. Another, *Parkia auriculata*, had bark as smooth as glazed chintz and high above, a canopy of round leaves. *Ceiba rivieri* did not look like our old friend in the *llanos* of Venezuela. I wished that I knew even what Pedro would have thought elementary.

The zenith of unreality was Plataforma I, a samba hall to which some friends invited us. It was a show based on the carnival, the dancers wearing some of the actual costumes and the musicians playing tunes of the recent carnival. We sat in awe, drinking a stupefying cocktail called a *caipirinha* – many *caipirinhas*. The music thumped its way into our bodies and the spectacle of a myriad girls in clothes of such extravagant fantasy stunned us. There were so many girls that all individuality was lost, their long, brown legs reminded me of a forest of camels' legs at a well where one cannot tell which limb belongs to which animal. The men danced with unsurpassed agility. Some of the choreography was imaginative, slave-dances being presented as rough fights. We stayed, enthralled once more by the rhythm, for two hours.

Of course the whole thing was bogus, designed for tourists. It was still the most colourful dance I have ever seen. The skills were real; the costumes were majestic masterpieces of tinsel and feather, which never

99

slid into tawdry. Somehow the grotesque become normal. For me, it summed up Rio.

* * *

The way west led us at first through country of little promise for about fifty miles. Then we were in wooded hills and below us lay the sea and the shore of the Baía da Ilha Grande. At once the folderol of Rio was forgotten. The coast is one of the most beautiful in the world. The hills rose like upside-down drips, ready to fall. The tropical forest was stippled with purple, yellow and the purest white. Small islands hovered in the secrecy of mists and further out to sea there were adumbrations of land, perhaps the Ilha Grande itself – once used by pirates, now a resort island despite being the site of a large prison.

The coast was a cross between Japan's Inland Sea and an undiscovered Italian Riviera. Later, as the sun sank, the hills and the islands lost all but shape, looking like monochrome cut-outs. In the last tracings of light, we saw a white church, with a tower, set on the beach.

The road was new, although a tempest had already snatched away a finely engineered bend. Not long ago, the land near the sea had been worked. Now the coconut palms stood neglected amid a greedy under-growth. The bananas had withered. The farmers have sold their land or it has been expropriated. The beauty has not long to run. Already there were marinas with poor copies of Port Grimaud sprouting beside them. At one point there was a nuclear power-station, with a fancy information centre to soothe the anxious. In thirty years or less, it will all be like Rapallo.

I was so pleased to be out of Rio that I was determined not to let such speculations spoil my enjoyment. We slept and, in the morning, went back to the lone church on the beach. It was as simple and pretty as I had hoped. It stood a little way out from the low cliff along which the road ran. It had green wooden doors and the windows were shuttered. Swifts were nesting by the bells in the square tower.

There were half a dozen houses, white like the church but with blue doors and shutters, under the cliff, nestling against boulders far bigger than themselves. Water poured from a rock face, as if struck by Aaron's rod. The colours were intense, the white of the buildings, the pale cream of the sand and the rich aquamarine of the sea. A little island offshore looked crisp and tempting.

There was no one about, except for a Venezuelan boy – Dilson. He was drifting, the vanguard of the hippies perhaps. He had worked at the gold mine at Las Claritas and was harrassed by the police for some reason. He had fled over the border to Brazil where no one, he said, needs an identity card. He told me that the church was 450 years old.

We came to Taratuba, a slightly larger village in a tight-curved bay. Each place was more idyllic than the last. Fishermen were coming with their morning catch in long multi-coloured boats – yellow and red, brown and blue. One, who had already landed, sat gutting his fish on an upturned boat. His eyes slid sideways and he rocked a little with each stroke of the knife. He was drunk. The fish was about three feet long with a very pointed tail. A barracuda, perhaps. 'Tuberão,' I think the fisherman said, laughing more than any apparent joke deserved. He pointed his knife at me and then at another fish. 'Cuvina,' he said and nearly fell on his knife with laughter.

As we came near to Parati, the houses were more prosperous. There were motor boats at anchor and villas were being built. Parati is a colonial town which, in the seventeenth century, was an important port for the export of gold. With no new road to it, the town was forgotten. Nothing spoiled it, rather it was enriched by soft decay. The streets are narrow, cobbled with large stones. The main church is an elegant building, but I liked the simple feeling of the church by the water. A couple of horses grazed by its plain doorway. It may have been the slave church, for in early colonial times each race had its own church, contrary to what the Portuguese like to claim about their lack of racial intolerance.

Parati has now been declared an historic monument. It was a little dead in feeling, but not precious even if the 'sleeping policemen' were cobbled. The town had a real life, but a monument always takes on something of the fly in amber. And, in season, the tourist hordes invade down the new road from Rio.

*　　*　　*

We had now been too long in Brazil. I wanted to head for Paraguay and also to avoid the city of São Paulo. So we turned north to Cunha, taking a laterite track that climbed through banana plantations up to undisturbed forest. These wilderness woodlands in South America were a repeated delight, forever surprising in their variety. The day had started wet, but the sun was burning off the clouds. Some still hung, defiant in the valleys, but by noon only wisps of steam remained. The hillsides gleamed with washed colours, purples mostly, some yellow and shafts of silver from the *cecropias*, shining among the infinite number of greens. There was one tree I had never seen before, bearing purple flowers and white flowers simultaneously. The silence was broken by a screech of parakeets and the falling of clear water. For many hours, we saw no one.

When we reached the top, we moved into the state of São Paulo. The land fell gently to softer pastures and cultivated fields. Here we saw some monkey-puzzles (*Araucaria*) for the first time.

There cannot be many trees which stir feelings of anger in people, but monkey-puzzles are widely detested in Europe. It cannot always have been so, otherwise there would not have been so many of them. The first ones in England, I long believed, were planted by Joseph Paxton in Cumbria, when he was gardener to the Duke of Devonshire. They fell down in a gale, but were pulled upright again by horses, and they still stand. They were soon to be seen all over the country. Perhaps snobbery had a hand in the matter, the cachet of a tree from a ducal garden triumphing over taste in suburbia. Now they are despised, perhaps snobbery is reversed, monkey-puzzles are thought suburban. Awkward authorities now assure me that they were introduced at least fifty years before Paxton's time. In their own habitat, they look quite attractive and when we came to a forest of them, I thought them splendid.

For several days, we drove through farming land which did not change much. In the higher lands there was coffee growing, and mining; in the plains there were fields of cotton and maize and endless sugar-cane. There was little forestry, apart from great stretches of eucalyptus. There were cattle ranches as big as counties. The enormous agricultural wealth of Brazil was inescapable.

More changeable were the people. The faces which stared at us from the roadsides would alter from one region to another. At first, faces that matched my old-fashioned idea of South American farm labourers, dark-eyed people with broad hats, riding in buggies. Further on there were many Japanese faces. The women in the fields were dressed as they might be in the rice-fields of Matsuyama. The men were more conventional. I saw one on horseback. He wore a broad-brimmed hat and no shirt – a far cry from a samurai. Beyond them were villages where I was struck by the neatness and cleanliness. Here the people were fair-haired – Scandinavian and German.

The immigration over the years has made it impossible to say who is a Brazilian. At the end of the last century, Pedro II was encouraging Europeans to come to work the acres of his empire. In 1888, for example, there were 131,000 immigrants, mostly from Italy. In this century, there came Japanese and Germans and Arabs.

In Marília, we had the only trouble with the car during the whole of our journey. The universal joint was rattling. We found a garage which was run by a Japanese. Most of his customers were Japanese, too, or of Japanese appearance. While they changed the joint, I sat in the sun talking to a farmer who had brought his car to be serviced.

Sadao Hino was fifty-eight. He stood with that apologetic stance of Japanese people who are uncertain about the status of their interlocutor. There was no question of bowing even when we spoke in Japanese, but he had no Brazilian swagger, nor any Japanese superiority when addressing the mechanics to whom he spoke in Portuguese.

He farmed, he said, three thousand acres in different lots. Principally, he grew coffee and maize, but he was especially proud of his mangoes. The particular kind he produced were Tommy Atkins or, as he pronounced it, achkins. 'Oishi desu,' delicious, he said.

'I came here as a child. We lived in Kyushu. My parents were simple peasants and there was not any future for them.'

Sometimes Hino-san looks at the prosperity of Japan and wonders whether the frightening upheaval, which he remembers clearly, was worth it.

'My parents had a better life here. They missed the war. The atom bomb fell on Kyushu, however . . .' He left the Japanese sentence hanging in the air.

'My life is probably better too. I would never have had three thousand acres in Japan.'

He and his wife speak Japanese to each other, but their five children speak only Portuguese.

'Sometimes my wife and I look at each other and wonder how it would have been and we used to talk in a foolish way of going back. Then we look at the children . . .' He laughed. 'They are pure Brazilians.'

On the road again, we saw flags fluttering at Herculandia. It was a circus. 'Cirque Wembley', it said in huge letters. The people of the circus were fine-looking. The pectoral muscles of the trapeze artists who came to talk to us were so highly developed that they looked like those alarming anatomical drawings of the seventeenth century. They were entirely nomadic and had no homes other than their caravans. They moved all over Brazil, except the far north, staying up to ten days in one place. I asked how the circus got its name.

'It is a good name for a circus and lucky. In London there is a very big circus called Wembley.'

'Ah, yes,' I said. We wished we could have seen a show in their lurid, red and yellow big top, but they were not performing that night. We drove on and for a long time could see their colourful flags in the breeze.

As we neared Paraguay the land was flat and dull. We were late getting to Dourados. The sun set with one of those immense displays that the wide skies of Brazil provide. Every cloud formation that the weather knows formed itself at one or other corner – a series of thunder anvils, cumulus, cirrus, nimbus, all at once, as if arranged for a lesson in meteorology, each illuminated in turn until the last red faded.

7

Paraguay

A CONTINENT OF MONEY-CHANGERS

At Ponta Porá, a straggling town, there were no signposts of any sort. Which was the way to Paraguay, we asked? They pointed and we wandered through quiet streets. We asked again for Paraguay. This is Paraguay, they said – San Juan de Caballero. We might have guessed, for a soldier with a fixed bayonet stood on the corner.

I thought it best to go back to try again, in view of the ruthless reputation of this dictatorship. So we did, and the same thing happened. We never found the border posts. Perhaps, as it was Good Friday, they did not bother. After three attempts I gave up and took the road to Concepción. Soon there was a checkpoint. I expected difficulties. The post was manned by sullen children with machine-guns. Glad to be rid of the struggle of Portuguese, I prattled at them. They did not answer. They asked nothing, but just waved us on. I wondered how they taught youth to be unsmiling when the rest of the people were noticeably forthcoming.

At first, we drove through deserted country on a good road. After sixty miles, the tarmac stopped but, perversely, the population increased. The farming was skimpy. The villagers sat on chairs under mango or banyan trees, chatting. The nearer that we came to Concepción, the more television aerials we saw. But there were pitifully few compared with

105

Brazil where, whether by design or not, television has done more than anything else to inspire a sense of national identity, uniting the north and the south, blending the Portuguese with the German, the African with the oriental.

As we came into Concepción, there was an army barracks. A notice insisted that we should not drive at more than ten kilometres an hour. This seemed so ridiculous that we ignored it. A hitch-hiker we had picked up begged us in tones of real fear to slow down. We might be shot, he said. Without doubt we would all be imprisoned.

I liked Concepción at once. It had that decaying emptiness that one imagines South American towns have and that they seldom do. There was a bleached movie-look to the houses, which were mostly white. There were some fine turn-of-the-century buildings, many dilapidated, often abandoned. The only well-kept ones were the administrative offices. The smartest of all was the bishop's palace – a sugary thing of the 1890s. There were some new houses, but evidently no one had the idea of doing up the crumbling, old ones which stood deserted.

There was hardly any traffic. People sat on the pavement, gossiping. Two young men had brought out a table and were playing chess. By way of contrast, some girls in trousers rode up and down on motor scooters, blowing kisses to Symon.

The hotels were nearly all full, because Brazilians come here for holiday weekends. Eventually we found one with a dark mosquito-filled room. We had become spoilt by Brazil where, on the whole, hotels in remote places were quite comfortable and there was always something to eat. In Concepción, it was a struggle to get a sandwich at three in the afternoon.

We sat outside on the pavement, drinking with a Brazilian doctor from Ponta Porá and with a Paraguayan lawyer from Asunción, the capital. It was hard to imagine why either should choose to spend Easter in this run-down hotel. The doctor was notably handsome. He had one hideous older child and two beautiful younger ones. He sat chain-smoking and every so often making offers for my car, the sums getting larger and larger as the afternoon darkened to evening. The lawyer, a stumpy, autocratic man, given to jerky, imperious gestures, became agitated when I said I was writing a book.

'Europeans have a poor opinion of South America. Will you not correct that?' he asked, pouting his lips and waving as broad a sweep as his short arms would allow.

I asked him which misapprenhensions he would like to see corrected.

106

He would not specify, but promised me many influential introductions in Asunción and, chopping the air, enumerated the places he thought that I should see.

I rather wanted to go to the Chaco, the lonely land to the west and north-west of Asunción, which makes up more than half the area of Paraguay. The lawyer spluttered, his arms whirling like propellers.

'What for? There are just Indians with bows and arrows, nothing else. What you must see is our civilisation.'

The idea that animals and birds might be interesting produced a look of utter mystification. And when I asked if he knew that only twelve years ago a wild pig, which was thought to have died out in the Pleistocene age, had turned up in the Chaco, the lawyer looked scandalised as if I had uttered an obscenity. Fortunately, he soon became so drunk that he had to go to bed.

Symon was shocked to find that in the evening we could only have the same kind of ham and cheese sandwiches we had had when we arrived. After this dinner we went into the sitting-room. A small television was flickering in one corner and most of the guests were hunched round it. Soon, at the other end of the room, a thirteen-year-old girl started to play the piano. She played a little Liszt and then tunes of Simon and Garfunkel and Lionel Richie. She could sight-read and could even pick up a tune that she had never heard, which Symon hummed to her out of key. Gradually she won. The guests moved one by one to her end of the room. Finally the television was turned off. Paraguay seemed agreeably old-fashioned after the future-loving Brazil.

The road from Concepión to the Chaco was impassable because of the rains and, in any case, opinions varied as to whether the bridge across the Paraguay river was finished. We set off instead for Asunción, although there was even doubt as to whether we would be able to reach there. In many places lorries had cut deep ruts in the mud, wider than the car, so that we travelled at an alarming angle for miles at a time.

The countryside was sparsely populated, a reflection even today of a genocidal war of more than a hundred years ago. From 1865 until 1870, the Paraguayan dictator, Marchal Francisco Solano López, led his people in a war against Brazil, Argentina and Uruguay. It did not end until he fell in battle, fighting side by side with his Irish mistress, Madame Lynch.

From this side of the border we saw a side of the genial Emperor Pedro II that was not so apparent in Petropolis. In this war, he was unyielding. It did him little good in Brazil to conduct so prolonged a campaign, yet it must have been pursued with an unforgivable viciousness. At the beginning of the war, the population of Paraguay was 800,000. At the end of the five-year struggle, 186,000 men and 120,000 women had died. Only 14,000 males survived, all but 2,100 of them being under the age of twenty.

We caught up with a large herd of white, brahma cattle. There were about two thousand head, filling the red mud track for a long mile. The five men driving them wore leather trousers, spurs and floppy straw hats. They carried long knives, but no guns. Their saddles were sheepskin and the bridles were made of flat metal rings rather than leather. They had eight spare horses and mules. They said that they had bought the cattle in Brazil. They did not mind Symon's taking photographs of them but were otherwise uncommunicative. I thought that they might have rustled the cattle rather than bought them.

Further on, we came to houses which looked different, wooden rather than mud, and tidier. The people, too, were surprising – fair-haired and dressed in a way that belonged to the 1930s. We stopped to buy petrol and talked to some of the young men. They were Mennonites, who spoke little Spanish. Among themselves they spoke a version of *plattdeutsch*, or low German, which has virtually died out in Europe. One offered to take us to his father who, he said, spoke English.

Pieter Neudorf was a man of about sixty-five. His features were sharply cut, his eyes set deep in his lined face. He looked strong, but tired with the fatigue of a lifetime on the margin of poverty. His wife was a majestic woman, who came out of their house with a measured gait. She was the only one of the family to have darker hair and brown eyes. Their elder daughters, in their early thirties, had none of their mother's presence. They were thin and meek. Their hair was braided and tied back; their faces were innocent of make-up. They wore small floral prints in browns and greys, their skirts long. One had a large cotton hat. They looked like people out of a pre-war, black-and-white film, set in the dust-bowl of America. The sons were better dressed, in trousers and western shirts, never in jeans. They wore broad-brimmed straw hats. Two smaller girls, granddaughters possibly, were shooed away.

Pieter asked us into his house. We sat in their bedroom and Frau Neudorf brought us water to drink. The room had a very high double-bed covered in pretty patchwork quilts. On the floor there were rag mats and the chairs had cushions of the same material. The furniture was very simple. Pieter told me that he had made it all himself, except the chest of drawers which his son-in-law had made. Cooking pans and an umbrella hung from hooks on the ceiling.

'Our founder was Simon Mennon, who came from near Holland. He did not believe in child baptism as it was not in the Bible. This caused difficulties in the Church and he was driven out. So he and all the people who believed in his teachings went to Friesland in 1575. Then they moved to Russia where they stayed sixty years or more . . .'

Pieter was a bit vague about dates.

'In 1875, my grandmother moved from Russia to Canada. I was born there, but when I was three we went to Mexico. Then, in 1969, we came to Paraguay.'

The Mennonites, in fact, were originally a branch of the sixteenth-century Anabaptists and, in particular, the Swiss Brethren. Menno Simons was a Dutch priest who joined the Anabaptist movement in 1636, and consolidated the scattered groups of Anabaptists in the north of Europe. Their wanderings were much as Pieter described them. At the end of the sixteenth century, there were 160,000 Mennonites in the Netherlands, but at that time the Swiss branch broke away to form the Amish church.

In the eighteenth century, they moved to the Ukraine, largely to escape military service. They acquired half a million acres and ran their own communities, with some autonomy, until the revolution. There had, much earlier, been some emigration to North America and those who fled Russia moved there. Gradually they have travelled southward, many settling in Brazil and Paraguay.

Pieter said there were two main groups of Mennonites in Paraguay, the Colonia Rio Verde who owned fifty thousand acres and the Colonia Mexico with seventy thousand. The *South American Handbook*, speaks of three colonies in the Chaco, numbering about ten thousand people, one of which comes from Russia, via Canada and Mexico, but gives them different names, so Pieter may have been wrong. There were, he said, some two hundred and fifty families in the Colonia Rio Verde.

When I asked how many children he had, Pieter hesitated: 'I have s-s-s six and one adopted.'

'So, seven,' I said. He looked pleased.

'Yes, yes. That is right. Seven.' And he smiled, nodding at his wife.

'Seven children,' he said to her in *plattdeutsch*.

Pieter and his family worked about one hundred and fifty acres. Their chief crops were soya beans and wheat. Apart from that, they kept a few cows. It was a hard life and Pieter looked older than his years, but he was content.

'It is a bit difficult for some of us . . . to be in the tropics. The heat and the mosquitoes. The insects that attack the people and the crops. But we are happy.'

There was nothing overtly sanctimonious or bigoted about Pieter and his family. Their clothes were old-fashioned. They rode about in horse-buggies. But, unlike the Amish, there was no absurd refusal to accept all change. They were happy to use tractors, if they could afford them. They had nothing against buttons.

At the same time, only a very firm belief could have enabled a community to preserve its language, physical appearance and traditions for four centuries of wanderings through foreign countries. Why, I wondered, did they move so often? Pieter slid away from this question.

No one, I decided, could dislike these mild, hard-working farmers. Most countries, however, require people to conform. In Canada, even in Mexico, officialdom would have asked why the children were not at school. Moreover, the Mennonites are pacifists and would never accept conscription. They do not believe in taking oaths or in holding civic offices.

In many nations, these views sit awkwardly with the views of authority. The Mennonites, determined to keep intact their singular traditions, would move on. In Paraguay no one would ask questions about children's schooling. As for the other points, when they first came here in 1927, they were given many promises of non-interference as well as cheap land. For Paraguay, they are perfect immigrants – an industrious, rural people who have no interest in politics and want only to be left alone.

* * *

The 'siege' had been lifted a week or so before we arrived in Asunción. This state of emergency had been in force for forty years. The BBC news had given an exhilarating account of this moment of liberation. Exiles were to be allowed to return. The press was to be free. It was no longer legal for the police to demand papers of people in the street for no reason.

We dined on our first evening with an urbane Paraguayan aristocrat and his French wife. They laughed when I mentioned the BBC's account of universal jubilation.

'That was very starry-eyed,' said Jeanne. 'In any case, it is not censorship or spot checks that keep people down. It is much more direct and simple than that. In the ways that matter, nothing has changed. Nor will it.'

Neither they nor anyone else was anxious to talk about the government or about General Alfredo Stroessner, who has ruled Paraguay since

1954. He is regularly elected every five years by a majority which is never allowed to slip below ninety per cent.

Asunción had a paradoxical ambience. At first, I was struck by its Rip van Winkle quality. There were advertisements of Odol, a forgotten name from my childhood when toothpastes sounded like a Greek verse – Odol, Eucryl, Euthymol, Kolynos. In the fine, arcaded, yellow and brown railway station there were old steam trains – one engine, still in use, fired by wood. There was an old-fashioned sense of peace. We had no fear as we walked through the streets at night. The violence of Asunción is not inflicted on strangers; it is done privately to those who live there.

At the same time, there was an equally unexpected feeling of activity, if not of progress. The traffic woke me at five in the morning. All the shops and the offices in the skyscrapers were open by half past seven. Although the mood of the city was provincial, there was a sophistication bred of corruption. Why, I wondered for a while, were there so many *casas de cambio*? How, in view of the proliferation of *casas de cambio*, did ambulant money-changers make any sort of a living? Why was every *casa de cambio* thronged with people throughout the day?

It is true that South America is a continent of money-changers. In remote towns in the high Andes, there is always someone who will change dollars at a rate, quoted without hesitation, enormously to one's disadvantage. To turn all savings into dollars is an obvious insurance against the preposterous inflations. In a month, the savings may double. However, Paraguay was almost a burlesque of this Latin-American trait.

It was soon apparent that at least half the economy of Paraguay was based on contraband. The streets were bright with new cars; most of them smuggled in, many of them stolen and then smuggled. Coffee is one of Paraguay's important exports but, I was assured, no one grows a bean of it.

Symon was reading Graham Greene's *Travels with My Aunt*. 'It is exactly as he describes it,' he said. Of course.

While Symon waited in the half-hour queue for stamps, I sat in the courtyard of the Post Office. It was painted in the same yellow and brown as the station and was pretty, with a garden. (I thought that all civic buildings might have been done up in those colours. Then I saw that the Legislative Palace was an appropriate shade of grey.) In the centre of the garden was a statue of Solano López, who had introduced the telegraph in 1864, the first in South America. His father, three years before, had built the railway, one of the earliest in the continent. Solano López was

111

the president who launched the War of the Triple Alliance. I sat speculating as to whether he might not have created a paradise of a country had not his *folie de grandeur* led to the death of half his people. Probably not; South America is made up of so many Edens.

In the courtyard, I met Cheli Dominguez and her American boyfriend. She was a vivacious, agreeably plump girl. Symon said she had the look of a college kid, but she was in fact twenty-six. She lived in America where she would soon qualify as a doctor. Cheli's father was exiled by Stroessner twenty years ago.

'From time to time, he attempts to come back with the maximum of publicity. He always manages to get beaten up at the airport and create a sensation.'

Cheli found that funny. She had lived long enough in a place of freedom to have lost the automatic caution of most of the people.

'This siege-lifting could be the beginning of the end, but not in a hurry. The exiles are supposed to be allowed back, but only if they keep their mouths shut and I don't see my father doing that.

'It is always hard to tell what's going on. People don't criticise the government openly, but maybe the mood is changing. Of course, there's not much protest. Why should there be? Things are peaceful, you don't see anything terrible. The gap between rich and poor is no worse than in any other country in South America. Indeed we were richer than many until two years ago, when things started to go wrong.'

Stroessner holds on to power partly through the military and partly through the Colorado Party to which all his civil servants are obliged to belong. The civil servants are naturally beholden to the President for their jobs. Despite the lifting of the siege, armed thugs still beat up opposition leaders. Radio stations and newspapers are still easily closed down. One was shut when its owner appeared on American television and made some minor criticism of the government.

Cheli took us to a family party given by one of her uncles. The older guests were mainly leaders in Asunción's medical profession. No one spoke of politics.

'Naturally,' said Cheli. 'Half of my relations are mixed up with the Government. You don't know how small this place is. If I see my uncle walking down the street with his concubine, I have to dodge into an alley and pretend I know nothing. What the hell, let's go to a night club.'

But it was too late. There was still a curfew at one o'clock.

'It's funny,' said Cheli. 'There is no sort of ending. They just bang on the lights. The music stops. And everybody goes obediently home.'

112

In any event, we had drunk too much. In the morning we left.

*   *   *

We had passed through gentle, green country. There were villages with some rows of one-storey houses, their front doors behind a low colonnade for shade, but mostly the houses, however small, were separate. Some were thatched, others tiled. All were neat and clean.

As we neared the missions, or Reductions as they were originally known, we came first to prairie land, then marshy country – not inhospitable, but not a place of plenty.

In 1549, Ignatius Loyola, the founder of the Jesuit Order, sent seven of his followers to Brazil to evangelise the Indians. Some fifty years later, the Superior General created a new province of the order called the Province of Paraguay. The Indians of the area were the Guaraní, a semi-nomadic, warrior group, who practised a measure of agriculture. Some sources claim that they were cannibalistic. Others point out that they had names for eleven hundred plants. Their chief god was Tupang, an all-pervading spirit, incapable of evil. They had many lesser gods; most were the guardians of nature, only one was wicked.

The Jesuits, in the most successful missionary enterprise in the history of the world, converted the people to Christianity. Whatever one may feel about missionaries, however much one may wish that they would leave people alone, there is for me no doubt that the Guaraní were happy to be converted.

The communities which the Jesuits created were, in the view of many people, the greatest experiment in community living in the history of mankind. Voltaire said that it 'appears alone, in some way, the triumph of humanity. It seems to expiate the cruelty of the first conquerors.' Robert Southey, who regarded the Roman Catholic Church as bigoted and idolatrous, declared that the Jesuits 'formed a Utopia of their own . . . erroneous as they were, the sanctity of the end proposed, and the heroism and perseverance with which it was pursued, deserve the highest admiration.' Arnold Toynbee called the Reductions 'an idyllic hiero-cracy'.

It was Toynbee, also, who described the destruction of the missions as a 'wanton crime'. The reasons for it were twofold. The first was, in a sense, the response to one of the motives of their creation. The Jesuits, quite apart from their primary aim of evangelising the Indians, wanted to protect them from the Portuguese *bandeirantes* from São Paulo and from the Spanish colonists, both of whom wanted a plentiful supply of slaves.

Secondly, the governments of both Spain and Portugal were suspicious of the Jesuits.

In Europe, comically enough, the Jesuits were regarded as having a sinister influence because in many countries they had become the confessors of the Queen. In South America, the grounds for alarm were more serious. Both the Spanish and the Portuguese governments were fearful that the Jesuits were planning to set up a separate state. The autonomy which they already enjoyed and their self-sufficiency were anathema to the authorities. They might pay taxes at the moment, but it was feared that they could arm the Guaraní and secede.

In 1767, the Jesuits were expelled from the whole continent. The Reductions were destroyed. The slavers moved in. Dr John Hemming in his recent *Amazon Frontier*, says:

> The Indians lived in tidy rows of small thatched huts surrounding a large rectangular parade-ground plaza. Each hut had a verandah and a large single room in which the family cooked, ate and slept in hammocks. The Jesuits had totally destroyed the native Indian culture and replaced it with daily regimentation and strict social control.

Even without going to the Reductions, I could not help wondering how sixty priests, with no support from the colonial authorities, could for 150 years have controlled so rigidly 140,000 warrior Indians (for Guaraní means warrior). In the whole history of the Reductions, not one priest was killed by a Guaraní, although several were murdered by other tribes. It seemed more likely that the Guaraní responded willingly to the teachings of the Jesuits. Once anyone has seen the ruins of even one of the thirty communities that the Jesuits established, nearly all suspicions melt.

We came first to San Ignacio, the earliest Reduction, founded in 1612. The original church had long ago disappeared. In a quiet street there was a long, low building, with a pillared verandah. It was once part of the *colegio* of the mission and is said to be the oldest building in Paraguay. Now it is a museum. The *colegio* in each mission served as the school and the administrative section, including the priests' living-quarters and guest rooms. The part which survives is simply built with mud walls and heavy beams, solid but plain. The museum consisted of four rooms filled with wooden statues, pulpits and retables.

The impact of these carvings is extraordinary. In the first moment that I saw them, I forgot all that I knew about them. I forgot that these statues were sculpted by Indian tribesmen whom the colonists would have called

114

savages. I forgot that they depicted subjects of which the original inspiration must have been at least bewildering if not virtually incomprehensible to the artists. I saw only an artistry infused with love and with understanding.

We cannot know how the Jesuits drew out from the Guaraní such skills, but we can see how much of themselves the Indians put into the carvings. The flowers which decorate the pulpits were their flowers, not acanthus or roses. The figures were themselves. The young St Stanislaus Kostka was no Polish nobleman's son. He could have been found that afternoon in San Ignacio, with his arched eyebrows and dark eyes and round cheeks. And he would have carried his baby brother in just the same way that St Stanislaus held the Christ child. The foreshortened, squat horror of a devil under St Michael's foot belonged with the shades of a tropical jungle. While some of the faces of the saints were obviously modelled on paintings shown to the Indians by the priests or copied from the Jesuits' own work, the eyes especially of the angels were usually Indian and the saints seen from behind had Indian, not European bodies.

The observation of movement was so wonderfully conveyed. The risen Christ seemed only to be pausing between rising from the grave and ascending to heaven. His face wore the precise look of fresh surprise that someone rising from the dead would surely have, though it had never before occurred to me. The Virgin Mary meeting Christ moved forward, her arms outstretched in tentative wonder, her eyes both startled and loving.

St Ignatius, pointing at the Jesuit symbol on his breast, was deeply moving. The fluidity of the carving was astonishing, convincing us of the Saint's restless energy, coupled with an intelligent, calm humility.

At Santa Rosa, too, the church had fallen. Only the crumbling base of the bell-tower remained, but the main square of the village was composed, on three sides, of what were originally the Indian houses of the Reduction. Far from being huts, they were stoutly built, with two good rooms. The roofs were tiled. A verandah or *galería* with stone pillars ran in front of the houses and women sat outside, talking to passers-by.

The priest of the new church, built on the site of the old one, came from Louisiana. He was a Jesuit, aged about forty-five. After sporadic relaxations of the banning of the Order and renewed expulsions, the Jesuits were finally allowed back into Paraguay in 1927. He was a nervous man, but welcoming. He said that he liked to talk English, although his first language was French.

'It makes a change from struggling with Guaraní, which is what most of my congregation speak.'

He unlocked for us the small chapel, known as the House of Loreto, on the same side of the square as the church. There had once been frescoes on the wall but they were not interesting. There was, however, a sculptured group of the Annunciation which was of supreme quality. The Virgin had a glorious expression of serene pleasure. I liked best the rather cocky archangel, delighted with himself for bringing good news.

When we went into the chapel, a shrill crowd of children followed us, chattering in Guaraní. Their faces were those of the dark-eyed seraphs of the carvings. Their lives were possibly no better than those of the models three hundred years ago. The priest had just come from burying a boy of four. Still moved, he held some of the younger children to him as we looked at the statues.

'Too many of them die,' he said. 'Often it is of diarrhoea. There is a clinic, but what can the man do? He has no equipment, no X-ray. He can do an appendix and a caesarian and that's about it. One of my parishioners was very sick. He had to go to Foz de Iguaçu in Brazil for treatment. It was so expensive that he had to sell his oxen.'

In the morning, we took a dirt road through what was once all mission land – flat, flooded country. Horses and cattle struggled, sinking in the mud, the reeds brushing their bellies. Storks circled overhead and we saw lapwings, herons and egrets, and many birds that I didn't know – a beautiful yellow-throated bird with a speckled back and ubiquitous, yellow and brown birds with a long cocking tail and a fierce chirrup, which I think were Guira cuckoos.

At the Reduction of Saints Cosme and Damián, we saw the first of the large, red-sandstone ruins. They were reminiscent of churches in Staffordshire and Cheshire, but lacking the grime of the Midlands. This Reduction, in the eighteenth century, was an astronomical centre, where the priests made observations, particularly of the planet Jupiter, important enough to attract notice in Europe. Little remained of the church and nothing of the observatory except for one carved sundial.

It was at the Reduction of Trinidad that I felt the real enormity of the destruction of the loving craftsmanship of the Guaraní. Trinidad spreads over a wide area and here one can visualise the life of a Reduction.

The central point was always the church, often big enough to hold five thousand people. To the south, attached to the church, would be the *colegio*, perhaps in two large courtyards, with the school, the priests' lodgings, and the workshops. To the east, there was often a mission garden; to the north a cemetery. Near the church, also, there would be a large house for widows and orphans and anyone else in need. Facing the west door of the church would be the main square, a 'parade ground' only in the sense that it was used for religious processions on feast days.

Round the square were blocks of houses for the Guaraní, and behind them streets with more blocks. These blocks, in the larger missions, usually consisted of six stone-built houses, joined by a verandah, each having two rooms.

Much of the life of the missions was communal. The fields were worked for the common good, the herds of cattle belonged to the group, though each Indian family had a garden of its own. There was nothing strange in this for their tribal customs would have involved a nearly identical system of sharing. The unexpected aspects of these singular communities were the religious devotion and the astonishing artistry, both sculptural and musical.

The huge church at Trinidad was begun in 1706. It had a vaulted central nave, eleven yards wide, and two vaulted side aisles. The building was destroyed within eighty years by the secular administrator who took over the running of the Reduction when the Jesuits were expelled. He removed the keystones of the arches and the building fell. Even what remains is impressive. An enchanting stone frieze runs round the surviving walls of winged angels playing musical instruments – bassoons, flutes, a Paraguayan harp, even an organ with another angel working the bellows.

There is a wonderful innocence about the carvings. One is certainly aware of the guiding hand of the priests, but also of the encouragement of invention, as in the flowers decorating the doorways of the Indian houses. It is plain that both priests and Indians must have shared in the enthusiasm of creation.

Trinidad was perhaps the most remarkable of the Reductions, but the wonder and sadness was with us for several days as we visited other ruins. At Jesús I sat with a crowd of children who seemed to speak no Spanish, but found me immensely funny, while Symon went to find a woman who had the key. She came with her small son who guided Symon into unknown crannies in the ruins. The façade of Jesús had trefoil Moorish arches, but it was unfinished when its builders were banished.

It was while I was waiting for Symon that I was assailed by a measure of doubt about the Utopian nature of the Reductions. I looked at the children, unable to communicate in the senior of the two languages of their country, and regretted their limited education. It then occurred to me that they would have been no better off under the Jesuits. In all the years that the Reductions existed, not one Guaraní had been ordained into the priesthood. They taught the Indians to build, to play instruments, to carve, but not to read or to write.

I began to wonder how the priests had thought of the people. Did they consider them really as human? Or did they think of them as some kind of sub-species? If the Indians were human, why did they not educate them? I began to fear that what they sought primarily was a headcount of conversions.

Later, back in Brazil, we went to São Miguel. It stood proud on a hill and was visible for miles. Its façade was better preserved than most, reminding me of the cathedral at Salvador. The carvings in the museum were almost more skilled than any we had seen, energetic and alive. I remember vividly a monkey.

To have destroyed such works of love and optimism must have needed a savagery beyond compass.

In 1750, the mission lands, including São Miguel and six other Reductions to the west of the River Uruguay, were transferred by treaty from Spain to Portugal. The treaty stated that the missionaries must move with all the Indians to Spanish territory. They could take moveable property but the towns, churches, houses, buildings and land were to be given to the Portuguese.

The Guaraní refused to move. The Portuguese and Spanish sent a combined army to put them out. The Indians marched into battle carrying their Christian images for protection. The armies of two powerful Catholic kings butchered fourteen hundred innocent believers.

When the Jesuits left in 1767, the communities in Spanish control were not immediately disbanded. For a while they were run by secular administrators, who had no real interest in the people.

The borders were, in fact, never settled until late in the nineteenth century, after the War of the Triple Alliance. Throughout those hundred years, the Guaraní suffered. The Portuguese behaved even worse than the Spanish. The population of the seven Reductions on the far side of the River Uruguay at the height of the Jesuit period was about thirty thousand. In 1821, it was three thousand. The slavers could now seize slaves and the settlers took the land.

Even Dr Hemming in his *Red Gold* concedes that: 'The Jesuits were the most determined and intelligent of the missionary orders. Their Paraguayan missions were the most successful attempt at conversion or acculturation of any South American Indians. Amid all the hypocritical claptrap about the benefits of Christianity, these missions demonstrated that in the right circumstances something could be done.'

The Jesuits did an unique thing. And in doing it, they held off the inevitable results of Spanish and Portuguese greed for 150 years.

* * *

We left Paraguay in much the same way that we came in. This time there was a border post. Some people stopped at it. Others, presumably locals, just drove past. I thought it easier to do this, rather than try to explain how we had come into the country. Nobody even looked up. On the Brazilian side, they were equally unconcerned.

So often borders in South America were prolonged bouts of bureaucratic dementia. I decided that it was part of the game of tormenting the neighbours. If any grounds could be discovered for refusing entry for somebody, thereby inconveniencing the country he was leaving, that was a point scored.

Each country dislikes its neighbour. In Venezuela people told me how disagreeable the Brazilians were. In Brazil they said the Uruguayans were dull. The Uruguayans hated the Argentinians and the Agentinians the Chileans. The Chileans were odious to the Bolivians and the Peruvians, while the Peruvians and Ecuadorans were in perpetual dispute. The Colombians were on uneasy terms with the Ecuadorans. We shall see later how it was at the Venezuelan border, by which time we had completed our circle. Everyone, of course, despised the Paraguayans.

We spent the day by the falls of Iguaçu. The water fell in broad and narrow ribbons, separated by promontories of rock, over a wide Y-head, so that some parts of the fall were at right angles to others or even facing them. I was surprised and, at first, a little disappointed to see that the river coming over the lip was brown with silt. The foamy lace of the tumbling water looked a little as I always imagined Miss Havisham's wedding dress. As we came closer, the sheer volume was so astounding that it overwhelmed any expectation of pretty whiteness. What must it have been like to come upon this splendour without any foreknowledge of its existence? Those murdering *conquistadores* never deserved so glorious a moment of discovery.

In useless speculation, I weighed the attractions of man-made or natural wonders. I had skipped the great Paraguayan dam at Itaipú, tall as a sixty-storey building, the largest hydro-electric scheme in the world, twice as powerful as Grand Coulee. According to the brochure, to go to it meant joining a tour, watching films, travelling in a bus, 'stopping to buy refreshments', spending half a day being guided and filled with statistics.

Of course, it would have been impressive. But only ten minutes in a hidden place near the natural fall, I knew, would give me as much pleasure. I sat on a jungled knoll from where I could see no one, but could watch the placid river start to fret as it came to the crusty rocks before the drop. Already ruffled, the curling water frothed caramel as it plunged over the lip and fell, with its look of an airy fabric, to the foot of the cliff. Then with a stupendous roaring the lace reverted to water and hurried, all calm lost, through narrow walls to join the Paraná and flow on to mingle with the Uruguay as the Río de la Plata and emerge into the Atlantic between Buenos Aires and Montevideo.

While I sat, butterflies like dancing leaves stuttered from tree to tree – saffron, crimson, purple, blue, some with silver dots, others with golden stripes. A kingfisher swivelled through the undergrowth. High above, a huge falcon circled in patient expectation. Beyond, a multitude of dusky swifts swirled tireless through the spume thrown up by the waterfall, in and out of the steady rainbow. What they found in the spray from the cauldron of furious water below is hard to imagine, but they were a pretty sight.

It was odd to find such peace in the midst of so great a noise, a thundering which carried for ten to fifteen miles.

We headed south-east, back in the rich lands of Brazil, but somehow the people were poor. The wooden houses had a German look, painted blue with brown shutters. The barns were of plain wood, with tiled roofs. The style did not change for many miles. On the rounded hills were windbreaks of standing maize which looked like contour lines on a relief map or even, when they were close together, like soldiers ranged for battle. They reminded me of a book by Glauber called *Furnaces*, which had once belonged to Oliver Cromwell. On the flyleaf he had drawn a battle plan. 'Me' he had written on one flank, 'Fairfax' on the other. Opposite he put 'Enemie'. How little it takes to make an historical figure human. And how peculiar the random nature of one's thoughts when travelling.

We slept and, in the morning, mist hung in the valleys like careful packing. For many hours the wooden houses went on, pink ones with blue shutters, white or unpainted ones with brown shutters. The tiles here were flat not rounded.

We stopped to ask the way of a fair-haired man with eyes of a fierce blue. He did not understand us and shifted his weight from one leg to the other in a restless effort at comprehension. Do you speak German? 'Alles,' he said, meaning everyone in the region. Whether *hochdeutsch* or *plattdeutsch* was beyond him. I asked if he himself was German. 'Brazilian.' And his parents? 'Brazilian.' He had no idea when his family came to Brazil, no idea really that they had ever come from anywhere else. He spoke two languages fluently, but seemed not to know why. Yet when we asked about the next village, called Frederico Westphalen, he said it was an Italian town. He owned no land, was in effect a *peão*. We parted in amicable misunderstanding. Even in Frederico Westphalen the political slogans painted on the rocks were all for German names – Müller, Biehl, Bender, Braun.

Later, we came to the Italian lands, where the houses had porches and verandahs. The people rode in bullock-carts. The children had round, dark eyes and the adults the lined, leathery faces of Calabria or Sicily. Then we were in the plains and we sped to Pelotas and a ranch in the flat coastal lands of Rio Grande do Sul.

The Granja Silvana belonged to Guilherme Echenique. Gui was a little over fifty, a shortish, strong man with a pointed nose. His face had a mischievous cast to it, borne out by his enkindling laugh. His wife, Leda, was attractive in a distinguished way, with large brown eyes and a beautiful skin which quite belied her industry. Complementing his sense of fun, a quiet current of humour ran beneath her dignified calm.

They had two daughters living at home. Mercedes had a languid, soft, rather serious air. She had studied art in Rio and now taught the subject in the local school. The younger daughter, Eliza, who was twenty, was studying to be an accountant. By contrast with her sister, she had a lithe, energetic figure and her eyes sparked with her father's mischief.

Their son, Guilherme, older than the two sisters, was away working on an oilrig as the farm did not interest him. He was coming home soon to be married, and preparations for the wedding were going forward.

The name Echenique is Spanish in origin. Gui's ancestor came with Pizarro to Peru. The family gradually moved south, at first to Argentina. Then Gui's great-grandfather moved to Brazil, having married a Brazilian girl from Pelotas. Gui inherited some two thousand five hundred acres and later bought a further thousand.

About 750 of these acres were devoted to rice. It was harvest time. The land is grazed for half the year, ploughed in November and the crop ripens in April. We went out into the wet fields to watch the combine-harvesters working. In the field where we were, there were three – two green, imported ones and one red, made in Brazil. There were eight in all working on the ranch, each new one costing $60,000. In principle, a new machine could fill thirteen hundred fifty-kilo bags a day, worth $7,800. In reality, because some of the machines were old, they cut about a hundred acres a day, each acre producing just under two and a half tons of rice, about half what they hope to do with new machines. During a week's harvesting they used ten thousand litres of fuel.

It was odd to see such different birds in a harvest field – ibis and limpkin following the tractors, predatory cari-cari waiting to catch fleeing mice and, overhead, storks whose interest I could not work out.

There was so much to learn about the farm. They ran 1120 Red Poll cattle, each cow needing two and a half acres, and a herd of five hundred Hampshire Down sheep. They had no milking cows except for two Jerseys which Mercedes kept to make cheese and butter, in order to supplement her meagre pay as an art teacher. Leda wished that they had more cows of different kinds. 'All cows are so beautiful,' she said.

Copses of eucalyptus patterned the land like clumps of bristle on a worn brush. Gui grew them for shade and for fencing-posts, cutting them every seven years. In two years, the new plantations grew thirty feet tall. The wood for fencing was soaked in water for two years, which made it more durable.

The rice-drying plant was a mixture of a factory and a laboratory. I was startled once more by the lavish wealth of Brazil when I saw that the hoppers, in which the rice sat after husking and polishing, were made of solid mahogany.

Behind the plant were the workers' houses – they were poor, untidy shacks. There were twenty people employed full-time on the rice and another four on the cattle. A combine driver earned $160 a month, a tractor-driver $100 and anyone else the minimum wage of $45. It was not surprising that their living-quarters were wretched.

One might, given the outrageous disparity between rich and poor in all of South America, have expected the Echeniques' house to have been luxurious, but it was not. They built it eight years ago. There was one large pleasant room with a big, stone fireplace, but apart from that the house was small compared to the farmhouse of a four-hundred acre farm in England.

Leda did all the cooking, in a country where anyone with money has servants. Indeed, she said that she found even this house onerous, because Gui liked to have large numbers of cousins and friends to stay, even strangers like ourselves. They wanted to go to Europe for a holiday, but they could not afford it – everything they possessed was tied up in land.

We all went to bed at nine, for Gui was always up by five.

In front of the house was a paddock, not more than half an acre, surrounded by trees. When I went out in the morning, there was a horse standing in this patch. The early, slanting sun illuminated the glossy coat of the horse so that it shone a deep, vibrant chestnut. The horse arched its neck, the curving muscles standing out from shoulder to ear in a lazy demonstration of strength. Its tail rose tight and narrow from its rump and fell in coiffed splendour. It was the most beautiful horse I have ever seen – a pure-bred Arab stallion.

This was a side of the ranch of which we had learned little on the previous day. In 1929, Gui's father had bought ten Arab mares and one stallion from Argentina. Now they had forty pure Arabs of which six were stallions. They also bred other horses of mixed blood and had just sold forty-four of these.

We went down to look at the stables, old buildings with pretty fanlights made romantic by the morning mist. Even the concrete silo, with a pointed roof and a weathercock of an Arab horse, looked like a Provençal tower. As we walked round, Mercedes and Eliza shared *maté* with their father. *Maté* is a kind of herb tea, tasting a little like hay, which people drink from a gourd with a silver straw.

The horses were superb. They danced round the paddock for us, but none could match Nunas, the chestnut stallion. I kept going back in my mechanical chair to look at him. I could not rid myself of the anthropomorphic idea that he was aware of his beauty. He was inquisitive and plainly fascinated by my chair, but mostly he struck attitudes and held them for bemusing minutes. Then he would trot a little and move on and assume another pose. There was something epicene in the apparent vanity of this supremely masculine horse. I longed to go in and touch so exquisite a creature, but Gui said he would bite.

The Echenique family were the most delightful people we had met in Brazil and we were sad to leave. As we went, I was intrigued to realise that the dull, flat land we had seen as we arrived had taken on new character.

The rich brown *Furnarius rufus*, known as João de Barro (Muddy Johnny), scuffled in the dust. They build their domed, mud nests on any posts, a habit that earns them their other name of oven-birds. A young colt shimmied down the field next to the drive, following us. A southern screamer and its mate, looking like a cross between a turkey and a pheasant, stood in the marshy field by the road. Our slight acquaintance with these fields, and the clumps of eucalyptus so transformed this drab country, spread in the morning with a quilt of sparkling cobwebs, that we could understand how Gui and Leda and Mercedes gave their lives to it.

8
Uruguay
TWO TIME-WARPS

Uruguay was clean and neat, as worthy and as unmemorable as Switzerland. This judgement, I was conscious, was both unjust and ungrateful, for the country is, in terms of humanity, the most sympathetic in South America. Both primary and secondary education are free. There are, in theory, pensions of all kinds, unemployment benefits and free medical care. The birthrate is low, the expectation of life is high – higher than in Britain for men and not much lower for women. Capital punishment has been long abolished. The Church has no link with the State. There was, in the 1970s, a depressing hiccough in these agreeable arrangements, when the military seized power. In 1985, however, near-proper democracy returned, although there are ugly signs that it was the rich who prospered and the poor who suffered from the dictatorship. And the economic circumstances that led to it are not much changed, so that the suppositious pensions and benefits are rarely paid.

Having travelled for so long in wonder and puzzlement at the persistent cruelties, instabilities, ineptitudes and perversities of South America, it was contrary on my part to find this relatively humane, equitable and safe country somewhat uninteresting.

Two things stuck out from the bland amiability – both twists of time.

We drove down the coast towards the tower blocks of Punta del Este. We came first to grand villas, built in a variety of golf-club styles. Nothing divided one from the next. Their smooth, prinked lawns ran into one another, a lonely shrub perhaps marking the boundary. They were all deserted. The shutters were closed on the lower floors, the blinds drawn above. No cars stood in the car ports. On one lawn, a solitary sprinkler dripped a limp shower on the too-green grass. No person moved, nor any animal. After the villas came the blocks of flats. Smart new blocks – all shut. Blank windows reflected the afternoon sun. The children's swings hung idle. Behind the locked glass porches, the lifts sat dark, their automatic doors open. No light glimmered. The car parks were empty.

Mile upon mile we went. It was warm and sunny, the sort of day we call perfect in England in June. Had it been Frinton, we would not have been able to see the beach for crowds, but here the sand stretched empty, save for some carefree gulls, the only living things.

At last we came to the city, an agglomeration of boutiques and restaurants and hairdressers, all shut, shut, shut. The traffic-lights stood mute, giving no encouragement or warning. In the very centre, there were a few lost people and a car or two. The door of one bank was open. I felt quite unnerved, as if we had leaped forward into a time soon after the neutron bomb. Symon was hungry, but he hardly dared to ask one of the 'survivors' where he could find some food. In any event, there was none to be had.

Later I learned that Punta del Este is largely an Argentinian resort. It is they who own the houses and the flats and they use them for only two months of the year. On 31 March they go home and for ten months this mass of expensive, luxurious, albeit hideous, property stands empty. Were Uruguay's population increase not so moderate, the affront might prove intolerable. As it is, it merely sours relations.

*   *   *

In Montevideo, the leap in time was backwards. At first, I thought we had somehow got muddled up in a huge vintage-car rally. Model-A Fords pootled past, then a Packard like one my uncle had in 1935, and a Buick from 1939. Nor were they just American cars. There were many from my English childhood. I saw a pre-war Hillman Minx, a twin to the one that I had learned to drive in 1945, and masses of those Vauxhalls with silver fluting on either side of the bonnet. Some long-forgotten 1950s cars had obviously been popular, Morris Oxfords, Austin Cambridges, an occasional MG or Austin Healey. Once a beautiful pre-war sporting Jaguar. It was like meeting a lot of old friends of whom one had not had news for years. And, similarly, some of their names had slipped my memory and I spent hours peering at bonnets to read Simca Cinq, Marmon, Wolseley or Humber Super Snipe.

The explanation for these relics was partly the formidable duty levied on new cars and partly that cars more than forty years old were exempt from road tax. Those more than forty-five years old were easily identified, because that was when Uruguay changed from driving on the left to driving on the right.

Of course, it had not escaped the notice of South American traders that old cars have a rarity value. It was a nice question as to when the rising price of an old car overtook its usefulness. In a showroom, I saw an impeccable 1929 Model-A Ford for $7,000. There is now a ban on the export of old cars but an engaging villain had a line of ancient models parked on the seafront, any one of which he promised he could ship to me in England. I was tempted by a 1926 Willy's Whippet for $1,000, but thought that it would be unlikely to arrive.

It was not only the cars which induced the same sense of twisted time. I chose the hotel that we stayed in for its improbable appearance. It might have been transported whole from the front at Nice. It was built early in the twentieth century in a French casino style. The entrance lobby was an oval hall with six pairs of stone pillars supporting an elaborately gilded, domed ceiling. The halls beyond stretched for nearly a hundred yards and there was, indeed, at the far end, a gaming-room, pillared and domed in a similar grandiose fashion.

There were six hundred bedrooms and, for a risible sum, I took a suite, furnished with a mixture of precarious French discomfort and solid Spanish ugliness.

Closing my eyes as I passed another resounding hall where a game of bingo was in progress, I indulged the time-machine fantasy and went to the casino in the mood of a 1920s playboy. I was rewarded by an encounter with Osvaldo Farnacci, a thin, hungry-looking man whose affected air of nonchalance was marred by his eyes which flickered with nervous suspicion. He liked to speak English, because he had lived in England for a while, until he was deported by the Home Office. He wore a dark suit of which he was proud, although it hung awkwardly and the stitching had loosened, making the seams look like ladders. 'I got it at the British Home Stores,' he said, as if this were a name to conjure respect. Osvaldo was a professional gambler. He told me that he made eighty dollars a day on which he could live. He confided his system to me. When I had lost thirty dollars, I forsook the playboy fantasy and left.

*   *   *

There was a *tristesse* about Uruguay that I found nowhere else in South America, a quite different kind of hopelessness. The beaches were, to my mind, far more beautiful than those of Rio, but they were lifeless – the price of respectability perhaps. In the older part of the city, the architecture, apart from some good 1930s buildings, was hideous. On the other hand, it was weirdly adventurous and exciting, though now grey and decaying. The newer architecture was uniformly tame and unimaginative. The spirit was gone.

As we drove away from Montevideo we passed the prison. It looked like a Victorian, Italianate country house. There had recently been an attempted break-out. The authorities learned of the plot because someone had ordered three buses to be waiting at the prison gates. Instead the police were waiting. There was a modest shoot-out. Two prisoners died. None escaped.

There was so much good sense about, which no other country would think of. It was forbidden, for instance, to carry a gun on May Day or Election Day. But what use was that, when the police were paid so little that they were easily corrupted and even the force itself was so short of money that it often could not afford to buy petrol for its patrol cars.

On the way to Fray Bentos (which I was amazed to find was a town of fourteen thousand people), we saw 750 or more new Zetor tractors, imported from Czechoslovakia, sitting in a compound. Next to them were thirty Fiat Combi vans. They must all have been there for at least a year, unused and rotting. A high fence ran round the compound which was marked as a prohibited area. At the gate, I saw that it belonged to the Ministry of Finance and Economics. Common sense was not all-pervading.

9
Argentina
GENTLEMAN RANCHERS AND
WILD WELSHMEN

An enormous sign soon after the border said *Las Malvinas son argentinas*. We were to see this declaration all over the country, at the approach to every large town. Yet we had had no trouble at the border.

'Why is your visa issued by the Brazilian Embassy?'

'Well, you see . . . er, we don't have an Argentine embassy in London.'

'Why not?'

'Well . . . er, there is, as it were, the question of the Malvinas.'

The immigration man laughed, stamped our passports and said, with no sign of irony, 'You are very welcome.'

I was relieved, as I had had some apprehension as to how we would be treated. He was pleased, I think, that I had said Malvinas. I found no difficulty in this, because I have always felt that those wretched islands were not worth the loss of one life, whether for territorial ambition or even a matter of principle. In any case, Malvinas is the older name.

It was not until 1690 that Captain Strong landed briefly on the bleak and windy islands and called them the Falklands. French sailors from St Malo had landed many years before and named them Malouines, which the Spanish corrupted to Malvinas. It was the French, too, who first occupied them when Admiral Bougainville planted a colony on the Malouines in 1764. Two years later, the French sold the islands to the Spanish who, it was said, had an equal claim. The British almost at once marched in and installed a survey post. In 1770, the Spanish closed the post; the next year, the British restored it, only to abandon it totally three years later.

The Argentinians moved into the empty islands in 1820 and remained for eleven years, when a German, who ran the settlement, imprisoned some American seal-hunters. The United States sent a warship to break up the community, but the Argentinians continued their occupation. In 1833, the British arrived and drove them out. The British claim to the islands is feeble, the talk of the inhabitants' being British is humbug.

After a few miles we saw rheas, huge balls of feathers running, their long necks like a spare leg on which they might do Isle of Man cartwheels. It was strange, too, after so long in the tropics, to see vines and willows, apples and runner beans.

It was odder still, after the bourgeois tones of Montevideo, to find ourselves in the orotund splendours of Buenos Aires. Here the old-fashioned quality was no time-warp of fantasy. It was a living presence. The grandiosity was not the faded nostalgic sigh of the Carrasco Hotel; it was fully-fledged pomp and circumstance. I found myself humming Elgar. There was nothing cosy about Buenos Aires.

Great mansions, with elaborate wrought-iron gates and grilles, in imitation of nineteenth-century France, were still lived in. The newer blocks of flats had roofs of Roman tiles. The grand shops were filled with silver photograph frames, seals, half-hunter watches and carriage clocks. The furniture was of ormolu and marble. There was an abundance of amber and ivory, and I came to feel that the air hung heavy with the smell of polished leather.

The smarter women wore skirts well below the knee and were dressed in shades of caramel. They had furs of all kinds and gleamed with gold. Nearly all covered their poor complexions with too much make-up. Their dark glasses were tinted a pinky-orange that matched the rinse of their hair, which they wore long. They had that imperious impatience which comes naturally to rich, Latin women. They deferred, however, to their husbands.

The men wore suits, which might have come from Savile Row, of light worsted with a faint check. Their shoes were rather pointed and highly polished, which agreed with their slicked-down hair, cut in military style.

They looked small beside their fur-plumped wives, but they spoke with crisp authority to them and to waiters.

Our hotel was beautifully run. It catered for country landowners on visits to the capital. Most of them spoke English and we exchanged courteous greetings as we passed in the panelled hallway. Many were of British descent and their voices and accents carried me back almost to infancy.

One was Rod Henderson, a friendly, bumbling man of about forty-five. His family had come out in the 1850s but, had I met him in Brown's Hotel in London rather than in Buenos Aires, I would have assumed he was up for a few days from, say, Warwickshire. In fact, he was unable to return to his family property in Sante Fe because of floods which were covering twenty-five million acres. The Hendersons had prospered for many years but their estates had now shrunk to eleven thousand acres, which Rod regarded as paltry. Their connection with Britain had never been broken. He and his brother were educated in England. Rod had undergone a course of Sufi in London, with a Turkish teacher who was an old friend of mine. His sister has a mime and dance school in Cornwall.

The ambience of yesteryear breathed over every aspect of Argentina, particularly politics. Gina Caranci was an attractive, hospitable person. I have a friend who divides women into two groups – gear-changers and non-gear-changers. Gina was undoubtedly a gear-changer; capable, intelligent and energetic.

'I prefer to live under a military dictatorship,' she said the first time that I met her. 'Either way we are going to be in an economic mess, it is better at least to have security. Since we have had democracy, the number of rapes and murders has gone up. Four hundred stereos are stolen every day in Buenos Aires. I know it is not as bad as it is in Europe, but nevertheless . . .'

I loved Gina for her forthright honesty. She paid no lip-service to ideas with which she had no sympathy. When I protested about the lack of human rights and 'disappeared' people, she made no pretence that such things had not happened. 'There are always brutalities in war,' she said.

In any case, she maintained, foreigners only heard one side of the story. Every day women stand in protest in the Plaza de Mayo. They are the mothers of the 'disappeared' people.

'My friend's young maid came to her and asked for the day off last week. What for? my friend asked, as the maid had had the day off the day before. "It is my turn to be one of the mothers in the Plaza de Mayo," the girl said. So much of it is lies.' We were to return to this discussion quite often.

It was not only the rich who held these right-wing views. Bingo was a businessman of modest means, funny and jolly and extremely macho. He was happily married with four children but told us many entertaining stories of experiences in the *hoteles transitorios* as the love-motels were called in Argentina – how he had scalded himself in a jacuzzi and of his mechanic friend who had all his clothes stolen and went home at three in the morning in a pair of borrowed overalls, to be told by his wife not to work so late.

Even when his sixteen-year-old son joined us for dinner, Bingo talked of his exploits in Brazil and told his son to give Symon the names of some submissive girls in a town we were to visit.

Bingo's view of democracy was jaundiced. 'I consider it more shaming to have to hand over twenty per cent of a deal to a civilian, who won't otherwise give me a licence, than to a military man who says he'll shoot me if I don't give him the money. At least it is not disgraceful to pay to save yourself from death. The other is less excusable. I prefer one man feathering his nest to three hundred supposed representatives, who represent nothing but themselves.'

Rather forgetful of these theories, he told me how monstrous he thought it, albeit amusing, that during the South Atlantic war, the Argentine soldiers were issued with medical supplies bought from Britain. 'Someone was getting a cut.'

Bingo had sympathy for the officers who were being prosecuted for their crimes and inhumanities in what is known as the terrorist war.

'Alfonsin was Procurator Fiscal during the terrorist war. He demanded "blood and more blood"; now he wants to prosecute those from whom he asked it.'

Bingo was, in reality, a most reasonable man, moved primarily by a belief that life was for enjoyment. He would never have wished to harm anyone. His views on the Malvinas were quietly reasonable. He believed, as did every Argentinian, that they belonged to Argentina, but he agreed that they had no claims to South Georgia.

'The only reason we are after that is to make the Antarctic wedge bigger on the map.'

On every map printed in Argentina, even a map of a small region in the north, there appears an inset showing the area of Antarctica claimed by Argentina. I could only suppose it was required by law. By showing South

Georgia as a possession, the segment of the Antarctic Circle is much enlarged.

*   *   *

As we drove north, there was a feeling of prosperity which was quite new to us – perhaps not prosperity, but at least none of the shrivelling poverty to which we had become so used, but never inured, in Venezuela, Brazil, Paraguay and even on the fringes of Uruguayan towns.

On a busy road some way out of Buenos Aires, two cars ahead of us drew level with each other. The driver of the right-hand one reached out his left hand and gripped the right hand of the passenger of the other car. For a half a mile they travelled, maintaining their handclasp. When we overtook them we saw that they were hippies.

The country was flat and monotonous. There can have been little to amuse the police who stopped us at a checkpoint near Rosario. I saw the young couple from the car in front of us, clutching a puppy, hand over a note to the men.

The police asked for Symon's driving licence. He had three which they shared out between them and then went a little way from us in consultation. Rather like people playing an after-dinner game, having prepared their questions while they were, as it were, out of the room, they came back. They asked for a number of other documents, which we had. Then:

'Have you a warning triangle?' Symon rummaged in the back and produced it.

'Have you a jack?' Symon found two.

'Tiene matafuego?' Symon played this one for quite a long time, looking anxious. He got out the dictionary. When he found the word, he put on an even more worried expression. The police looked triumphant. Then Symon, like a conjuror, pulled a fire-extinguisher from under my seat. They looked crestfallen.

'Put on your handbrake.' Three of them went to the back of the car and pushed, hard. The brake held. They waved us on with wry smiles.

In the town itself, it was different. Map-reading, I made Symon take an illegal left turn. More police, this time unsmiling. We must pay a fine.

'How much?'

'Three hundred and fifty dollars,' they said.

'I haven't got anything like that kind of money.'

'How much have you got?'

'Sixty dollars in all.'

'That'll do.'

I always feel degraded when I give in to this kind of corruption, but the alternative is three hours of argument in the police station. It was late. And, anyhow, the police are wretchedly paid. I handed over sixty dollars, having difficulty hiding the rest of the money in my wallet.

We went on by a quieter road through country where they were harvesting beans. The combines and the trucks set up a dust which hung in long thin streaks like mist over the land. The sun set dry and glowing, casting no patterns in the broad empty sky. The rains had stopped and it was cold.

As we travelled further north, I wondered again about attitudes towards the British. The effect of propaganda is always startling. Even someone as intelligent as Gina could be lured into cloudland by its nonsense. She had assured me that Chile and Britain were on the point of joining forces in order to seize Patagonia. If she, who was half English and had many relations in England, could believe that, what might someone who had lost a son or a brother in the South Atlantic war believe about us? A cynical friend in Buenos Aires had told me that most of the troops who had fought in the war were from the north, from the areas where people were darker with Indian and Negro blood.

A man was standing by his car which had broken down in an empty place. He said he lived a couple of miles down the road. He came along with us to fetch some tools from home. In fact, his farm was five or more miles away, so we talked. He did not look like a farmer. His hair was neatly oiled, his beard and moustache were trim. Eventually he asked what nationality we were. When I told him, he fell silent for long minutes and his knuckles went white.

When we got to the turning to the farm, he made as if to get out, but we insisted on taking him to the house another mile and a half down a lane. I plied him with more questions. He had 110 acres on which he kept ninety cows which gave him 370 gallons of milk a day, which seemed quite good, for the soil was not rich.

At the farm, five dogs barked and two newborn Friesian calves struggled to get up. The house was built of a mellow, red brick with large sash windows. Round it were the ubiquitous eucalyptus, but also *Cupressus sempervirens* and casuarina trees, looking as always out of focus.

His old mother came out from the house, disconcerted. Suddenly, he smiled – a shining, handsome smile. He squeezed my shoulder and shook hands warmly with Symon, and we left relieved.

The sierras rose ahead and we climbed. For several days we roamed in these foothills – our first sight of the Andes which were to lend such varied wonder to the rest of our journey.

From Jujuy we followed the Rio Grande. How many of those can there be? And Rios Negros, Rios Verdes, Rios Blancos – few of them, as Paul Theroux observed, of the colour specified.

The river was wide and gravelled, the bed of pale pebbles scored with thin rivulets of dark brown water. Willows grew at the water's edge and, later, poplars. The hills rising on either side were covered in scrub, which dwindled as we went higher, giving way to candelabra cacti and those tall, fat ones like spiky cigars.

Rounding a bend, we saw ahead two spurs of land, both of which had suffered slides down to the river, exposing the rock. The first scar was a sharp red; the second, not two hundred yards beyond, a lustrous grey-green. It seemed impossible that they should be side by side, such diverse colours, until we came to Purmamarca, a village in a hidden valley off the main road. Behind the white, colonial houses was a rounded lump of multicoloured rock, perhaps three hundred feet high, striped purple, yellow, pink and green. Behind it the mountains soared in brooding red. Above, the sky was photographic blue.

The little church with one white tower was simple. The roof was made of mud and grass and gravel. Inside it was unexpectedly light, despite there being only three small windows. The ceiling, the pews and the semi-circular pulpit, reached by a shaky stair, were all made of cactus wood, soft with dark knots, almost holes, where the spikes once were. The floor was brick. There was an old confessional, painted green and white and decorated with flowers in relief, made with gypsum, in the same way that the little shrines in Indian homes are made. Inside was a sheepskin for the confessor to kneel on. There were small, crude paintings done by the Indians; what little interest they may have held had long since faded.

The valley of the Rio Grande, known here as the Quebrada de Humahuaca, was part of the early Spanish route from Lima to Buenos Aires. The missionaries, Franciscans and Dominicans, came in the mid-seventeenth century, moving south from Bolivia. Along the way, they built scores of tiny churches.

We stayed in Huacalera. The hotel had once been the main house of a large *estancia*. The owner had evidently been a good farmer. In the hall hung many framed certificates of prizes he had won for his crops, and row upon row of rosettes testified to the quality of his Aberdeen Angus cattle. His sons sold and the estate was split up. No one won prizes any more –

least of all for running a hotel. The beds were racks and the lavatory bowl fell apart at the first touch, having been propped together by the last guests. The visitors' book revealed that that must have been more than a month ago.

The tall, fair-bearded 'manager' was charming and his wife was pretty. They were not hoteliers, but friends of the owner who had gone away for a holiday. Ernesto Gerrard had soft, blue eyes, which conveyed a warm interest and sympathy. He was a sculptor and, although less than thirty, he had achieved a certain recognition which had not disturbed his modesty.

Ernesto showed me photographs of his work, some of which were grand civic commissions. He had done a fine statue of the great soldier of independence for the town called Libertador General San Martín. In Jujuy, the state capital, he had carved a large relief for the wall of a bridge. It was a map of the Malvinas, with the date Agosto 2, 1982. I asked if he felt strongly about the islands.

'Gerrard is an English name,' he said. 'My grandfather was English and he married an Argentinian.' And we left the matter in the air.

Ernesto took us to see the minute church of Huacalera. A portly, middle-aged Indian, José-Maria Mamani, had the key. He came with enthusiasm, at once needing answers to questions about English football, which I was ashamed not to be able to supply. Then, it occurred to me that a little fancy would be just as pleasing to him as strict fact, and surely more satisfying than silent ignorance.

The church, which José-Maria said dated from 1601, was quite dim, particularly as there was a wide, darkening porch at the entrance. As at Purmamarca, the walls were painted a creamy yellow, the floor was brick and the ceiling of cactus wood, but here the paintings were more interesting. José-Maria said that they were Peruvian in origin. There was a beautiful Annunciation and a very touching Marriage of Mary and Joseph, which Ernesto maintained was worth half a million dollars.

José-Maria, when I had answered another question about Liverpool to his satisfaction, produced a collection of small silver votive offerings to the Virgin of the Immaculate Conception. They compared well with the hideous offerings I remembered at the Bomfim church at Salvador.

Discovering in myself a talent for the invention of imaginary football games, I was rewarded, in the capricious shade of a spreading willow, with José-Maria's account of the passing of General Lavalle in 1848.

The General was the enemy of the tyrant Juan Manuel de Rosas. One may see in Jujuy a copy of the doorway through which Lavalle was shot.

(The original, being a national treasure, has been removed to Buenos Aires.)

'Lavalle's friends,' said José-Maria, his face composed with an appropriate expression of dolour, 'wanted to take the body to Bolivia. Hurry as they might, by the time they reached Huacalera, the General was beginning to go off. The smell was unbearable. They could not continue with the General in that state. So here, on this very spot, they tore the flesh from his body, till there was nothing left but the skeleton. The bones of the General . . . and his heart. They put his heart in a casket. And they took the skeleton and the heart to Bolivia. Then they took him to Chile. Then when Rosas fell, they brought him to a final resting place in Buenos Aires. The General is at peace.' José-Maria looked happy.

We left to look at some of the other churches. At Urquia there was one about a hundred years later than Huacalera. Its bell-tower was detached. The altar was more eleborate and gilded, but nothing much had developed. The greatest charm again lay in eight paintings of winged angels, all of whom were dressed as soldiers. One carried a gun, all the others swords. They had the look of young men painted by Nicholas Hilliard, their long legs bending in epicene languuour. They, too, had been painted in Peru. It was the custom for the missionaries to request from Lima paintings to decorate their churches. They were painted by Peruvian Indians under priestly guidance.

These churches were a far cry from the Reductions. The missionaries can have found little response from the Omaguaca, the Indians of the Quebrada, to compare with the enthusiasm of the Guaraní. They were proud people, who had driven back the Incas when they tried to expand southward, down El Camino de los Incas, a little to the west of the valley. The Guaraní were forest-dwellers; the Aymará, of which the Omaguaca were a branch, were mountain people.

At Humahuaca itself was a huge monument which I was told was a tribute to the Indians, though the *South American Handbook* says it is an Independence monument. The largely naked figure I took to be a representation of an Indian, Argentinians being usually overdressed. If so, it was puzzling that he should be bearded. In any event, it was hideous and thankfully not the work of Ernesto.

We crossed the river at a ford and took a perilous road beside a tributary, because I wanted to see a staging post on the old road, the new one having taken a different route.

La Cueva was a hamlet, hanging uncertainly above the stream. The rocks were an angry orange in the evening sun. The church, reputedly very old, was shut. A woman of about twenty-five was tending a flock of thirty or forty sheep, which grazed the unpromising slopes above the hamlet. The colours of her clothes stood out from the harsh background – a bright, purple skirt and a vivid, green jumper. Her beautiful teeth shone white under her broad-brimmed hat. On one arm she carried a baby; another child ran beside her, its cheeks so rosy under the brown of its skin that they looked painted.

A lamb had just been born and the woman was trying to persuade the ewe to take an interest in it. Another lamb, a few days old, nibbled at Symon's trousers. The woman said that only five people lived in the village now – her parents, herself and the two children. It seemed indelicate to ask where the father of the children was.

As we drove back, the last of the sun softened the hills on the east of the valley. The scars of landslides that had earlier stood out like flattened oyster-shells now looked like beautifully manicured nails. The reddish-purple stones, among the tufted scrub, smoothed by the light, might have been Scottish moorland. When night fell, the cold was steely and we shivered in our shirtsleeves.

*   *   *

At Posta de Hornillos was another staging post, a pretty place on the main river. Here Jorge Stande ran a small museum, which he had managed to make extremely interesting. The crowds of schoolchildren were brought primarily to look at General Belgrano's bed and his desk, which he had used in his campaigns for independence from the Spanish, rather than the local artefacts that I found more interesting.

The Agentinians are obsessed with history. Every town in the country has a street called after the military heroes of the past: Rivadavia, Belgrano, Lavalle, San Martín, Alvear, Urquiza. In the state of Buenos Aires alone, there are seventeen towns and villages called after generals. I came to long for Brazilian indifference to the past and to wish that Argentina would show a keener interest in the future.

What made Jorge Stande's museum so good was his concern to preserve a record of the Indian culture of the region. He showed us ropes made of cows' tails, and small figures made for festivals out of strips of peach. He explained that a particular woven belt must have come from Chile because it had grey threads; the Omaguaca used every colour except grey. A woman, wrapped in cloth, found in a grave, must have been a stranger, for her skull had been squeezed back in childhood, rather than upward which was the local custom.

He had made a collection of foods. There were many varieties of potato – *chuño, morada, runa, oca* and the silk-skinned *lisas*. There were dried vegetables – tomatoes, broad beans, peaches and toasted-maize biscuits. Here I first heard of *quinua*, the Andean grain now become fashionable among vegetarians in New York. It was an Incan staple.

Jorge, alas, was soon leaving the museum. The state government, he said, were quite useless.

* * *

Our wanderings took us up to the plateau above the valley – the *puna* de Atacama. They were lost days in which we saw few people. We were at roughly the same latitude as we had been in Concepción and as we would not be again for a long, cold month in Patagonia and southern Chile. We saw our first llamas as we rested at a deserted mining village, by a salt lake. An old man came out from a stone ruin, but he spoke only what I took to be Quechua, the tongue of the Incas.

Across a long, flat, sandy plain, we came to San Antonio de los Cobres, a glum mining town, twelve thousand feet up, yet we could see peaks far above, topped with dunce's caps of snow. We canvassed opinion as to whether the road to Molinos, recommended by Jorge, were open. Three people said yes, two were doubtful. We took it. After a few yards, a sign read *Ruta Intransitable*.

Instead we drove to Salta, through a narrow, windy gorge and on to Cafayate. At first, I regretted the barred road and the beauties Jorge had spoken of, then the country changed abruptly from the uninteresting farmland around Salta to spectacular scenery.

We plunged into a valley beside which the colours of the previous week faded into drabness. The permutations spun the imagination in a frenzy of pigments – the pink of Petra, the richest rust, sulphur yellows and copper greens, one after another, blending, mixing; the strata sometimes almost on end, at others flat like a file of the millennia. What happened, I wondered, to make that thin, white streak between the coral pink and the solemn umber? What glum period formed that grey-brown slice, thick as a doorstep?

The oyster-shells or fingernails now looked like the moiréed endpapers of a precious volume. There were towers and castles and cathedrals of erosion. Single columns stood like sentinels or like fat squaws. And there were rows of upright rocks, clustered before a cliff

face, their tops pointed, their middles rounded, like so many plump
missionaries in their cowls, all turned to stone.

The patterns multiplied and interbred and burst out in new configu-
rations, so many and so many – the only constants were the river below
and the wind above, the two creators of these designs. Apart, that is, from
the monster blast which threw the world asunder, spewing out burning
boulders, turning centuries on edge. Now it was all so calm in the
sunlight, with cotton clouds throwing shadows on the roseate cliffs,
varying their colours still more.

At Cafayate it all changed again. The valley widened to a desert of
thorns and sand and grey blocks of stone, interspersed with oases, not of
palms but of aspens and vines. There were grand domain houses, one
boasting of producing 1,700,000 litres of wine. Wildlife appeared. An
armadillo ran across the road; hawks and harriers hovered. There were
flurries of birds migrating north for the winter, among them a large skein
of geese.

*   *   *

We turned east away from the Andes, up into country that was bare and
green, over a pass where there were stone houses, thatched with coarse
grass. A few thin cattle grazed, but mostly the herds were of proudly
bearded goats. On the far side, we dropped again to a lake and a dam. On
a round knoll, a military governor had collected 129 menhirs from all over
the region. Some were carved with pre-Colombian patterns, which to a
lay eye looked little different from northern or even Carib interpretations
of faces. Then we were in the plains again and our aimless wanderings
were over.

Much of Argentina's history and character was focused in that north-
west corner – so much trade, so many battles. We had passed a place
called Alemania where men died, whether in the war of independence or
in a civil war I did not establish. Either way, the killing seemed to me so
pointless in that barren land. It made me wonder anew at that passion for
history. This hotchpotch of a nation thrilled to names which might be
Italian, French or English just as well as Spanish. Half the people of
Argentina have Italian blood. How can they be so nationalistic? How,
indeed, can all South American countries be so nationalistic, made up as
they are of such a kaleidoscope of races and nationalities? I wrote in my
diary again, of the dislike each country bears for another, of the countless
wars they have fought against each other. Yet they are all such delightful
people. They all hated each other; I could hate none of them.

In that colourful valley we had found a lone obelisk. It stood near no village. For once, it was not a battle marker, nor a tribute to a general. It said just this: *Solomon Trunsky. Un amigo de humildad.* He rather cheered me up.

* * *

When we arrived at the *estancia*, the Carancis had just finished a count of cattle. Here, at La Catalina, they had 27,046 head. They had more at their three other ranches in San Luis and in Cordoba, but the land in those states was permanent grass and the cattle could not be finished there. This was the main ranch with seventy thousand acres. The others amounted to a further sixty thousand. It sounded a lot until I realised they had barely more than one cow to the acre. And there are people in Britain who own more land than that.

They had, in addition, one thousand horses and, by coincidence like the Echeniques, sixty-five pure-bred Arabs. They had three sheep to keep an old mare company and three llamas rescued from a zoo.

Helios, Gina's husband, was a man of surpassing good looks, like the hero of a western, always immaculate even after a day in the dust or the mud of the farm. They had two young daughters and a small son.

The old house, where Gina's parents had lived, while not enormous, was impractical, so they had built a new one. It was a one-storey, white building with unpainted, wooden shutters and a grey-tiled roof. Inside, it was extremely comfortable with a deceptive air of simplicity. While every fitting was in perfect taste and made of the best materials, there was not one ostentatious thing to mar the unaffected temper of the house.

Except for the hundred or so acres round the house, where trees of splendid dimensions grew, the land was empty and flat. With Gina, we went to look at the animals and the husbandry. As before, the bleak, eternal pampas took on an interest one could never have guessed at.

Huge bulls paced up and down the length of stoutly fenced paddocks. 'In the old days, they kept the bulls in houses on stilts like that one over there. The wind blew through making them cold, so that the animals grew more fur. They fed them on soup and milk, so that they became fat, so fat that when they were sold they could not "marry" for a month.

'Now we exercise them. We put their food at one end of the paddock and their drink at the other and that is why they walk up and down. At the end, they are fit and strong and can cover a cow as soon as they arrive.'

The breeding was highly technical and efficient. 'We have a greater success with artificial insemination and embryo transplants than they do in the United States, probably because we can afford enough staff to maintain hygiene.'

The *estancia* employed 140 men. The housing for married men was excellent and that for bachelors simple, but far superior to anything I had seen in any other country. There was a club for the *peones* with a swimming pool, a large colour television and a video recorder. A tractor driver earned $230 a month, and the lowest-paid man got $160.

With Gina we drove out across the wide fields. Burrowing owls sat on the fence posts staring, reluctant to move unless we came very close. Some rheas ran, stirring up clouds of dust the same shape as themselves and, on the far side of one field, we disturbed a herd of antelope.

The fields were separated by electric fences and we drove through curtains which hung in electrified strips. In one field the Hereford cattle looked strange. When we got closer we saw that their heads hung low, and that their eyes were blear. Their thick tongues stuck out from between their lips and from their mouths dripped a revolting, yellow mucous. I had never seen foot-and-mouth before. In field after field, the poor creatures dribbled from their blistered tongues and trod with ginger steps.

'What can we do? We cannot slaughter twenty-seven thousand animals, which is what we would have to do if we wanted to eliminate the disease from Argentina.'

Foot-and-mouth is endemic in Argentina, so that its effects are mild compared with what would happen in Europe. In fact, it was only a small proportion of the herd which was affected. They would make a complete recovery from the disease, so there was no need nor point to slaughtering any of them.

If there is a serious epidemic, movement of cattle is restricted and herds in the surrounding areas are vaccinated. In Patagonia and Tierra del Fuego, which are supposedly free of the disease, they do have a policy of slaughter. But no one in Argentina hesitates to eat the meat of an infected animal, for it is harmless to humans.

In the afternoon, Helios paraded for us his best Arabs. He seemed to have some especial sympathy with them. They might come from the stable looking beautiful, but not imposing. Then Helios spoke to them and all at once, they assumed a princely magnificence, their necks superbly arched, their tails dancing like the plumes of an hussar. For a whole hour he ran with these exquisite animals to amuse us. Then Symon went riding with the daughter and her friend. They chased the llamas, which very properly spat at them.

This happy weekend drowsed on, and I reviewed the impressions I had formed in Buenos Aires. This family was rich certainly, but they were rooted in the land. They did not hesitate to work beside the *peones* when it was necessary. It would be hard to say that someone with a private aeroplane lived modestly, but Gina and Helios were well aware of how other people lived.

'Paraguay is dreadful,' Gina said. 'It is quite different from here. There the gap between rich and poor is much too big. They have no middle class at all.' Her disgust was genuine, but she found a failure of imagination in me when it came to Argentina.

They knew what I felt about the kind of regime they preferred, but our differences were, I began to realise, the impediment to my understanding of South America. The most difficult preconception of all to eradicate is that of believing what suits oneself must suit everyone.

Gina's tolerance was, in its way, quite as great as I believe mine to be. When I asked how British residents were treated after the South Atlantic war, she laughed at me.

'Of course people can go on being British if they want to. There are hundreds of British people in Argentina and nobody asked them to become Argentinians. They have their chintzes, and their early-morning tea is brought to them in bed. They are waited on by lots of servants and live a life they could never have in England.'

I thought of those voices in Buenos Aires, warbling with the modulations of my childhood.

Some people came for tea and we talked again of the 'disappeared people'. It was hard to sift the fact from fiction, the truth from echoed propaganda.

One visitor said, 'You know, on the morning after the junta took over, three thousand cars were found abandoned. They belonged to people who skipped the country, knowing they'd be in trouble. Many of them are now living abroad and they are called "disappeared". I know one "disappeared" person living comfortably in Spain.

'Amnesty International just don't want to know the other side of things. Those two Irish women who came here . . . when asked if they would like to meet some of the terrorists' victims who had been tortured, flayed, burned with cigarettes, they said they weren't interested.'

It seemed pointless to say that Amnesty concerns itself only with the actions of governments, legalised inhumanities.

Gina was clearer. 'The terrorist war was a civil war. One day we had a letter saying we had been removed from the kidnap list and put on the assassination list. You see, in a civil war you do not know who your enemy is.'

It is a fault of mine when I fall among sympathetic people, to expect them to share my prejudices; when language is no barrier, to forget the circumstances and history which have shaped their lives.

Why, I had wondered for much of this journey, did South America have so different a history from North America? Both were colonised from Europe at roughly the same time. In both halves of the continent the indigenous populations were brutally treated. There was, of course, the difference of religion, but that did not seem to be the root of this divergence. Much of the United States and Canada had been settled by Roman Catholics. Catholicism was not of itself a prescription for instability, nor an inspiration for dictators.

I was coming to the conclusion that the answer lay in the motives of the colonists. Those who went north did so to escape from tyranny. They went to work and to found a more just society. Those who came to the south came for greed. 'I came for gold not to till the soil like a peasant,' was how Cortés put it. The northerners came to settle; they brought their wives and families. The *conquistadores* came alone, to take what they could and to return home to Spain. For three centuries, the two Iberian kings ruled South America by force as absolute monarchs. It is a legacy hard to eradicate.

The Carancis flew to Buenos Aires on Sunday afternoon, leaving us alone in the *estancia*. In the morning when we left, the buxom cook and Claudia, the pretty maid, the only two servants, kissed Symon and myself goodbye.

*   *   *

Puerto Madryn was grim. As we crossed the pampas, the country stretched blank in unremitting flatness. The only thing to hold the eyes was the profusion of birds – white-tufted grebes which dived under the flood waters as we got close, fierce peregrine falcons, lovely red-backed hawks and enchanting white monjitas (*Xolmis irupero*), pure-white birds, the size of sparrows, white all over except for black primaries and black tips to their tails.

It is not far north of here, at Viedma, that there is talk of building a new capital. There could be no purpose to such a move unless, as Gina said, it was to cut down on civil servants, for who in his right mind would wish to exchange the temperate climate of Buenos Aires for this gloomy shoreline?

Puerto Madryn was grey – the outskirts shanties, some new grey houses, each with a tall, ugly water-tank on its roof, a cluster of posher, suburban villas and some not very high, high-rise horrors. The infertile land around it sprouted only dusty scrub and sage. We had not seen a tree for long hours.

If Patagonia was dismal in our sight, how must it have looked to those 153 Welsh people, led by Parry Madryn, who landed here in 1865? They had left their green valleys for the promise of a new land, free of English domination. They were faced, in the cold of July, with a forty-mile trek across thorn-strewn desert to the Chubut valley, the homeland that they were given by the Argentine government. This valley was far from green and its name in Indian meant mud.

For three years they struggled, with the inimical, dry, cold climate, with the Araucanian Indians and with their own ignorance. Then Albert Jenkins's wife noticed that the river flowed higher than some of their land. Why not lead the water down to irrigate their crops? From then on it was better. The Tehuelche, enemies of the Araucanians, taught them to hunt and it was better still. They had good flour to bake their teacakes and the valley was splashed with green.

We paused at Gaimán, where Bruce Chatwin had stayed thirteen years before. The pink brick houses, of which he wrote, were still there but, even in those few years, much of the Welshness had faded. We pushed on up the valley, crossing the river at Las Plumas after which it ran through a wide canyon, pink and yellow with high cliffs. At the foot of one, there was a gaggle of eleven upland geese that let us come almost close enough to touch them before they took off. There were groups of elegant-crested tinamou (*Eudromia elegans*), a dozen burrowing parrots (*Cyanoliseus patagonus*) and some bustling rhea. The male rhea has a paradoxical existence, combining the pleasures of the harem with the duties of the nursery, for it sits on the nest in which several females lay their eggs.

It was not until 1884 that the Welsh travelled this way, over the Paso de Indios to found Trevelin, in a softer valley below the Andes. Fred Green told me the same story about John Daniel Evans, who had discovered the place in '83, that his son Milton Evans had told to Bruce Chatwin.

John had been three years old when he came on the brig *Mimosa*, with the original party under Parry Madryn. So he was just twenty-one when he went over the Paso de Indios with three companions, exploring. He had been brought up with Indians, so he knew how to cover tracks, how to evade pursuit. But some Northern Indians caught them. Only John survived. His horse El-Malacara leapt a three-yard ditch. The Indians could not follow. (In Milton Evans' story, the ditch was a crevasse and more than twice as wide.)

Within a week John was back at the scene with forty other men. They found the bodies of his companions. Their hearts were missing and their severed genitals were in their mouths. Two Indians lay dead beside them. The following year, Evans moved to Trevelin and later, when El-Malacara died, he buried the horse in a grave which can still be seen – a tribute for saving his life.

Fred Green's house was one of the most substantial in the valley. It was here that Richard Llewellyn used to come to stay on visits to his relations. It lay a mile or so outside the small town. We went up a drive, past some wooden farm buildings where a huge bull grazed at the roadside. Some buff-necked ibis chortled in a field – friendly birds that come back to the same nest every year. We crossed a stream and the last part of the drive climbed steeply. The name of the house was Ty Pennant – the head of the brook.

We sat in a room with a large, stone fireplace in which a wood fire flamed. Fred stood in front of it, a distinguished, elderly figure in the *bombacho* trousers and crumpled, leather boots of the gaucho. His sandy hair was thinning but his moustache grew vigorously. He wore a silk neckerchief held together by a ring.

'My family came from Llangollen. My father travelled out by himself when he was thirteen. He did it to please his mother because his older stepbrother, who was meant to come, had vanished, and he thought she was disappointed.

'When he arrived at Puerto Madryn, a *peón* met him leading a thin horse and he was put to work at once. He looked after two or three hundred sheep, camping out with them for most of the time. He took bread with him; otherwise he foraged for food.

'By the time he was twenty-one, the flock had grown to two thousand and he was given half. Then he got married and they travelled west. My mother was a good shot and we had a good life.'

They had lived in Gaimán but, after the great flood of 1932, they moved to Paso de Indios. Fred Green still had land there now, which one of his sons looked after. It was Fred's father-in-law who had come to Trevelin and, when Fred married, he joined him. His other son, Charlie, now worked the land at Trevelin.

'I have two thousand five hundred hectares a league from here and twenty thousand at eight leagues,' said Fred, in an anachronistic combination of measures. It was not clear how much land his son looked after at Paso de Indios, which was some sixty leagues away. There, in the higher land, they just kept merino sheep. At Trevelin, they had cattle and grew timber. Over a century, the Welsh had thrived, but life could still be hard.

'Three years ago my son lost three thousand sheep, half his flock. I have lately lost two hundred hectares of timber in a fire that burned about four or five thousand hectares round here. The whole area was wooded once, but it has either been cut or burned.'

So much had changed in Fred's lifetime. Fewer and fewer people now spoke Welsh and the newspaper came out less and less often. Maggie Freeman died in 1981. She had been born only thirteen years after the Welsh arrived.

'There was a man living until last year in Sarmiento who remembered the Indians hunting on foot. They ran in two columns like a V. Then when they had enclosed a guanáco they threw balls joined by a cord – not round their legs as you would think – it was best on the neck.'

The guanáco is a wild relative of the llama and alpaca, a little smaller than the vicuña.

'The Welsh and the Indians got on very well. They found each other's languages very easy, but they also liked and trusted each other. The Indians had a saying – "Get drunk with a Spaniard and you wake naked in the morning; get drunk with a Welshman and he puts you to bed."'

Fred still talks every Sunday afternoon to friends in Llangollen, on the ham radio that sits in the corner of his living-room. But I doubt whether his grandson Brian, 'who rides like a cowboy just like his great-grandfather', will give much thought to Wales.

'The Welsh chapel closed three or four years ago. There are lots of new chapels – Pentecostal, Assembly of God, even Bahai. Like the upland geese, which have all been killed by the mink, we will soon be gone.'

There are those who cling defiantly to Welsh customs. Vincent Evans and his wife lived in a prefabricated house with a corrugated-iron roof, painted a sickly cream, through which the rust was breaking. The house, called Nant Fach (Little Stream), looked over the broad, misty valley coloured by yellowing willows and the sumptuous red of the wild rose-hips. We went through a gate of gothic pattern, made of bamboo and painted green, into a tiny patch of garden, safe from the cows. We sat in the cramped living-room.

There was a bookshelf, full of *Readers Digest*s in Spanish, a round table and a Bandoleon or automatic organ, made in Germany. On the walls were old photographs of Vincent's relations – he was one of eleven children – a framed article about a gaucho, and a horsewhip. Propped on a shelf were some circular pictures painted on stone.

Vincent was a powerful man with dark hair and bright Celtic blue eyes. His *bombacho* trousers were kept up by two belts, one a wide cummerbund of cloth and the other, outside the first, of puma skin. Mrs Evans slid round the wood-patterned, linoleum floor on two bits of cloth under her tennis shoes. Her neckerchief was held on by two gold rings.

They both spoke only Spanish and Welsh. Vincent had about fifteen hundred acres on which he mostly kept beef cattle, though he did grow a few crops. He liked to talk of the days when there were only horses to work the land. Even today, he did some of the tasks with oxen. As a hobby, he made watchstraps of puma skin and calf, with buckles of cowhorn.

'My father's six-year-old brother was eaten by a puma, the only case in the Chubut of a puma killing a human.'

I remembered a picture in the museum of a plump child. The puma must have made a good meal.

Even with the Evans family, customs are being slowly adapted. We had come really to hear Vincent's tape of the Eistedfodd, which is still held every year. We sat in solemn silence while 'The Men of Harlech' and 'Cyfrir Geifr' (Counting the Goats) resounded. Every so often the rhythm changed and Spanish voices took over, some of the singers, surprisingly, being from across the border in Chile. About half the songs and poems were still in Welsh. In another generation, there will be none.

10
Chile
A LAND OF CROSSES

Here was such a different beauty from the bare mountains of the *puna*. Instead there were high, sharp peaks with snow and, below them, forests of trees, fine firs and larches, green on the steep slopes. Lower still, the willows were orange and the poplars yellow in the valleys where the water scrambled.

From Trevelin over the Andes to the Chilean coast was little more than a hundred miles. Chaitén lay in a scallop of land through which the Rio Blanco coiled to the sea. Immediately behind rose the forested range we had just come through. We had been joined by a road which led southward to an indeterminate conclusion, amid the islands and lakes of southern Chile. Otherwise, there was no way out of Chaitén except by sea. Across the water, we could see the island of Chiloé, which at sunset grew spiky, low and dark, seeming to be a short dinghy ride away but actually fifty miles.

Chaitén hardly merited the title of town. In the 1930s there were only a couple of houses here but, in 1938, a boat started to call once a month and, by local standards, the place took off. There were now 2,500 inhabitants, and it rated as the capital of the province of Palena. The houses were small, hung with shingles of plain wood. The grid of roads, many of them innocent of houses and tarmac, revealed that some planner's optimism had not been fulfilled. There were television aerials on most of the houses, but a miasma of poverty hung over the place.

There was a park area with benches and young trees, prematurely stunted. No one sat there. Perhaps they did in the summer. On the east side was an ugly church, happily of modest proportions. In large letters running diagonally across the front was a message: Glory to God in the highest. On the north side stood an administrative building. At six in the evening, some twenty soldiers paraded there in the dusk and a bugler tootled. The men wore camouflage and, on our first day, Symon nearly ran into them.

We had been told in Trevelin that there was a ferry to Chiloé on Fridays. At Chaitén they laughed. Sometimes on Mondays; who knows? There were three hotels. One was shut. The Schilling had no restaurant, so we settled for the Continental, if only because there was nowhere else to eat. Like all the other buildings, the hotel was made of wood. There was no heating, but a stove glowed in the dining-room. In any case, we comforted ourselves with the thought that the sun shone. It should have been raining, for May was the season of rains, but the *puelche* was blowing from the south, sweeping the sky clean.

The hotel belonged to Edmundo Bradanovich Valle. He looked Slavic with a long, grey face, shrouded in the grizzled beard of an archimandrite. His manner was grave, but when he smiled the priestly austerity dissolved in charm. Edmundo said his grandfather was Yugoslavian and had come to Chile to work in a saltpetre mine. His mother was Italian. Edmundo's wife was of Irish extraction, with red hair and blue eyes.

'Her maiden name was Braniff. Have you, it may be, heard of the airline of that name? It belonged to her father's uncle.'

They had a son, who had inherited his father's long face and his mother's red hair. As a mark of his own individuality, perhaps, he had acquired a high, absurdly squeaky voice which virtually precluded sensible conversation. Nonetheless, he had managed to get engaged.

We had arrived quite early in the day and, when we had broached the question of lunch, Señora Bradanovich had somehow deflected us into having sandwiches. Being rather hungry, Symon tried to find a bar of chocolate in the shops. There appeared to be little food of any sort in the town. He came back with a packet of dry biscuits. With them, the woman in the shop had given him a calendar, the size of a playing-card, with a nude photograph on the back. She gave us one of these each time we bought anything, accompanied by a little simper.

We lived in the dining-room, as it was the only place where there was any hope of being warm. A long series of windows ran down one side of the room, so that one could see all that was happening in the town, which was not much.

The stove stood half-way down the room. Edmundo spend most of the day beside it. When dinnertime arrived we were pessimistic. Edmundo came and asked if we would like *locos* for dinner. *Locos*? Madmen? I became even more gloomy. 'You know – *avalon*.' I had wild thoughts of King Arthur. Then I remembered that this was the Pacific. It was abalone.

I had let slip that it was Symon's birthday. With the abalone, Edmundo brought a bottle of champagne as a present. It turned out that Señora Bradanovich was an excellent cook. We all drank more, and we had three happy days.

But it was so cold. When we went to bed I shivered for hours. I remembered Jorge Stande in the museum in Northern Argentina. He had said that when the missionaries had come to Patagonia, they had found the Indians naked and had dressed them, and that they had died of infections which clung to the cloth. I could believe anything, except that anyone could ever have gone naked in this climate. And it was only the autumn; winter was yet to come. On the next nights, I slept in my sleeping bag.

The household did not really stir before nine-thirty in the morning. Edmundo stood by the stove. He was diffident about interrupting us when we were reading or writing, but he liked to talk, in rather vague, melancholy terms about insubstantial matters. It was never really clear why he ran the hotel in this lonely place. He spoke obliquely of having been in lumber. There was a Chekhovian aura about his affairs.

'I have an idea to take fish to Trevelin and Esquel. It is only 150 kilometres away. Otherwise they can only get fish from the Atlantic and that is six hundred kilometres. We have to wait for the customs arrangements to be sorted out, and then we shall see how things will be.'

I felt somehow that they never would be, due more to his inertia than to any difficulty with Argentina. Everyday relations with the people over the border were cordial enough. This was also the nearest place for the people of Esquel to find the sea. In the summer, many came, or so Edmundo said.

'Most of the Argentinians that come here think that to try to take the Malvinas was a mad enterprise. Galtieri had two possibilities to distract the people. He could try to take either the Malvinas or Chilean Patagonia.

151

He thought Britain was far away and so safer. It was the wrong choice.'
Edmundo's long features assumed a look of wry pleasure.

We never spoke of Chilean politics.

In the afternoons, when it was warmer, Symon and I sauntered in the
town. Everyone always paused outside the house where they sold tickets
for the ferry, to read the news of any sailings, which was written on a
blackboard. Not that most of the people were going to go anywhere. It
was a contact with the outside world. Whenever we went past, they shook
their heads.

At the far end of the town, where there were few houses to fill the grid,
Carlos García and his fourteen-year-old son, Sergio, were building a
fishing boat. It was to be twelve and a half metres long and three metres in
the beam. Sergio stoked a fire under a copper, which puffed steam up a
tube. Carlos moulded the pliant planks of cypress in the steam as if they
were plasticine. His craftsmanship in getting the wood to obey his hands
was entrancing to watch, and our interest made Sergio giggle, until his
father reproved him. It took Carlos three months to build a boat but,
despite his skill, he said he never built a boat for anyone else.

Or we travelled up a track to the north. There was a little village, a few
miles up the road, with a stream spilling out on to the beach of black sand.
Then the track went inland to a dark lake in the forest, where Symon
swam naked in the icy water. Beyond the lake, the military had barred the
road.

The military, quite apart from the twenty who performed the evening
ceremony, were numerous. I had talked to Edmundo about my interest
in, and distant connection with, Lord Cochrane. He had mentioned this
to some soldiers, one of whom was determined to meet me. I had not yet
realised how different the attitude to the Chileans was to that of the
Brazilians about the admiral. In Chile, he was a hero. Every large town, I
saw later, had a Cochrane Street and to the south of us was Lake
Cochrane and a provincial capital, even smaller than Chaitén.

José was a plump and somewhat bombastic young man. He came with
three or four fellow-soldiers. He talked loudly of Cochrane's exploits,
showing off his knowledge to his companions, but in the course of each
pronouncement, his nervous eyes skidded to me to check that I was not
about to contradict him.

He ordered champagne, declaring that it was his duty in return for the
privilege of knowing us. As the first bottle began to take effect, José
switched from discussing Cochrane with me to one of those recitations of
the names of pop groups which Symon encourged. After toasts to many

renewals of Symon's birthday and to the charms of José's girlfriend, another bottle was needed for the long life of the Eurythmics, Fleetwood Mac, and the inevitable Madonna.

José became expansive, but I got the impression that there was something he wanted to say to me that he could not manage to bring out.

'The army is a perfect life, but I would like to know about other lives. I am so happy in the army, but you must tell me of the things I don't know, although I know many things.'

His companions drifted away. He claimed that he was paid $140 a month. (When he had gone, the regulars at the Continental laughed a lot at that suggestion.) On the strength of the thought, he ordered another bottle.

'I would like your opinion of the way of life in Chile. It would inform me to know how you see my country.'

It was easy to avoid that by pointing out that I had only been in the country for three days and only in Chaitén.

'This is the most beautiful place in Chile. It is so pretty and so tranquil. It is the last perfect place on earth. I shall live here always.'

José was to get married in a month's time to the girl from Santiago whose long life we had toasted earlier. I asked whether she too liked the south.

'Not at all. She loathes it down here. She does not like the fresh, clean air. She only likes the city. She will go on working in Santiago.'

I suggested that this might not make for happiness in the marriage, if they lived hundreds of miles from each other. José just giggled. Eventually he became so drunk that he could hardly stand. He shambled to the door and stood swaying. Symon gave him a tape of Queen and José left crying. The regulars sat silent and embarrassed.

At last, the blackboard said that the ferry would come the next day. With some difficulty, I persuaded Edmundo to prepare the bill before we went to bed. He had left off several items and charged less than his list announced for whisky. He was reluctant to alter the bill.

'But you like whiky,' he said, losing the *s* as do most South Americans, and looked bemused when I insisted. How this charming couple survived was a mystery.

*   *   *

The *Cai-Cai* was a largish landing-craft. It was overcrowded with four lorries and our car. I looked with doubt at the lifeboats – one old, wooden rowing-boat and a new, inflatable Beaufort life-raft. But the sea was calm and there was no wind. As Chaitén receded, a band of smoke from the newly lit morning fires hung motionless, twenty feet above the houses. The smoke was lit from behind by the sun which illuminated, too, the peak of Corcovado mountain, rising behind, the shape of Mont Blanc, to 7,500 feet.

We sat in the sun. The other passengers crammed into a tiny room, uninterested in the black beaches, the dark green of the mountains and, as we went further, the snowed ranges of the Andes. One truck was loaded with bull calves, with no food or water for a six-hour journey.

The sun was low when we reached Chiloé. The ramp was lowered, but no one was allowed to go ashore. The passengers huddled in the cold at the top of the ramp, expecting to go at any moment. We were waiting, they said, for permission from the navy to disembark. A couple with a baby had planned to go to the end of the island that night. Now it would be too late and they had nowhere to stay and no money, except for their bus fare to Ancud. The mother and baby came to sit in the car, and a shivering woman whose eyes were watering with the cold. We waited more than an hour. Then a man in naval uniform came. He checked nothing, and said at once that we could go. It was an appropriate introduction to the second dictatorship of the journey.

*   *   *

Chiloé, if Bruce Chatwin's sources were to be believed, was an island of hobgoblins and of the *Brujería*, a brotherhood of male witches. Somewhere not far from where we landed was the cave of this evil sect, guarded by the *Invunche*. This is a human being, scientifically deformed in childhood so that his head faces backwards and his right arm emerges from under his right shoulder-blade. When fully grown, he feeds on human flesh, a diet supplemented in times of shortage by billy-goat.

The island seemed a little like Ireland, Donegal perhaps, with rocky bays and inlets. The air was soothing and damp, feeling as if you could cup it in your hand. Narrow roads wriggled between small fields of soft green and mellow brown, where men in hats ploughed with oxen. Blackberries swelled among the red-leaved brambles on the wooden fences, and apples hung in the orchards.

The similarity with Ireland was, of course, enhanced by the thought of witches. We ate a picnic on the shore of Lake Huillinco, its surface so still as to be almost eerie. Sitting, a little sleepy, by this lake, I thought of a lough I knew as a child, in the depths of which lived the banshee. The little people had taken her there, away from her cruel father who had caught her lover in a man-trap. They burnt his castle later, when with great impiety his grandson put an unexpected guest into what had been the banshee's room. The old woman in whose cottage I lived reproved me for striking a hawthorn tree with a stick – a profanity. She was fearful lest the little people should take a similar revenge on her house as they had upon the lakeshore castle.

But, here, the birds which skimmed the water, their wingbeats ruffling a wake on the sheen, were not mallard, but neotropic cormorants. And the girls in the capital, Castro, wore ponchos over their jeans.

The contrasts were unsettling. At breakfast, I cursed Marshal McLuhan's 'global village' as, yet again, the shrilling of Madonna came over the hotel's loudspeaker. Yet, when we walked into town, I was struck by the quiet. There was so little traffic that all one heard was the sound of footsteps. Chiloé had always been old-fashioned. It was the last strong-hold of the Spanish. Even Cochrane had failed to capture the fort at Ancud in the north and, when the royalists saw that all hope had gone for them in Chile, they offered the island to the British. Happily, Canning refused.

Despite the jeans, the people of the island were unsophisticated and poor. An old woman to whom we gave a lift was terrified. She had mistaken us for a bus. She had never been in a car before and had never spoken to a foreigner. Although deeply superstitious, she was intelligent and friendly.

The land, she told us, once she had decided that we were not hobgoblins or marked with the evil eye, was owned in very small parcels – not that she thought they were small, this merely became clear from her pointing out what this or that person owned. The spirit of community, she conveyed to us, was very strong. If someone were building a house or had some big project in hand, then everyone else would naturally help. Nonetheless, she was plainly surprised when Symon helped her to carry her heavy parcels up the path to her house in Chonchi.

Apart from the soft-aired beauty of the landscape and the instinct charm of the people, much of the interest of the island lay in its architecture. The early housing was built at the water's edge on stilts. These houses, called *palafitos*, were originally to be found in all the ports, but now the only ones that remain are in Castro. Many are quite large, some have fine windows in the weatherboarding, all are held up by an inordinate number of pillars. I could not make out why they should have been built in this fashion. One book said it was 'to take greater advantage of the shore'. Some were so big that they may have been warehouses, and thus accessible to larger boats at high tide, for the loading of grain or wool.

The houses built on land were nearly all hung with shingles. While the shingles at Chaitén had all been square, in Chiloé there were six different patterns to that part of the shingle which overlapped the one below it. They were used singly or in combinations, each arrangement giving a different texture to the appearance of the houses. Some patterns were associated with particular villages or districts. Often the larger houses had grand classical windows and many of them were painted in bright but natural colours.

Most remarkable of all were the churches. The Jesuits were the first missionaries to the archipelago and, by the time of their expulsion in 1767, they had established seventy-nine small communities, each with a chapel. They also built *residencias* with more substantial churches. We crossed to the island of Quinchao to see the earliest of these, which was built in 1735 at Achao, and was the model for all those that followed.

It was entirely built of wood – cypress and larch. The shingles hung a gentle grey, like pewter. A portico with six pillars ran the width of the front. The four outer arches formed by the pillars were round, the centre one slightly flattened. Above the portico was the choir with three Palladian windows under the wide-pitched roof. A square tower with one more window rose, again with no break in the façade. Above that, after a short, narrowing roof, was a hexagonal tower with a steep, pointed roof topped by a cross. The sides of the building were plain, with comparatively small windows.

There was something about the exterior which was reminiscent of a New England or a Scandinavian wooden church. The interior was unlike anything. The first two pillars of the nave rested on living rock and were fluted, the rest must have been solid trunks encased in planks of smooth wood. After that everything was a wild frenzy of fretwork, curlicues and carving, painted in blues and yellows. The roof was extraordinary and ingenious. An overall barrel shape, it was vaulted with planks going in different directions. The planks were thinly painted in a dark blue, but the segments of vaulting were edged with a fretted pattern of unpainted wood. The altar, the retable, the pulpit, and the side chapels were covered in fripperies and filigrees, festoons and fancywork. It was more astonishing than beautiful.

The other churches followed the same general layout – while their interiors were not so elaborate, their façades showed amazing variations. The portico of Dalcahue had nine arches, five of them very narrow gothic, three of them nearly rounded; Chauchi was yellow and orange picked out in blue, much of its triple tower was made of corrugated iron; Tenjaún was unique in having three towers and its portico consisted of three wide, nearly square arches and two needle-thin pointed ones.

I was sorry to leave this enchanted island.

*　　*　　*

Valdivia lies ten miles from the sea up a wide eponymous river. It is more a bay than a river, into which five other rivers flow, but the mouth of the bay is narrow – less than a mile across. Settled by the Spanish in the middle of the sixteenth century, it became strategically the most important port on the South Pacific coast. After an Indian raid, which temporarily disabled the town, and later a threatened invasion by a Dutch squadron, the Spanish, in 1645, sent a large expedition to begin the fortification of Valdivia against attack by land or sea.

To protect the entrance to the bay, they built eight forts of varying sizes. In case any invader got past those, they set around the first widening area of the bay three powerful batteries. To defend the entrances to the Rio Valdivia proper and to another waterway, the Rio Tornagaleones, which could also lead to the city, they put five more forts, one on the island of Mancera. The three most important of all these were El Castillo de la Pura y Limpia Concepción de Montforte de Lemus at Niebla, finished in 1671, on the north-eastern point of the narrow mouth of the bay, the Castillo San Sebastián de la Cruz opposite Niebla at Corral, and the Castillo San Pedro at Alcántara on the island of Mancera.

The city was, by any sane estimation, impregnable.

'Cool calculation would make it appear,' said Lord Cochrane, 'that the attempt to take Valdivia is madness. This is one reason why the Spaniards will hardly believe us in earnest, even when we commence. And you will see that a bold onset, and a little perseverance afterwards, will give a complete triumph.'

Late in January 1820, Cochrane, now Admiral of the Chilean revolutionary navy, set off from Valparaiso on this lunatic enterprise. He had already made a reconnaissance, sailing into the bay under Spanish colours, demanding a pilot whom he seized and persuaded to help him in mapping the bay and its defences. On the way out, he had boarded an incoming sloop which was bringing $20,000, the pay for the garrison.

The beginning of the actual attack did not go so well. On their fourth night at sea, while Cochrane slept on board the *O'Higgins*, his lieutenant gave the ship over to a midshipman and went to bed. The ship ran on to a reef, ripping off the false keel and holing the bottom. The pumps failed. The ship's carpenter was a farmer with no experience of pumps. Cochrane himself had to mend them. Everyone, except for Cochrane, was for turning back. They went on. The water poured in, but the pumps held.

Out of sight of the forts of Valdivia, Cochrane transferred all his troops to his other two smaller vessels. He had decided to land at La Aguada del Inglés, a beach to the west of the bay. The beach was protected by the Fuerte Inglés. How could he land his men?

We made our way along a good track, following the far banks of the Rio Futa and the Rio Tornagaleones. It was misty and the mountains to our left were lost in cloud. The track rose and fell steeply as we had to cross numberless streams running down through the forests of pines. There were few houses, merely a shack or two beside an occasional clearing where a scattering of cows grazed. To Cochrane it might have looked like Scotland.

The little village of Corral had a neglected charm. In the small shop, the old woman asked if we would like postcards. These were home-made, just photographs taken with a cheap camera, stuck on to a plain, thin card and captioned in ink in her shaky, careful hand.

'The road is new,' she said. 'Until two years ago you could not have come in a car, only on a horse or by sea.'

At the mention of Cochrane, she nodded, baring her few yellow teeth in a spasm of a smile. But she knew no details of the battle, which she called the *toma*, the taking of Valdivia, rather than the battle.

The castle was huge in extent, but it lay low, not far above the sea. It had been the most powerful fort of the bay, with twenty-one cannon and quarters for two hundred soldiers. Across the water we could see the Isla Mancera, perhaps a thousand yards away. No enemy ship could pass between the two forts.

Beyond, we came to a pretty beach sheltered by a promontory on which was the fort of Amargos. This was the mouth of the bay and on the far, eastern side we could see the castle of Niebla on its high cliff, promising disaster to any invader who tried to sail between us.

On again and there was San Carlos, a small compact fort on a rock separated from the mainland by a fifty-yard channel. There was now a little village, a mere cluster of houses, which seemed to be populated only by young girls who ran beside the car shrieking and flirting. It was the first intimation I had of the phenomenon of there being far more girls than boys in Chile.

From travelling north we now turned sharply to the east so that the shore faced the open sea. There ahead was La Aguada del Inglés. It was a rocky, shallow bay quite invisible from any of the forts except its own. Today there is a farm on the flat land above the beach, but in 1820, the cover would have been good for concealing the troops.

The next stage of Cochrane's assault also started badly. His two ships came in as close as possible to the shore, flying Spanish colours. The ships' boats, filled with soldiers, were hidden on the seaward side of the ships. The commander of the Fuerte Inglés came to challenge the vessels. A Spanish-born officer of Cochrane's explained that they had come round Cape Horn and lost all their boats in a storm. They were hoping for a pilot to guide them into Valdivia, maybe in the morning.

The commander was not altogether convinced. The last stranger to ask for a pilot had been El Diablo, Cochrane. His suspicions were soon confirmed. One of the boats behind the ship broke loose and drifted into sight. All hope of waiting until dark was gone. The cannons of Fuerte Inglés opened fire. Forty-five marines landed first, routing the Spaniards on the beach with a bayonet charge. Most of their powder had been soaked in the *O'Higgins*. It was still an hour till dark. The remaining 250 Chileans came ashore. Then, splitting into two parties they moved in, one group clattering and shrieking in a blind, frontal attack. The purpose of the noise was to cover any sound made by the other half, who crept round the back of the fort and scaled it from the rear. The commander was so surprised by this move that he and his men fled.

Running away, they were met by a force of three hundred other Spanish troops, who had been alerted by the firing. Those fleeing advised the newcomers to run too; their counsel was backed by the wild howling and wailing of the Chileans who chased them.

At San Carlos, the gates were opened to let in the fugitives. Cochrane's cacophonous horde rushed in behind them. So all fled from San Carlos to Amargos. Once again the gates opened; once more the fort was abandoned. The trembling Spaniards piled into the *castillo* at Corral. This was a harder proposition. All the garrisons of the western forts were now in this large fortress. Cochrane had virtually no powder left.

But his luck had turned. Colonel Hoyos, commandant of the *castillo*, was drunk, largely from drinking to overcome his shame. Moreover, Cochrane had sent a detachment of men up to the Fuerte Chorocamayo

159

on the heights above Corral. They had captured it easily. From there, they could shell Corral. Some of the Spanish took to the water and went to Valdivia, there spreading alarm and fear.

Colonel Hoyos surrendered. One hundred Spaniards had died. Another hundred were captured. Cochrane had lost seven men and nineteen were wounded.

Niebla was ten miles from Valdivia. We drove along a road which hopped from island to island and travelled along the north bank of the Rio Valdivia. In the river a sunken ship was witness to the trickiness of navigation. The last part of the road was steep and muddy and the village itself was lonely, with rather disconnected groups of poor housing. The *castillo* must have been extremely impressive, but little now remained. We stood on the top of a two-hundred-foot cliff. Below us, a lone albatross wheeled in the soft rain. We could look across to the forts we had visited the day before and to the Isla Mancera, again only a thousand yards away. It gave one almost a sense of power just to be in this commanding place, the gun-metal sea breaking beneath us in a thin line of white along the coast. No one could seize this fortress, much of it using the actual rock as floor or wall, its batteries, in Cochrane's day, accessible only by a tunnel or by scaling the sheer cliff.

On the day after Colonel Hoyos' surrender, Cochrane decided to tackle the eastern forts. There was nothing for it but to sail in under the guns of Niebla and past those of Mancera to pick up his troops from Corral.

So much of Cochrane's tactics were psychological. He embarked his troops on the two vessels and at the same time brought the *O'Higgins* to the mouth of the bay. The garrisons of Niebla and the other eastern forts had heard accounts of the previous day's fighting, the numbers of Cochrane's men doubtless much exaggerated by way of excuse. They now saw a fifty-gun ship, presumably bringing formidable reinforcements. They had no means of knowing that there were no troops on board and that she was nearly sinking. They abandoned the forts and the castle with its long proud name without a shot being fired.

The *O'Higgins* had to be beached for repairs. The *Intrépido* ran aground near where I saw the sunken ship. It was of no consequence. As Cochrane advanced towards the city, he met the dignitaries of Valdivia waving a flag of surrender.

*   *   *

Santiago was far grander than Buenos Aires, which I had thought grandiose. It was also superficially more congenial. Of course, Buenos Aires was at least three times larger and lacked the mountains which, rising behind the splendid buildings of Santiago, gave them a majestic background that preserved them from empty ostentation. There was an intimacy and a warmth which I had not found in the Argentine capital.

The centre of the city was more open and, even in autumn, very green, as well it might be for it rained more than it did not. I was struck by two immediate curiosities – first, how many people were carrying musical instruments, and secondly, how beautiful the women were. There was a further peculiarity in that there seemed to be so many more of these beautiful women than there were men. The people had high sing-song voices and their Spanish sounded softer than Argentinian Spanish.

I would have warmed more to Santiago, but it was not long before I began to feel that chilling incompleteness that pervades all dictatorships. People's eyes are restless; conversations have abrupt endings. Strangers search to read your meaning, but barricade their own thoughts against you. At the same time, the strangling nature of the poverty impressed itself upon me.

Women crouched on the pavements, selling one cigarette at a time, one sweet, two safety-pins. Men with hideous twisted limbs, others with no legs sitting on boards with tiny wheels, pushing themselves along with their knuckles, one dignified old woman, with a ravaged, patrician face – all begging with a cringeing politeness which spoke of grim harassment. Lewdly flirtatious children made unspoken suggestions, when asking with absurd hope for ten dollars. In the red-light district, hundreds of those pretty girls gazed helplessly from behind grilles. We had seen worse misery in Brazil and were to see far worse in Peru, but in Santiago there was a condemned and lifeless quality to the squalor.

Maria was a student. 'No one speaks of politics, even in whispers, unless you get to know a real left-wing young man who trusts you. There are too many plainclothes police.

'Most protest is subtle. The buskers sing political songs. They are very sweet, the buskers. Often they get on the buses and they make a little speech, saying, "I'm honest, I do not steal, I have no money and my family is hungry. For the love of Jesus Christ our Saviour give me alms." Then he sings and quite often the songs are very naughty about the Government. And everyone on the bus laughs, because who can be arrested for laughing?'

161

Maria told us about a rock concert at Viña del Mar. 'The bands came from Argentina. There were hundreds of police, many standing between the audience and the bands, so as to cut us off from them. But they sang political songs and the police could do nothing.'

The measure of protest seemed so inadequate, while the threats were ever present. One had only to see the street-traders when the police took a whim to harrass them. Suddenly two hundred people would vanish from the street, rushing with their pathetic wares into the nearest church – for in this old-fashioned country sanctuary fortunately still applies.

We drove with Maria up into the mountains behind the city. Once we climbed above the slums, the way was pretty. At the roadside, people sold big walnuts, damply fresh, and honey in old wine bottles. There was a road up a valley marked on our map. A long way up in craggy, grey terrain, daubed with snow, there was a military barrier.

'I hope you've got your papers,' said Maria. We hadn't. She spoke to the young soldier guarding the barrier. No one was allowed any further, so he did not ask for any papers. We went back. Maria was nervous. 'We may be stopped anywhere and without papers . . .' She left it to us to imagine.

As we went through a village, a flint-smart policeman waved us down.

'There is no overtaking in the village. Licence?'

We had overtaken nothing. I decided that he wanted to look at the car. They were rare in Chile.

'Good evening,' I said and was about to try to explain. He looked surprised at my accent, expecting from the Venezuelan licence plates a better Spanish.

'Which country are you from?'

'Inglaterra.'

'Ah, tenemos buenos relaciones con el pueblo de Inglaterra. Continua.'

It was so courteous, again so old-fashioned in its way. But this old-worldliness in Chile is just a part of the pattern.

'We do have fun you know,' said Maria. 'And it is good that we don't have any drugs in the university.'

Then she talked, with no awareness of any contradiction, about her friend of twenty-five, who belonged to a farming family. She had had an illegitimate baby, by an eighteen-year-old boy.

'Her father has disowned her. He wants her to go away, but she is still living at home and they get their revenge for the disgrace by making her work so hard that she is ill. She loves the boy and would like to marry him, but he is an alcoholic.'

Isabella was older, a married woman with three children. She belonged to the old ruling class, a descendant of the *conquistadores*. She had a commanding beauty and an aristocratic confidence. Her house was not large and what I took to be her ancestral furniture was too big for the rooms. Grand photographs stood on desks and bookshelves. The atmosphere was one of formal intelligence. Her husband was a lawyer and she had an academic position of some sort.

It was hard to get a clear picture of what life had been like under Allende, the extreme left-wing President of Chile in the 1960s. The people of the right spoke with such venom, and those of the left with confused nostalgia and disappointment, having to admit that the economy was now more stable. Isabella's account was probably the most reasonable that I heard.

'Of course there was a momentary uplift when Allende came to power, but it was soon destroyed by six-hundred-per-cent inflation. Then we had shortages and queues. There was a ridiculous system by which, if you wanted to buy one thing, you had to have a package of others. If you wanted bread, you had to buy some floor polish as well. It was hopeless for poor people with no floor to polish, only mud.'

Isabella's floors gleamed, as did everything else in her house.

'The police were just as savage then as they are now. They were run by Cubans. Allende's daughter was married to the head of the Cuban secret police.

'At the time it was a split of an ideological kind. Many of the upper classes had been in the guerillas and many of the lower classes were against him. People predicted civil war, with one million dead, but it didn't happen. I know the take-over was rough, it had to be. What is wrong is that it goes on now. People still disappear.'

Isabella's approach was one that would have been, if not acceptable to all, at any rate perfectly respectable sixty years ago in Britain. It was informed by a genuine concern for the poor, but also by a certainty about the limits of liberty. She pointed out that there was no direct censorship and that there were opposition newspapers published, but she rather glossed over the fact that the editors of such papers were often thrown into jail for insulting the President or the army, which seemed to me a very direct form of censorship. The larger papers, of course, exercise self-censorship.

'Before Allende we had liberal governments who did much to benefit the middle class, but very little for the poor. Allende was entirely impractical, in his land reform for instance. No one was to own more than a hundred acres. It destroyed farming, but I must admit it made people use their ingenuity to make a living from such a small piece of land.'

I had seen, south of Santiago, the rapidly expanding fruit business which was a direct result of this policy, but I had heard, too, of completely disorganised ranches, which had been chopped up into useless sections and on which co-operative ventures had collapsed in acrimony. There was now no land ceiling.

Isabella believed that Pinochet's government spending had been for the benefit of the poor. There were, she said, many new schools. Much had been spent on clinics for small communities, rather to the disadvantage of large hospitals. There ran through her exposition an unvoiced thread that life under Pinochet was better than the likely alternatives.

'The Pope's visit was an odd turning point. For the first time in years, there were six hundred thousand people in one place. The Communists forged five thousand tickets and came to yell and shout anti-Pinochet slogans. The Church, which is rather left, urged their followers to shout. But when the Pope spoke, there was absolute silence. There were a lot of people arrested, about eight hundred, but no one was wounded.

'This was the first time that young people who have grown up since Allende have been able to express themselves. They did so, but they did nothing wild.

'You must remember Allende's government had only thirty-four per cent of the vote.'

Patricio was a rather beautiful man of about thirty with gentle, cool eyes and a soft beard.

'Allende's time was not bad, except for landowners. It was very lively, though there were food shortages.'

He looked a little worried at this last thought, as he was cooking lunch.

'It was perfectly dreadful,' said his mother, a woman of great elegance. 'Those awful Communist salutes and all our land was taken.'

The flat was modern but large, with wide windows leading on to a balcony overlooking the city to the mountains beyond. The furniture was in perfect taste and unusually comfortable. There was some Lalique glass and oriental china and superb Victorian silver.

Their surname was Basque, but Patricio's mother's family were

Italian. They had owned a silver mine, and used to send silver to England to be made into grand pieces for their dining-room.

Patricio was making Sattwic food, laughing at himself. He had travelled a lot in India and now taught yoga. His mother obediently did the breathing and other exercises. And she ate his very limited diet.

'We both feel well on it,' said Patricio. 'The desire for meat and other things leaves you. Drink left me. Coffee hasn't left me yet. Garlic has some good properties. It is good for the blood, but it makes you lethargic. The thing to avoid is onions. Onions make for desire – all desires, for a new car, for instance.' He laughed again.

We ate and it was good. Then Patricio's mother spoke in a wistful way of the high price of fish. 'The Japanese take it all,' she said. Fish had evidently not left her. Perhaps she had been at the onions.

*   *   *

Santiago appeared to be on some meteorological dividing line. It had been raining ever since we left Chiloé. A few miles out of the city to the north we found the sun.

We paused at Valparaiso in order to see Cochrane's house. The city buzzed with a vitality that we had not sensed since Brazil. The land rose so steeply from the shore that the port was visible from every one of the city's many levels. Down at the bottom were grand mercantile buildings, often in an art-deco style. Then came elegant houses, many built of close-rippled corrugated iron, with classical, pedimented windows. So steep was the hillside that each house looked over the roof of its neighbour below it. The roads had to wind by long routes to reach each level. Cobbled and stepped lanes were the shorter, wearisome way of getting home. These eventually withered to clambering mud tracks that led to shacks on near cliffsides, some on stilts so rotten that nothing would have tempted me in.

Cochrane's house was shut. It was a low, white, colonial building with a small verandah on one side and a balustraded walk in front, from which one could look down over the harbour far below. The museum was under repair, reasonably a low priority after an earthquake.

We passed Viña del Mar, a very Mediterranean-looking resort, with a huge floral clock, which actually told the time, next to a plaque which said that Garibaldi anchored at that point in 1851.

At one pretty fishing village we looked at a small colony of penguins and at another we lunched. The little hotel was run by a blowsy woman with bleached hair and a red slash of lipstick. The dining-room was done up in the aspidistra style. The ceiling was immensely high and sloping. Huge green leaves obscured the patches of damp. The wallpaper was patterned with red and yellow diamonds. On it hung dreadful pictures of the Andes. Dried pampas grass and fake flowers sat in ugly vases on the closely crowded tables. We were the only diners.

The woman had none of the dishes advertised on the blackboard outside, but we could hardly complain as lunch for two of us including beer cost $4. She told us that all four of her children lived in Perth in Australia. She visited them every year and she loved Perth. I asked if she could speak English.

'What would be the point? All my family can speak it.'

The further north we went the drier it became, until it was near desert and the land was divided by fences of prickly-pear and the corrals were of drystone walls.

*　　*　　*

The Elqui valley ran inland from La Serena. Fed by waters from the Andes, it started wide and lush, with great fields of potatoes and cabbages. The vines were trained to grow very tall and then to flatten out and spread across the rows. Now, when the grapes had been harvested and the leaves had turned, the flat tops looked from above like patterned carpets, red and yellow. In their shade, goats and sheep grazed. The people were pruning, leaving neat lines of vine trunks, like matchstick soldiers.

The valley narrowed, the road hardly seeming to climb, but the mountains rose higher, striated a dullish red and dusty green in some places, often merely grey, always bare of vegetation, so that the band of green by the river, sometimes wide, sometimes pinched to a mere hundred yards, grew more and more startling.

We came to Vicuña, the birthplace of Gabriela Mistral, a pretty little town where, in the Plaza de Armas, there were beautiful trees growing thick and tall, their tiny leaves hung simultaneously with minute pink flowers and small green berries. A woman said they were *Pimientos sipreces*, and wrote the name on a piece of paper for me.

Gabriela's life was profoundly gloomy. She was born Lucila Goday Alcayaga, in 1889. Her family was poor. When she was three, her father wandered away. When she was only fourteen, the local paper in La Serena printed several articles by her. They were always signed with morose pseudonyms – Somebody, Soul, Loneliness.

By the time she was fifteen, she had already got a job as an assistant in a village school near La Serena. Two years later she fell in love with a clerk on the railway and she was promoted to being an inspector at a school in La Serena. When she was twenty, the railway clerk killed himself.

In 1914, she won the most important Chilean poetry prize for her *Sonnets of Death* and she started to call herself Gabriela Mistral. At the age of thirty-three, she published her most famous work, *Desolation*, and was established as South America's greatest poet. In 1945, she won the Nobel Prize for literature – 'the great voice of mercy and motherhood'. She died in 1957, unmarried and childless, her favourite nephew having committed suicide when he was seventeen.

Soon we turned off the main road towards Paihuano. This rough track rose well above the river, and we could look down on the rich cultivations. Everything was alive with colour – the yellow poplars, the orange willows, the saffron and red vine leaves and the bright silver bark of the bare fig trees. Even in the river, under Gabriela's 'sweet, sharp and rasping water', the large, rounded pebbles were all of different hues – red, purple, pink, green, grey. And the people made walls of these, which looked like piles of cushions.

Round each corner we found a still wilder landscape, always with this sumptuous band of richness, defying the dead grandeur of the arid mountains.

On each side of the valley there ran, high up, thin stripes of green which puzzled me until I learned that they had been, or in some cases still were, canals cut or built on the mountainside to catch any rainwater or melting snow, and to carry it along to irrigate each field below on the slopes. The newer ones were built by Chileans, but the older, often vestigial, ones were made by the Guarita Indians centuries ago, the greater height at which they irrigated the valley slopes speaking of their greater industry.

We gave a lift to a boy out for the weekend from La Serena, exploring the valley.

'How do the police treat you?' he asked, apropos of nothing.

'Very well,' I had to say. 'And you?'

'They are terrible to us.'

Even here, we could not forget politics. He was too young to remember life under Allende, but his family often talked about it.

'The shortages were severe. There was nothing to buy in the shops and people were hungry. The only difference now is that there is everything to buy in the shops, but what is lacking is any money to buy it.'

After Monte Grande, a small village where the spire of the church looked ready to topple, and where stood Gabriela's tomb, with its despondent statue, we turned again, up another valley towards Cochiguaz and the one place where politics could be forgotten.

The Comunidad Hermana Gladys consisted of a low, mud building with a corrugated-iron roof set in a green but rocky slope, through which minute streams trickled according to an erratic plan of irrigation. There were some eight acres soon to be enlarged to twelve. Fruit trees grew around, and there were vegetable patches and small crops of pulses, even a few vines. Beside the house were bright flowers, violets and I seem to remember dahlias.

Sister Gladys was a matronly figure of considerable presence. She introduced us to her husband Ernesto, to Juanita, a pregnant woman of about thirty-five and to a handsome, round-eyed, hippy youth whose loose mouth was fixed in an unchanging, meaningless smile.

We had come unannounced, but Sister Gladys was most welcoming. She asked if we would like lunch. We sat at a long table which could have held twenty people. On one wall was a picture of Jesus, on another a paper dove and a picture of the Andes, identical to the one we had seen in the blowsy woman's hotel.

'I studied twenty years in the esoteric schools in Santiago. Now, the Hermetic writings are open to everyone.'

I goggled at Sister Gladys. Surely this staid and portly person could not have studied all that stuff. Hermes Trismegistus was the name that the Neoplatonists gave to the Egyptian god Thoth. The Hermetic writings consisted of forty-two books, supposed to have been dictated by Thoth. They propounded that the world was made out of fluid and that nothing could ever be destroyed. The soul was the union of light and life, and it transmigrated.

But she had, and she believed it, together with a great deal more.

Seeing my surprise, perhaps, Juanita tried to help.

'We lead a balanced life, equalising the spiritual and mystical with the practical. Never are we dogmatic.'

Whereupon, there came a stream of remarkably dogmatic 'facts' from Sister Gladys.

'The magnetic centre of the earth moved here from the Himalayas in 1954, and the axis moved forty-five degrees. It is a vertical column standing around here, starting a little to the south and reaching up to Lima.'

This circumstance, of course, was important to extra-terrestrials. The other 689 planets in our galactic universe were extremely worried because ours was the only one to have wars. UFOs are their way of keeping an eye on us, to see that we do not blow up the earth and upset the equilibrium of the universe.

Sister Gladys produced fuzzy, black-and-white pictures of three extra-terrestrials. She told me their names, but I can only remember one – Link. He was green; another was bronze in colour. I got muddled between someone called Siracusa and another writer, but one of them had encountered extra-terrials near Lima.

Before lunch, Sister Gladys said a form of grace to nature and naturalness. It ended: 'Keep the world safe.' In the summer, they said, eighty pupils camped here and ate in rota at this long table.

The lunch was delicious – carrots, potatoes and maize with coriander and then semolina pudding. Juanita sat rather closer to me that I thought necessary, sincerity overbrimming from her faintly Indian features. She told me how she had forsaken the unnecessary comforts of Santiago, and how much better it would be for her baby to be brought up in this pure ambience. As she never mentioned any father for the child, I remembered Maria's friend and wondered whether there might not be other reasons for abandoning the middle-class morality of the capital.

I wondered also about Ernesto, who was amiable but never spoke. He was from the valley and had never ventured far from it. Did he believe all this? Or was the marriage one of convenience for him? It provided him with a living which he might not otherwise have hoped for.

After lunch, the conversation became wilder yet.

'The Americans have had a time-machine for ten years. It was built by NASA and Siracusa is able to use it for trips to Jupiter.'

Sister Gladys was well informed about developments abroad. I rose in her estimation by having a hazy recollection of a television programme about Findhorn, where a couple grew outsize vegetables. I was less knowledgeable about the British police who, Sister Gladys said, now had a camera which could photograph dramatic events, which left an aura, for anything up to two hours after the happening. They could photograph the scene of a crime and there would be the criminal, or an accident and you could see who was to blame.

Of course, there should be no crime. All that was needed was for us to alter our endocrinal systems and make a few other small adjustments and we would all be more intelligent, love peace and be like the extra-terrestrials. She produced a drawing of a ray shining down on a group of people standing in a circle. In this simple ceremony, all these things could be achieved. I rather think Siracusa was able to conjure it from outer space, like Glendower with his spirits from the vasty deep.

Juanita gave me a slobbery kiss as we left and said, 'Peace.' Sister Gladys stood grave and dignified at the door and as I looked back I noticed for the first time a painting of an extra-terrestrial on the porch.

No great distance away was the most important observatory in the southern hemisphere. They had heard nothing there of any untoward movement in the earth's magnetic field.

*   *   *

Then we were in the Atacama desert. Sometimes we were by the shore and the sea fog rolled in. At first, this desert was bright with flowers – some blue, a little like morning-glories sprouting from a succulent, others a rich saffron. Looking for some promised rare formations, we found only contorted rocks over which blustering waves broke in a spitting froth. In a hollow rock, a little back from the shore, someone lived. There were piles of cans, broken shells and rubbish. A coat hung on a line. The cave-dweller had put stones spelling 'no entry' on the sand. We could discern a rough bed, but there was no one there. I wondered who he was. A little further along the road, we saw a sign saying *Playa Hippie*. Perhaps that is what he was.

At other times, we climbed higher through valleys of pink and purple rock which I imagined laden with silver, for this was mining country and there were spoil-heaps. To our right we could always see the Andes rising high and cool while, in the day, the desert round us shimmered with useless heat.

I was reading *The Return of the Native*. I found it hard to feel the menace of Wessex, when surrounded by the lofty hostility of these majestic mountains. I could make little of all the classical allusion, irritating enough at any time, when travelling through this stark land. The Druids, I thought, had had it easy compared with the Aymará Indians whose crouched mummies lay under the parched sands, wrapped in exquisite needlework. The Roman invaders I felt were child's play compared with the *conquistadores*.

There were no diversions on the long straight roads. On the verges there were crosses, memorials to drivers who had died at that spot. Sometimes there were elaborate shrines with several crosses, decorated with headlights and old number plates. There were piles, too, of broken glass, tributes to popular lorry-drivers who met their end there. Their fellows, every time they passed, would fling another bottle from the cab window in memory of friendship. One morning, I started to count these crosses. In one hundred kilometres, there were forty-nine and four more in the next kilometre.

Then we were in the country of the nitrate mines, mostly long since abandoned. Each had its graveyard, pathetic squares jammed with wooden crosses. At the first one we came to, I could read but half of only one name, Peño de V . . . from your family. 1914.

At Humberstone, which was worked until 1960, I had heard that there was a British cemetery. I could not find it. There was a small village just after the deserted mine. I asked a policeman. He said he knew nothing of it, but judging me to be of a ghoulish turn of mind, recommended me to the site of the Battle of Pisagua.

'It has scores of graves,' he said with enthusiasm.

Never had there been so lifeless a desert as this. Usually I love deserts, but here I was depressed. This desert was one huge graveyard – of soldiers killed in pointless battles for useless territory, of miners who dug for chemicals that no one wanted, of drivers who die literally of boredom, falling asleep at the wheel.

11
Bolivia
MASKS, LLAMAS AND DANCING

The border with Peru was both silly and unpleasant. We had had quite an agreeable day in Arica, the northernmost town in Chile, once gratuitously attacked by 'the pirate Drake' as the locals called him.

We had looked at the cathedral and the customs house, both built by Gustav Eiffel after a great earthquake in 1868. They did not reveal Eiffel as having been an architect with many aesthetic gifts, but both buildings stood firm through a new castastrophe – a huge tidal wave, which the Chileans called a seaquake, in 1877.

Then we had been to look at the narrow strip of land which Bolivia was hoping that Chile and Peru would give to her, to provide that landlocked country with a corridor to the sea. The Bolivian outline plan had been announced only three days before. The filthy stretch of beach and the desolate land behind it was of no value to Chile, but it struck me as an ill omen, possibly deliberate, that the proposal was made public on the day when Chileans commemorate, in a fever of patriotism, their hero, Commodoro Rivadavia.

We had stared at the statue of Captain Arturo Prat who, in the 1879 war against Peru, when his small, wooden vessel was rammed by the big, ironclad *Huáscar*, boarded the Peruvian ship and fought on until he died.

Chileans, like all South Americans, love a hero but, looking at the plucky Prat, I decided that they nowadays lacked the vigour of those they admired. Pinochet had lost his support. He was aging. Even his fellow-officers had lost faith in him. The buskers might sing, but no one did anything. The people were pathetically accepting.

We had drunk *pisco* sours with Pedro, an engaging Mexican. He was the manager of a Mexican circus which we had seen on the road. It was a big affair with sixty people, ten elephants, ten horses and eight tigers. They had spent four years on the road.

'The best country was Argentina. We spent eighteeen months there.'

We were now both moving on to try Bolivia and Peru. The direct road from Chile to Bolivia was said to be so bad that we decided to cross into Peru and to take the marginally better one from Tacna.

On the Chilean side of the border, we had to buy forms from a small gift-shop, and to fill them out in septuplicate. On the Peruvian side, the officials were brisk with us, but odious to the poor. A middle-aged woman, carrying a baby on her back, was in front of us at the customs. She had two or three bundles wrapped in cloth and, quite openly, a radio, which did not look new. The man ripped apart her bundles, scattering their contents with contempt. Then he took the radio and, without any word, broke it in half on the edge of the counter. The *campesina* first picked up her clothes from the floor. Next, with a hesitant hand, she took back the two halves of the radio. She stood for a moment. Then she moved on, her face impassive.

Arica had felt busy for Chile. Tacna was humming by contrast. It was not an attractive town, though I was fascinated to see scribes in the street, sitting at tables with typewriters. The cathedral here was also designed by Eiffel, but was built of stone rather than metal. Although he was less fussy in this material, the building did have the look of an ecclesiastical railway station. The barrel roof went unbroken from one end of the church to the other. The high windows were circular, glazed with the too-bright stained glass of which Eiffel was evidently fond.

We left the coast and climbed on an exceptionally rough road towards the *altiplano*. It twined through narrow valleys where dour-faced people gouged a living from the steep, ungenerous mountains. The terraces clawed their way upward, sometimes as many as seventy, one above the other, so that the supporting wall was often greater in height than the terrace it held up was wide. These were Inca terraces, many of them still in use after centuries. And where they were neglected, we could see the same green thread that we had seen in the Elqui valley, running like a contour line far above any cultivation.

There were many police checkpoints where every detail of our passports was entered at each post, often by men to whom writing was a sorry labour. There was hardly any other traffic on this lonely road. By afternoon, we were among high hills with the peaks of the Andes showing above. There were llamas in small herds, pecking at the scant grasses of the empty plains. And in the evening, we came to a sombre town with grey houses. Darkness fell and we were beside Lake Titicaca, a name which conjured legends of lost Inca treasure, a place that I had always longed, but somehow never hoped, to see.

My excitement was great and I looked in amazement at the cold, gleaming water, striped with the reflection of a perfect full moon, so clear as to seem shrill.

Then I spoilt it by listening to the British election results on the BBC World Service. And the same moon shone bright on Mrs Thatcher.

In the morning, I regained as much of my enthusiasm as my breathlessness from this altitude would allow. At dawn, the sun could not relieve the steely quality of the water, though it glowed on the brown hills stippled with a fading, yellowed grass.

We travelled along the shore towards Bolivia. The grim villages of the night before looked little better by day; the houses were mostly built of brown, mud bricks with grey, corrugated-iron roofs. At the water's edge, reeds grew and boats made of those reeds paddled over the shallows with unexpected buoyancy.

In some of the villages there were grand, baroque churches built of andesite, a kind of red granite. Many of these curiously inappropriate buildings were crumbling. One at Zepita, with a splendid west front and superb wooden doorway, was just shut and abandoned, grass growing from its dome. At Pomata, restorers were at work and proud to show us their carvings of flowers and animals, but somehow I felt no association between the florid buildings and the high, rarefied landscape, with its rolling hills, all brown and yellow, and still less with the cluster of minute, mud huts with thatched roofs, set on a tufted plain where llamas and alpacas grazed.

The border was at the point where the Río Desaguadero flowed into the southern end of Lake Titicaca. A bridge of about eighty yards in length spanned the river. The scene was chaotic. For about a quarter of a mile on either side of the bridge, the road was thronged with people, pushing and hustling. We eased our way forward until we reached the first administrative building. The bridge would not be open for cars, they said, for at least three hours.

On Fridays, it appeared, there was an exchange of natural produce between Bolivia and Peru. Indians, laden with vast packages, streamed in both directions. The men nearly all wore baseball caps, reading Coca-Cola, Amoco, or the name of some other foreign company. Many of them came with barrow-bicycles, which also served as taxis. The women wore the traditional Andean dress – great, billowing skirts of every colour, with three underskirts, neat bodices, heavy shawls and pale-brown bowler hats. They carried their goods in vast bundles wrapped in striped cloth. Their cheeks glowed red under their brown skin, as though rouged.

Despite the thousands of people, there was curiously little noise. Everyone was quietly intent on his or her own business. Of course, while an exchange of natural produce sounded a wholesome affair, the *campesinos* interpreted the opportunity differently. Everyone was trying to smuggle something. The customs men were overwhelmed. I was amazed by the produce coming out of Bolivia. Boxes went past marked: sardines, Chilean fishmeal, Argentinian oil, auto adhesive, margarine, pumpkins, condensed milk. Hardly natural produce.

'What does it matter?' one of the customs men said. 'After all, at night the lake is buzzing with boats going to and fro with far worse things.'

The Peruvians send over radios and television sets. The Bolivians send cocaine. The customs men took these more seriously. I noticed a small boy acting as an informer on the bridge. He pointed to a woman's bundle. This the man tore open and, finding something, tugged the woman, like a peasant pulls a donkey, to the customs shed. A man asked me whether I had seen a customs van with particular markings between here and Zepita. When I said I hadn't, he said, 'We should get away with this then.' On the bridge, which served as a no-man's-land before a cleared space in front of the customs shed, little girls crouched waiting to dash across unobserved. It was like a very serious game of grandmother's footsteps.

At last the bridge was open for cars. The Peruvian formalities took far more than an hour, and the Bolivian not much less. Then we drove on a narrow, intolerably dusty road. Each time we came to a checkpoint we would have to have our papers examined, while all the local buses we had struggled to overtake, driving blind through a squall of dust, clattered ahead so that we would have to fight past them all over again. The journey to La Paz was perhaps a hundred miles. There were seven checkpoints.

We had moved now into the countries where the police intruded. The eastern half of the continent, while bureaucratic, had not been tiresomely interfering. Even Paraguay had recently abandoned its suspicious spot-checks of people's papers. The western countries were bedevilled by security.

*　　*　　*

The crowd was so polite, so restrained, so quiet. The parade did not start until late morning, our first in La Paz. The sun shone fiercely, but the wind was cool, blowing down from the snow-covered mountains that surrounded the city and, when it gusted, one could muster a shiver. The main road was steep and Symon was breathless as he pushed my chair up the hill, for the air in La Paz was meagre at 12,000 feet, the highest capital in the world.

Before the parade started, the mostly Indian crowd sat on the pavements, waiting with a patience that bordered on serenity. There was plenty to amuse. Vendors walked up and down the route selling oranges, beer, biscuits, peanuts, sandwiches, sweets, what looked like macrobiotic popcorn, toffee-apples, sausages, plastic bags filled with drinks of horrendous colours, ices, frozen juices on sticks, candy floss, eyeshades and peaked caps of cardboard.

No one pushed or even wandered into the road. If they did, it was no great issue. The police politely, not even firmly, asked them to go back to the pavement.

Next to me, on the ground, sat a *campesina*, who had brought a picnic for her three very small children. She produced, from her striped bundle, plates and spoons, even napkins. The middle child, who looked from her size to be about two, but was probably more, wore a miniature bowler hat. Her brother ate his bowl of grain in solemn silence and wiped his hands carefully on his grandmother's shawl.

People came past collecting litter in bags and gave to anyone who was interested a leaflet which explained that, after the festival, they had to collect four hundred extra tons of rubbish. Did that include the leaflets, I wondered? At last, we heard the music coming – a steady rhythm, enlivened by whistling pipes.

It was the Entrada de la Festividad del Señor del Gran Poder, and the *campesinos* had come from great distances to join in the parade. In a very modest way it was like the carnival in Rio. The groups of dancers, roughly a hundred and fifty strong, came from all over the country, as one could see from the differing cast of their features. The men as a rule formed the bands and the women danced in front and behind, but in some groups the dancers, too, were men.

The costumes were either traditional or fantastical and gaudy. The traditional ones for the women followed the pattern of their ordinary clothes, but were new and in unexpected colours, often bright pastels. The women in each group were always correct, their billowing skirts, their bodices and neckerchiefs and their bowler hats all identical, even their shoes. The men in the bands wore suits and ties. They, too, tried to dress identically. Usually they could manage the shirts and ties but, in some groups, one or two obviously could not afford the new suit that the others had saved for. One dancer still had the price on the lens of his dark glasses. I worried for those odd ones in blue among a matching group of browns. But nobody minded.

The wilder costumes looked as if they were made of boxes, covered in cloth of vivid colours. They were patterned with sequins, and finally wrapped in a transparent polythene. The men dancing wore elaborate masks, some of them looking Thai or Chinese. There were cardboardy animals, somehow reminiscent of Tenniel's Red Queen. There were many bears, some of them in fluffy costumes, one with explicit, furry genitalia. It was hard to remember that this was supposedly a Christian festival.

In general, the women looked matronly and serious, though there were younger girls in short, swirly skirts or flouncy dresses. Alas, none of them was pretty and they wore bad make-up over their red cheeks, chapped by the chafing wind of the *altiplano*. The men were short and, as they blew on their trumpets, one was conscious of their big-ribbed chests, enlarged by the need to breathe deeper to wrest enough oxygen from the skimpy air.

There was great variety in the energy of the dancers. Some shuffled by, doing the simple step of the dance, not unlike a Morris step, almost as it appeared by accident. Others danced with a furious verve, stamping their feet. I remember one group of men in rather sober clothes, but wearing heavy clogs with outsize spurs attached to them. They clanged enough to dim the band.

Another wholly unexpected group of men wore only tights. They had blackened the rest of their bodies. In their noses they had ring-pulls from tin cans. They went barefoot and beat on tom-toms. One of them, wrapped in a chain, rolled and rolled in the dust of the sloping street. Whenever he rested, another of the group stood over him with a whip.

It struck me as extraordinary that underprivileged Amerindians should act out a scene of Negro slavery. I could not judge the spirit in which it was done, but learned later that it was satirical rather than sympathetic.

177

There were no floats, but occasionally a group would have decked out an old car with a mass of flowers and an assortment of objects which presumably had a special significance. On the top there might be a portrait of Nuestro Señor del Gran Poder in a shrine, a stuffed baby llama, or a plastic doll. On the flat of the bonnet and the boot there were spoons, bells, a teddy bear, odd shapes made with sequins. The windscreen and windows were obscured with flowers, so that the driver had to hunch down to peer out of one small hole left at the bottom of the screen. Often the old car would boil over and then the group would push it until it cooled.

The music had about it none of that seizing of the senses which had made the sambas in Brazil so compelling. One could wander away from this quite without effort but, at the same time, there was no sacred tincture to it.

Although Nuestro Señor del Gran Poder might look like Christ, this was a Christian festival only by superimposition. The symbols, such as the baby llama, belonged to the old animist religions of the Andes. And on the following morning there would be a ceremony at dawn to greet the rising sun, the great power of the Tiwanaku and Inca religions.

The parade went on for eight hours, by which time twenty thousand dancers had shimmied by. It was a fine introduction to Bolivia.

*   *   *

'Everything in Bolivia has two or more meanings,' said Lupita de Krsul. She handed me a stone figure, smooth and pleasurable to hold. It was Tiwanakan.

'You see that face. But it could be a hunchback kneeling, or a potato. We have two hundred varieties of potato. Here could be another face. Then again, it could be a breast – there are so many images in this one carving.'

We had stopped in Tiwanaku on our way to La Paz. The ancient remains of what was once a large city were awe-inspiring, although fragmentary. There was little left of the huge complex of stone palaces, pyramids and temples. There had been buildings six hundred feet long and the pyramids had risen to fifty feet, constructed with andesite blocks, some weighing more than 150 tons, brought in reed boats from quarries on the far side of Lake Titicaca. The lake at that time was larger and had come closer to the city, where there now stood only a scrappy village.

Half a mile away at Puma Punku, there were the remains of another vast temple and pyramid – splendid gateways, said to be the finest examples of stone-cutting in South America; and a floor flagged with stones weighing thirteen tons, laid as evenly and closely as a mosaic.

Little enough is known of the Tiwanakan civilisation because, like the Incas, they had no writing. Their empire, ruled by hereditary emperor-priests, lasted for at least a thousand years, and came to an abrupt end at some time in the second half of the twelfth century AD. When the Incas conquered the area, in the fifteenth century, they found the Aymará living among huge ruins about which they knew nothing.

To me, the ruins were virtually meaningless, but they raised a multitude of puzzles. How did a people with no wheel move these immense blocks of stone? What was the inspiration for the carved face with negroid features? Or for the moustachioed figure, when the Amerindians have remarkably hairless faces?

The Tiwanakans must have been people of extraordinary ingenuity. They were great astronomers. Near the main Kalasasaya temple, an archaeologist found a stele carved with a solar and lunar calendar of amazing accuracy. Their greatest skill lay in their farming. In the plains around Tiwanaku and much further away, one can even now see what were, until very recently, inexplicable undulations. Dr Alan Kolata, an American anthropologist, decided that they were the traces of a system of cultivation involving raised fields, separated by irrigation channels.

The principle was far from simple. First, the Tiwanakans laid down a bed of large cobblestones. This they covered with a layer of impermeable clay, to prevent any salty water from Lake Titicaca seeping up to their cultivations. Then came two layers of gravel, one coarse, the second fine, followed by rich topsoil. The finished surface of the field was about five feet above the normal level of the ground.

The system gave protection from two likely hazards – drought and flooding. The irrigation channels were full of water; the raised fields were above flood level. There were several incidental advantages. The water in the ditches became warm by day. At night, when the temperature dropped drastically, the warmer water spread a coverlet of protective fog over the fields, which were not more than fifty feet wide, though they might be two hundred yards long. As the sun beat on the water of the channels, the algae thrived and the fish grew fat on the algae, and duck cruised the surface. A glorious compost formed at the bottom of the channels, made up of algae, duck droppings and fish mess. The Tiwanakans scooped this up and spread it as manure on their artificial fields.

All this was forgotten when whatever it was befell the Tiwanakan

Empire. Dr Clark Erickson, a colleague of Dr Kolata's, has managed to build some raised fields in Peru, at the other end of Lake Titicaca. He has coaxed sixteen tons of potatoes from a hectare, while the present-day farmers are lucky to get three.

Lupita de Krsul was both an intellectual and a woman of energy and charm. Her office was in a building which had once been a big hotel of the American kind, but which now appeared largely deserted. I rather think the site belonged to her husband. Anyhow, her office was a cultural oasis in the middle of empty modernity. Vivaldi was playing on the sound-system and archaeological objects and weavings stood and hung around the room.

She explained how much of the old culture remained just below the surface or even above it. What was important about the parade we had seen was not any real Christianity, but the image of Christ which had absorbed the sacredness of the place where the church of El Gran Poder stood.

'It is the place which is very important.'

At Guaqui, we had seen two marvellous stone figures from Tiwanaka outside the huge church, which contained, incidentally, a huge silver altar. Plainly, it was the place that was sacred.

'Whenever a house is built, a llama foetus is put into the earth in a ceremony called *challa*.'

I had seen these embryos for sale in one of the markets and wondered at them.

'In the hole they dig, they make a bed of white wool and aromatic herbs. They put in the foetus and cover it with coloured wools, llama fat, a little gold and silver, sweets and nuts. On the top of those, they put cut-out tinfoil men, cars and guns. After them two kinds of incense, four sugar plaques and tiger fur.' (I took the last to be some kind of wild cat.) 'Finally they add coca leaves and alcohol and set fire to it.

'For some really important things, like churches, factories or mines they need a live sacrifice. First, the priest says mass and blesses the place, then the *yatiri* takes over. He kills two llamas and buries them in a kneeling position, facing the sun. The burials in Tiwanaku were precisely the same.'

Later, Peter McFarren, an author and photographer, who was born in Bolivia and went back there to live nearly seven years ago, told me of complicated myths cherished by the miners, that had their origin in Inca legend.

The guardian of the minerals was originally an Andean devil with a dual nature, half bad – Supay, and half good – Huari. The latter was identified with the vicuña, a free spirit. Supay was banished underground by an Inca princess, Anusta. Supay sent out toads and devils and ants, all of which were beaten back by Anusta. Now known as Tio, the guardian must always be placated, needing offerings on Tuesdays and Fridays. He liked coca leaves, alcohol and cigarettes. Being choosy, he preferred Marlboro. Twice a year there had to be a sacrifice.

At one private mine, which Peter knew, belonging to four men, their mother had always offered a bull to the mine, in August and in February. The year after their mother died, the owners sacrificed only a sheep. Soon, six miners died in an accident. No one would work in the mine. The following year, one of the owners was killed in a car crash. The miners went back to work, happy that the debt to Tio was now paid.

Peter had a collection of masks, like the ones we had seen in the parade. Some were old, others quite new. Tio, it was said, came to dance once a year and it is for this reason that the masks were made.

In the rural tradition, the masks were made of any material, often a kind of parchment. In the city, they were made by constructing a plaster-cast mould, putting hat-felt soaked in cow-glue over the mould and then painting on several thin layers of plaster of paris. The designs were Indian, Negro and Spanish in origin – a whole mixture of styles, which even included Chinese dragons copied from tea cartons.

One of the most intriguing was a mask of death. It came from a district in north La Paz. In their festival, the most beautiful and healthy member of the group was given anything he wanted for seven days – food, drink and virgins to caress. At the end of that time, he must dance and dance and dance, until he dropped dead. Peter assured me that this custom, which came originally from Spain, was still practised today.

Thor Heyerdahl's pale, Scandinavian face was lined only by smiles. His eyes had that pure blue of the north. It was the face of a contented man of achievement. We had arranged to meet early for breakfast and he was there before time, eager to eat up the whole day.

He was in La Paz with a film crew, making a film of his life and his discoveries. Knowing almost by heart how he had started out on his remarkable career, I feigned ignorance. I wanted to hear him tell it – the story of his rejection and near ridicule by scientists, the amazing feat of his famous journey and, finally, the gradual acceptance of the theories to which he had stuck in the face of received, expert opinion.

'It first came to me on a Polynesian island. I had studied biology at Oslo University and I was living alone on this island collecting specimens of insects and plants. I lived exactly like the natives, going out in a boat to fish for my food. One day I realised what it meant that I could only fish on the windward side of the island, for otherwise I would never get back. It meant that the people who populated the islands must have come from the east.

'Then I noticed that many of the plants – the reeds and the sweet potato and so on – were South American species. I managed to find out that the name by which they called the sweet potato was the same as the name the Incas had used.

'There was an old man on the island, who used to sing to his granddaughter about the origins of his people. He sang of Tiki, the god-chief, son of the sun, who brought them to the islands.'

In Peru, Thor Heyerdahl found that, according to Inca legend, Kon-Tiki was the high priest and sun king of supposedly white men who had left the huge ruins on the shores of Lake Titicaca. In their represen-tations of Kon-Tiki, he was bearded and moustachioed. In a battle on an island on Lake Titicaca, between the chief called Cari and the white men, nearly all the latter were killed, except Kon-Tiki and a few close companions, who fled to the coast and sailed westward over the sea. Some Inca mummies have been found that appear to belong to a different race. They had reddish skin, were taller and had larger heads than the Quechua and Aymará.

'I knew that no scientists could agree on where the Polynesians came from, but they were all agreed that it could not be South America. I believed that it could be nowhere else.'

The war came and Thor Heyerdahl served in the Free Norwegian air force. It was not until after the war that he managed to finish writing his theory. No one would read it. He was jumbling disciplines, the scientists said. He should stick to biology, not roam around mixing cocktails of botany and anthropology and archaeology. In any case, there was one irrefutable objection. Whatever the Incans or pre-Incans may have done, the one thing they did not have was ocean-going boats.

'They had balsa rafts,' said Thor Heyerdahl.

The scientists looked at him with pity. They even suggested that he try crossing the Pacific on a balsa craft. So he did.

The Kon-Tiki Expedition was one of the most exciting, courageous and entertaining adventure stories ever written. By his astounding journey, he proved at least that his theory was possible. Gradually over the years more and more evidence has come to light. Thor Heyerdahl had concluded that the Tiwanakan Empire had spread down to the coast. A whole network of Tiwanakan roads was discovered which bore out this belief. Now it is calculated that the civilisation encompassed six million people and endured far longer than the Incan Empire.

'Tiwanaku stretched south to the north-west of Argentina and north to Colombia. Everyone now accepts that. It all came to an end in the twelfth century, but the beginnings get pushed back further and further in history, all the time.'

The film that they were making was meant only to be retrospective but, even at the age of seventy-three, Thor Heyerdahl was thirsting for more and more news of that history. The film crew were exhausted after scrambling over a hillside at 14,000 feet to look for a new road.

'Yesterday I found some balsa rafts on Lake Titicaca still in use. They were identical with ones that the Spanish recorded as having been in use on the coast.

'I am going down to Arica to see some mummies which were discovered this year. They were wrapped in textiles which match those found in Tiwanaku. It connects in a way with the Bolivian request today for a corridor to the sea. In fact, they have even asked for the mummies.

'Later, I want to see a "lost city" in Colombia which has just been discovered.'

The film crew raised their eyes to the ceiling. Thor Heyerdahl's face crinkled in smiles of anticipation. I thought how happy this man must be to have had a theory which everyone scorned and then to have been proved right. I looked at him again and changed the emphasis of this judgement. Never had he indulged in any joy in triumph over others. His happiness came from having looked for something and found it.

*   *   *

Of course, the Chileans with abrupt rudeness refused to give the Bolivians their access to the sea. The announcement was made while we were in La Paz and we felt the whole nation wince.

I sat with Walter Montenegro, a quiet, humorous man who had once been Bolivia's ambassador to Peru and had recently been there on a visit.

'They told me there that negotiations were going well. It looked very good. This sudden reversal can only mean that Pinochet is in trouble. It is not really important of itself, and it would have cost millions which we have not got to build a port and so on, but psychologically this corridor is vital to the nation.'

Bolivia's history is a sad one. The second president after independence formed a federation with Peru. Chile and Argentina, fearful of too powerful a country, combined to destroy this arrangement.

In the War of the Pacific, in 1819, Bolivia joined with Peru against Chile. Peru lost and Chile seized the whole of the Atacama desert for the minerals. Since then, Bolivia has never had any access to the sea. By way of some sort of compensation, Chile built a railway from Arica to La Paz.

In 1903, Brazil chiselled off another chunk of Bolivian territory in the Amazon basin. The Brazilians promised another railway from Porto Velho to Riberalta as compensation. It never reached into Bolivia, stopping at Guajará-Mirim on the summarily-chosen new border. It cost 6,208 lives in building.

In 1938, after two wars with Paraguay, Bolivia was, by arbitration, compelled to surrender to Paraguay some three-quarters of the Chaco. She is now a shrunken nation, with the largest proportion of her population living in the stern uplands in the north.

'Like all South American countries,' said Señor Montenegro, 'Bolivia is at a precarious point. As the President said, predicting six months ahead in Bolivian politics is like entering the cloudy world of futurology. But I think democracy is winning. The people won't accept a military government.'

How the country can sort itself out is impossible to say. It is the second-poorest country in the western hemisphere. Tin prices are low, the oil is not as abundant as was once hoped.

'Something like sixty-five per cent of the economy is black market. Since 1948, we have had one thousand political parties.'

None the less, Walter Montenegro had great faith in the capacity of Bolivians to resolve things peacefully. Certainly, I felt safer in La Paz than in any other capital in South America. There was an innate gentleness about the people, perhaps because nearly three-quarters of them were pure Indian.

'When the miners held a march and demonstration of eleven thousand people, it lasted a week. They let off loud bangers to show that they could handle dynamite as we might handle tea. The government sensibly did not provoke them. When they left, not one person had been hurt, not one window broken.'

As I left, Señor Montenegro said of his country: 'There is a Spanish saying: "With money, poverty is bearable." '

I was not quite sure what he meant, but decided that even in its dire poverty, Bolivia was extremely civilised. When I got back to my hotel, I found that my car had been clamped. I was not sure what that meant either. Perhaps it was the zenith of civilisation, for it was the only country where clamps had arrived.

*   *   *

In the morning, I had the clamp removed for less than the price of the hotel car park, and we set off for the day to the Yungas. To get out of La Paz the road climbed steeply. At the outskirts, we had to get a document, stating where we were going, which we had to have stamped at police posts in every village and at some which were not in villages. I asked what would happen if we decided to alter our route. The man gave a non-committal smile.

We went higher still, to about 15,500 feet, where the air seemed as insubstantial as a spectre, and the clouds engulfed the black peaks and eventually the road. Soon the road narrowed and plunged, writhing down a maze of valleys, in a series of hairpin bends which hung over sheer cliffs of a thousand feet. The road was rocky and waterfalls purling on to it grooved the surface with perilous ruts. There appeared to be some esoteric rule of the road which we could not fathom. Time and again we rounded a bend to find ourselves face to face with a lorry on the wrong side, which hooted at us in furious reproach. We worked out that on left-hand hairpins going downhill, one must drive on the left. We tried it and nearly went head-on into a climbing bus.

In twenty-five miles, we dropped 9,700 feet. The valleys were now deep and lush, and we found ourselves back with bananas and citrus and many old friends of flowers from the tropical forest. There were fields cultivated with a bush that I did not recognise. We crossed two fords and, at the second one, found booths selling bundles of fruits and vegetables. There was a restaurant which called itself El Numero Uno On The Bolivian-Amazon Highway. 'Highway' bordered on hyperbole, as we had never managed to exceed fifteen miles an hour. I wandered down the row of booths and discovered that they were selling polythene bagfuls of leaves from those bushes I had noticed. They were coca. I bought a bag, the size of a small pillow, for two and a half US cents.

We went on a few miles to the small town of Coroico. It was sleepy and poor. People sat in doorways and stared at us. No one said anything spontaneously, but they answered questions with civility, though they were reluctant to discuss cocaine.

185

It was not until I got back to La Paz to talk to Peter McFarren that I got any idea of the importance to Bolivia of the cocaine trade.

'All the legal exports of the country do not add up to the income from cocaine. There are three or four hundred thousand farmers growing coca, and a hundred thousand middlemen, who win a livelihood from it.'

The Yungas, where we had been, was probably the most innocent of the three main growing areas. Half of its production was for everyday use in tea or for chewing, all of it legal. The tea is good for alleviating altitude sickness and chewing the leaves, while uplifting, is a harmless pleasure. The Incas used the leaves for increasing their endurance and also for relieving thirst. The best leaves for these purposes are from a less bitter variety which yields smaller amounts of chlorohydrate.

Domestic production of this sort amounts to only a tenth of what is produced for the making of cocaine. The other two main growing areas, Chapari and Beni, are far less accessible than the Yungas. It is impossible to get to some parts of them even by helicopter.

Originally, Bolivia produced only leaves, but the temptation to move to the next stage of production, which is the making of the paste, was irresistible. As the rewards for making paste are so much greater than for growing, laboratories sprang up in large numbers.

The process is simple. They put the leaves into pits, lined with plastic. They then pour kerosene over them. That produces a thick, brownish liquid which is dried in the sun on paper.

Three hundred pounds of coca leaves makes one pound of paste, and from three pounds of paste one can extract one pound of pure cocaine. So, at fifty cents a pound, a farmer earns $450 for producing the raw materials needed for a pound of cocaine. A paste-maker can earn anything from $2,000 to $10,000 a year. What the farmer produces for $450 sells on the streets of the United States for $7–10,000.

'To try to stop the traffic is a hopeless battle. A hundred and seventy troops of the US enforcement agencies came and broke up twenty-two big laboratories. It interrupted production, but it did not stop it. In fact, cocaine prices are down because of overproduction.'

Peter McFarren was anyhow ambivalent about the rights and wrongs of the traffic.

'What do you do about the three or four hundred thousand farmers? To talk of crop substitution is unrealistic when they make ten times more from coca than they would get from any other crop.

'What, though, do you do about the thousands of kids who are addicted?'

It was after talking to Peter that I began to feel that America was approaching the problem from the wrong end. It was not their business to stop the Bolivians from growing coca. It was their business to stop Americans from importing cocaine and selling cocaine and to dissuade their children from snorting it.

12
Peru
HIGH DANGER

At Desaguadero, the border was again shut. We reached it at about ten in the morning. It would not open until four in the afternoon, they said. For a matter of twenty dollars on each side, we were into Peru by eleven.

The journey to Cuzco took two days. We travelled the length of the lake again and slept at Juliaca. It was a poor town, reputed to be dangerous. I later met a man who told me that he had taken a taxi when there. When they had gone a few hundred yards, the taximan drew a gun and demanded all his money. It was the third time that he had been robbed in a fortnight. Nobody threatened us as we walked, looking for a hotel.

The only comfortable hotel was full. In the square we found another, supposedly with heating. There was none. The night was cruel, for we were at nearly 13,000 feet. In the bar of the hotel, men sat watching television, their scarves drawn across their mouths against the cold. Symon set off round the town to get a hot-water bottle filled at a café or a restaurant. They were reluctant, as all water was turned off in Juliaca at seven in the evening.

In the morning, we strolled in the square, buying alpaca jumpers. The women selling them were surprised when we rejected so many on the

188

grounds that the wool was mixed with man-made fibre. They thought them new and therefore good. 'Machine-knitted,' they said with pride.

At the railway station, where we went in search of breakfast, there was a row of barbers. The platform round them was ankle-deep in glistening, black hair. The Indians save to get the fare to Lima where they expect to find riches. Hoping not to look like country bumpkins, they have all their hair cropped short. And outside the station I saw a man singeing the bristles on his face with a cigarette, by way of shaving.

The bigger towns of the high Andes were depressing, overhung with a dark gloom of poverty. Always, it seemed to me, a people of little humour, the Indians' charm lay in their dignity. Robbed of that, they filled me with sadness. The countryside, where their natural way of life persisted, had about it a crystal beauty.

We hurried through Pucará, pausing only to look at the enormous church, filled with incongruous paintings in heavy, gilded frames. The road climbed higher to over 14,000 feet, where there was a research station for studying llamas, alpacas and vicuñas. We found an alpaca lying on the road, bleeding from its ear. When we went to it, it moaned. Someone had hobbled its back legs. It looked dazed. Then it shook its head, spraying Symon with blood. We drove on, hoping to find someone to help, and met a pick-up. The men said they were on their way to fetch the animal. It had been hit by a truck.

Down again into a wonderfully fertile valley that spelled the history of Peru in relics. The Inca terraces, ever fertile, made brown and yellow patterns far up the high sides of the valley. On a knoll at the entrance, there was a monastery, deserted and for a time evidently used as a farm, then deserted again. Lower, there was one of those huge, stone churches which I was beginning to see as an affront. While the Jesuits had their success in Paraguay, what kind of achievement was this? Their legacy was irrelevant. It did nothing and never had done anything for the people. In Paraguay, they had at least provided sanctuary and security from the slavers. Here the Spanish had done their worst already. They had destroyed the Inca civilisation, they had stolen the treasures of the people, they had raped, butchered and betrayed the Indians. It was an insult to make them build great monuments to the invader's god, towering above their huts.

It was harvest time. The people were in the fields cutting the barley, as pale as the hair of a Saxon child, with sickles. And, by their huts, they were threshing in different ways. At one place, women were beating the crop with poles and brushes; at another, three horses abreast trotted in a ring, their brisk hooves doing the work in no time; at a third, a pair of oxen plodded their thorough way round and round. Left undisturbed, these people looked happy, content with their produce – neat fields of onions, radishes, beans, quinoa and the rice which was yet to ripen.

Further on, we saw people in strange costumes. I hoped for a moment that it might be the festival of the muleteers, for we were now back on the old route, the camino de los Incas, which we had travelled in northern Argentina, at Tucumán and Humahuaca. In the seventeenth century, the Tucumán muleteers used to bring several thousand mules here to sell at Yanacota Fair. Today, they are remembered in dances in which the people dress in high boots, hats and special ponchos and wave lassoes in imitation of the *tucumanos*. Instead, they were dressed up for Corpus Christi.

Shortly before Cuzco, we looked at the church of Andahuaylillos. It was built in 1580, almost certainly on the site of an Inca temple. The exterior was not striking, apart from a frescoed porch, but the interior was exceptional, with large murals, one fine one of a battling St James and another of the Annunciation. There were also paintings in elaborate frames of St John the Baptist and Jesus on the Sea of Galilee. The altar was impressive and gilded, with a large silver centrepiece. The roof was curious, having a rippled effect from the plaster's being put over the beams, and painted with abstract motifs.

*   *   *

Cuzco was *en fête* for Corpus Christi. When we went to the station to buy our tickets for the train to Machu Picchu, the manager of our hotel offered grave warnings about pickpockets and footpads. Already, Peru grated with menace.

We walked back, enraptured by the beauty of Cuzco. For the first time, I found pleasure in the fusion of the two cultures. Forgetting the iniquity of the destruction of this great Inca capital, the rather sombre Spanish, colonial architecture grafted well on to the vast stones of the original city. We looked in awe at the neat, mortarless seams of the immense blocks, which are incorporated into the base of so many churches and houses.

In the Plaza de Armas, we found a crowd. This square had originally been the Inca forum for festivals, known as Haucaipata. On the east side, where the cathedral and the church of El Triunfo now stood, was the site of the Palace of Viracocha. On the north was once the palace of Inca Roca.

The images, brought from all the churches of the town, had been put

190

into the cathedral on the day before. Now, they were being brought out for a parade. The images were big and were carried on long frames, borne by the young members of each church. In front of the figures came the other parishioners, many carrying lighted candles. Behind each group was a rather feeble band. In one group, each musician had pinned his music to the T-shirt of the man in front of him. First came San Antonio, carried by twelve young men in jeans. Then San Cristóbal, Santa Ana and Santa Bárbara, San Sebastián, who weighed three or four tons and needed twenty or thirty men to lift him, San Bals and San Pedro and finally San Iago on his horse, carried by sixteen men.

An old woman in a thin dress stood next to me. She said that she came from Arequipa every year for the parade. She offered me some bread from her bundle, though she looked hungry and poor. She told me that she would like to go to Machu Picchu, but she could not afford the journey. I started to offer to take her with us the next day, but when she only half understood what I was about to say, she broke into tears, protesting that she would pray to Santa Ana, who would take her if it were right, and hurried away in the crowd.

The festival seemed, in the morning, to be very tame compared with what we had seen in La Paz, the crowd dense but listless. We went away for lunch. When we came back the whole note had changed. The images had been put back into the cathedral, where they would stay for a week. The bands were now playing the same music that we had heard at the festival of El Gran Poder.

People in masks appeared, and men wore cheaper versions of the costumes the Morenos had worn in La Paz. In the centre of the plaza, people were dancing, holding white handerchiefs. They moved in a snake, weaving aimlessly, pushing the crowd aside. There was now the familiar mixture of Christian and pagan, but there was a new element – violence, or at least roughness. Two pairs of tourists told us that they had been robbed, and four youths bore down on Symon in a side street, but he was quick to get away.

By the middle of the afternoon, the people were drunk and the streets near the centre were running with urine. Men and women dropped their trousers or lifted their skirts and excreted on the pavements of the narrower streets. One man passing another, who was peeing through a railing, shook him by the hand, as the stream of piss trickled warmly round his feet and on down to where people were sitting on some steps.

Nothing, even the acrid stink of the late afternoon, could spoil the beauty of this town. We walked in the quieter lanes, admiring the balconies, the carvings in the churches, the masonry of the Incas. By eight in the evening, all was calm and we strolled in the empty streets, littered with the chewed stalks of sugar-cane.

*   *   *

The cafeteria at San Pedro station was packed at six in the morning. Behind the bar, there was a display of goods for sale – statues of the Virgin and Child, Inca symbols, whisky, chewing gum. It was hard to tell what nationality any of the tourists might be, until they spoke, for they all wore new, alpaca sweaters.

An American voice said: 'I got just the best peanut butter at my hotel.'

The tourist train for Machu Picchu left precisely on time, weaving out of Cuzco through grievously poor housing, only a matter of inches from the walls of trembling mud. In a window, a woman was combing her hair, oblivious of the inquisitive trippers' faces barely four feet away.

The way was so steep that the train would go forward for a quarter of a mile, pause while the points were changed and then reverse up the next quarter of a mile, pause and go forward once more, in a series of eight zigzags. Everywhere, among the houses which clutched the hill, lay rubbish. We scissored up some thousand or more feet, gazing down on the roofs of Cuzco which looked like a tumbled house of cards.

From the heights, we coasted down into softer country, where the plain of Anta and the hills around were dappled with browns and greens. In the fields, the cyan of the onion patches and the clumps of eucalyptus looked almost shocking. But nothing was so unnatural as this shining yellow and orange, metal train, dieseling its way along the trail of the Incas. Dogs rushed at its intrusion, barking with fury. People stared, with no trace of expression, from cottages so small that the hollyhocks grew higher than their roofs.

We followed the River Urubamba. At times, the valley narrowed to a gorge, so tight that broom brushed the windows of the train; at others, it broadened out and I marvelled as always at the terracing and the irrigation. As the day progressed, the feeling grew in me that the beauty of man's ingenuity lay more in the ability to squeeze a living from this inimical land than in the making of a silicon chip.

The journey lasted three hours and was spectacular throughout. We were threatened at first with a tape of the Beatles over the loudspeaker system, but gratefully this changed to Andean pipe music that enhanced the taciturn and powerful landscape.

Next to me sat an English couple, silent in their matching alpaca *chompers.* They spoke to each other once on the journey. He pointed something out to her.

'Yes,' she said, in the flat accents of Essex, 'it is amazing scenery, I suppose.'

I noticed an 'Indian' train, waiting in a siding for the tourist train to pass first, with its foreign trick of punctuality. It was full of people carrying great loads of produce, vegetables, sacks of grain, chickens, even a small goat. It looked fun.

How is it that the world's wonders always both disappoint and surprise? From other people's descriptions, I was expecting something quite different. Everyone had always told me of the huge blocks of stone, fitting mortarless together so perfectly that a penknife blade would not go between them. They had spoken of towers and temples, palaces and fountains. I had expected grandeur, more complete and larger buildings.

Nothing, on the other hand, had prepared me for the imposing glory of the situation. I sat at the highest point that I could reach and lost myself in the splendour of the position. It was too beautiful, somehow, for one to be able to imagine the Inca life once led here, even if anyone could have been certain what that life was. It did not matter much – the extraordinary thing was that anyone of any kind had ever chosen to build a city here.

City was, in any case, an exaggeration. The number of people who lived here had probably never exceeded one thousand, although guidebooks speak of '250 homes'. Hiram Bingham, who discovered Machu Picchu in 1911, believed that he had found Vilcapampa, the secret refuge of the last four Inca emperors, said to be an exact copy of Cuzco. Naturally, everyone tried to make the facts fit this theory. Only twenty-five years ago, Gene Savoy discovered, further away, larger and more extensive ruins, so far not excavated, which are now thought to be the real Vilcapampa.

That made it more likely, it seemed to me, that the theory was correct that Machu Picchu was a kind of convent for the so-called Virgins of the Sun. These girls were chosen at the age of eight or nine for their looks and family connections. They became either the concubines of the Inca and the priests or ceremonial cooks and weavers, producing robes for the nobility. Occasionally, one might become the wife of a favoured noble. The theory was postulated because, when the graves at Machu Picchu were opened, three-quarters of the remains were female.

It was the impracticality of the site which lent such majesty to the place.

193

To my right, about forty terraces etched their way down the precipitous slope, until the drop to the river, two thousand feet below, became sheer. Ahead of me, Huayna Picchu shot up, sharper than a mountain in a Chinese painting, hazardous to climb, yet worked with terraces near the peak. Puffballs of clouds wafted overhead and occasional wisps cruised beneath. Coronilla grew a rich yellow in crevices and orchids sprouted through the grass. A fat, lone llama stared at me. The only thing that was missing was a condor, which a girl had told me she had seen the day before. Never have I sat in a more stupendous place.

Once I had slaked my astonishment, I changed my view of the actual buildings. They were not as impressive as the remains at Cuzco, the blocks were smaller, but they were still unimaginably large for the place they were in. No wheel, no iron tools to work the stone. The Incas were a remarkable people; but still, what I would return for would be the place rather than the buildings.

As we left to go back down the five miles of road, the bus zigzagging through fourteen hairpin bends, a small Indian boy wailed a plaintive goodbye. After a zig and a zag, there was another boy identically dressed, who wailed in the same way, and two bends further down another. Then I realised that it was the same boy, who ran straight down the middle. It was a good joke, but none of the other tourists gave him anything for his enterprise.

The journey back was equally breathtaking in reverse. Another American voice said: 'You know, I make wonderful peanut-butter bread.' Does American youth think of nothing else?

On the way, I read in Hiram Bingham's *Lost City of the Incas* about irrigation and agriculture. I already knew something about the irrigation. However, I had not realised that the soil for the high terraces was originally carried up from the valleys below, and was so carefully nourished and tended that it remained, and in some cases still remains, fertile for centuries.

To preserve the fruitfulness of the soil, the Incas used guano from the islands off the coast. During the breeding season, no one was allowed to go to the islands. The penalty for killing a cormorant, a gannet, a pelican, or any other fish-eating bird was death.

Inca skills, although limited, so that their word for work was the same as their word for cultivate, were so well directed. They had the ingenuity to breed from the free-spirited vicuña two domestic creatures with such different purposes. The llama is big, its legs comparatively sparse of hair, and its wool is coarse so as to bear the chafing of a pack load. It can carry a hundred pounds on sure feet. The alpaca is smaller. Its wool is soft and covers even its legs. It cannot carry anything, but yields pounds of warmth.

Recently, I heard that modern potato-growers have found that the best repellent for a grub which attacks tubers can be made from the ground dried leaves of a plant called lantana. The Incas grew it for just this purpose.

They were an attractive people. Their everyday greeting was, 'Don't be a thief; don't be lazy; don't be a liar.' The response had a quality which socked the Pharisee. 'And don't you be either.'

They perished at the hands of the *conquistadores* – indolent thieves, practising every form of treachery.

*   *   *

The girl who had seen the condor was Katy, an eighteen-year-old American, the daughter of a brain surgeon. We said we would take her with us to Lima. At Abancay, we talked to the police about the road to Ayacucho.

'Don't go there,' they said. They did not forbid us to go, but counselled us strongly against going. 'There are deaths all the time. If you must drive to Lima, take the road to Chalhuanca. That way you will be safe by day, but don't drive at night. By Ayacucho, it is dangerous by night and by day.

Rueful, I remembered Hiram Bingham, only eighty years ago. The prefect of one department gave him a military escort. 'I never discovered why he was so insistent. There was no danger, and highway robbery is unheard of in Peru.'

We could hardly risk it with Katy, though I was sad not to see the cathedral and old colonial houses of Ayacucho. But in the end I was glad. The road from Cuzco had been beautiful enough, rising and falling in glorious valleys, flecked with patchwork fields. At one point, a whole wold was covered in white – the flowers of anise. On the banks, as we came down to Abancay, there had been wild, scented lupins. The road we now took was quite different and astonishing.

Chalhuanca itself was a grim little town, a few hours up the Río Pachachaca. We put up in an inn that made Katy cringe with horror. The other guests were drunk and the lavatories unusable without treading deep in excrement.

We ate in a bar opposite. Katy travelled with unending supplies of pots of bubble-blowing soap to entertain children. The barkeeper's little boys

195

were entranced, but their twelve-year-old sister wriggled with uncertainty when Katy tried to persuade her to join in. Her expression volleyed between girlish yearning and the need for dignity. In the end, after a nervous, searching glance up the street to see that she was unobserved, she blew, her cheeks puffed out like a trumpeting seraph. The bubbles flew up in a rainbow fountain and, at last, she laughed like a child.

It was Symon's turn to be horrified. The only dish was rich, goat stew. He always had that gaping hole, the opposite of the widow's curse, in his stomach that gnaws at all young people. But he was also conventional in his tastes. Goat was beyond his compass. He suffered miserably. And the night was made hideous for all of us, by lurching figures invading our rooms, as if by accident, whom we had to repel with curses.

In the morning, we heard shots, but it may have been the troops amusing themselves, or some Peruvian military custom, for in Cuzco at seven every day we had heard a splatter of gunfire, coming from the army post near the hotel. We were all glad to leave Chalhuanca early and to wash in the spark-bright waters of the river, before starting to climb the ridge of the Andes.

Here the mountains showed their youth, being spiky and crumbly, with narrow valleys to the sides of which the road clung with uncertain hold. Occasionally, it had given way altogether and we had to spiral up a provisional track to get round the gap. Eventually, we came out on to high, lonely plains. In the four hours of climbing, we had seen no other car. There was a strange, grey quality to the land, even in the sunlight, so that the boulder-strewn grazing was the colour of German army field-grey. Herds of llama and alpaca raised their long necks, turning their heads like periscopes to look at us.

The rare villages of stone, thatched with grass, were almost invisible among the tumble of rocks. Some curious animals hurried to hide as we came close. They had the head of a rabbit, but their long bodies ended with a rat-like tail. I asked an Indian what they were. His eyes widened with disbelief at my ignorance. He made me repeat the question three times, not because he had misheard, but to make sure that I was asking what anyone but a moron must know. At length, he said, 'Biscacha.' Hoping to correct the impression of idiocy, I said that in my country we had animals like these, but without tails. He laughed, to humour me perhaps, and I could see that I had merely confirmed his suspicions. They were indeed mountain viscacha (*Lagidium peruanum*), as I learned later – a long-tailed Andean rodent, a close relation of the chinchilla, fortunately a little less soft-furred, so that it has not yet joined in probable extinction its fluffier cousin.

We climbed still higher, to more than 14,000 feet, and here there were no villages. There were royal-blue lakes, with highland geese and coots and duck. And we saw our first vicuña. They were so much more graceful than the lumpy llamas that, at first glance, one might have taken them for deer. I enjoyed the improbable colouring of llamas, browns and whites and blacks in impromptu patterns, each creature an individual, but the regular, silky caramel and white of the vicuña, with their long, glossy shirt-fronts, was so much more elegant. It seemed apt that the most beautiful of this family should be untameable.

Another hour had gone by. Still we had seen no other vehicle and now there were no people. I was suddenly filled with the most wonderful sense of privacy. We had been in more remote places, in the Amazon jungle, for instance. But, for the moment, at this breathless height, the snow peaks around us, the vicuñas running, the geese sedate on the glinty lake, I felt as if the whole world were mine. I drew another breath of this pure and precious air and have rarely felt so fortunate.

*   *   *

The Nazca lines, those puzzling drawings on the floor of the Peruvian desert, whose purpose no one will ever be able to state with certainty, provide merriment for cranks and scientists alike. Are they a map, a pre-Colombian whim of early balloonists, messages from outer space, a decorative running-track, weaving patterns? The theories are manifold and ingenious.

Seen from the air, the enormous drawings are clear and indisputably what they are said to be, a monkey, a spider, a lizard, a tree, hands. From the ground they are shallow grooves and one must climb a hill to see that they depict something.

In the hotel there was a lecture. For at least thirty years, Maria Reiche, a German woman, has studied the lines. She has battled for their preservation. It is due to her that it is forbidden to drive or walk across the desert. She paid for the tower beside the Pan-American Highway, from which people can see the hands, the tree and the lizard.

Her lecture, which she gives every evening, is free, but any donations she passes on to the guards who protect the lines from intruders. With her step-ladder and on hands and knees, she examined every inch of each drawing; with her brush she cleaned any of the depressions which had been sullied by car tyres. She has given her life to the lines.

There were about thirty people to listen to her. She looked to be about eighty and she moved stiffly but erect, supported by her sister. Her face was gaunt, her hair cropped short. Her eyes were without light and, I imagined, almost unseeing.

She sat in an upright chair, gazing straight ahead, over the heads of her audience. In firm, almost arrogant tones she said: 'I can speak in German, French, English, Spanish and Italian. Raise your hands for the language you prefer.' The choice that evening was for German and Spanish.

As she spoke, she rocked, her gnarled hands moving ceaselessly forwards and backwards on the arms of the chair. Her face contorted, seemingly in pain, and her words came with automatic flatness.

The German finished, she changed with no pause to Spanish. No one moved. Those who had asked for the lecture in German sat on, uncomprehending. It would have been too rude to leave.

In her own language, it had all gone well enough. Whether age or illness had dimmed her mastery of a foreign language one could not tell, but in Spanish the lecture became a nightmare for the audience. She was speaking words that she had spoken a thousand times by rote. But now they came out in jumbled order. Sentences followed each other inconsequentially. Twice, long paragraphs were repeated with unvarying emphasis like a replayed tape. Sometimes the words just failed.

It was an agony to sit through, impossible to leave. Yet it was a wonder of a sort, almost a parable of dedication. But the audience was the real wonder – a mixture of nationalities, all respectful of another's dignity.

*　　*　　*

Grey hangs over Lima like a flannel. For six months of the year, the sun cannot penetrate the dense layer of shapeless cloud. I hated it. I disliked most of the cities of South America, but Lima filled me with a special horror.

As Carolyn Walton, in a guide to Lima called *The City of Kings*, has pointed out, it has been declining for nearly three hundred years. A French scientist, in 1713, wrote: 'The city now is poor compared with how it had been before.'

That was before the earthquake of 1746, which flattened all but twenty of its three thousand houses. In 1777, Hipólito Ruiz complained of its 'incredible poverty'. Alexander von Humboldt, in 1802, wrote of 'the filthiness of the streets, strewn with dead dogs and donkeys'.

Charles Darwin, in 1839, saw 'a wretched state of decay . . . heaps of filth are piled up in all directions, where the black gallinazos pick up bits of carrion.' The vultures are still there, and the filth. The dead body that I saw was that of a man.

Every so often Lima surges forward. First, it was the mines which brought early prosperity. In the last century, it was guano. Early in this century, it was cotton, sugar and wool. But after each surge, it sinks back into ever deeper squalor.

I could find nothing to like. The pompous plazas, painted dark pink and yellow, had a hollow grandiosity which repelled me. The blue and red, chocolate soldiers guarding the Presidential Palace were merely laughable. In the museums, I felt that the crocodiles of children were not being taught anything, they were being indoctrinated. They moved in lines, each child with one hand on the shoulder of the child in front. 'Eyes right, eyes left.' They processed blankly past the exhibits.

'You will love Barranco,' people said. 'It is so pretty.' I hated Barranco; it was a decaying resort with a grubby beach. Its houses were pretentious but peeling. The streets were dirty and we were forced off the road and made to wait while a squad of soldiers ran past us.

There was endless talk of muggings, not just of the rich, but of the poor as well. A man might be held up for his boots. A knife at his throat, he would be forced to take them off and to go home barefoot. A young friend wanted to go by bus. It was crowded and he stood. Five men pressed round him and ten hands felt all over his body for anything to steal.

The other talk, in smart houses, was of a kind that curdled the spirit.

'You know, she joined the Red Cross. She had her uniform beautifully made. The cut of the jacket was perfect and Maria did the hat, so cleverly. Oh yes, she went to all the classes about bandages and so on. She rather enjoyed those, I think.

'But when the earthquake happened . . . oh dear. She told the butler that if they telephoned for her to come to help, he was to say she was abroad.'

Butlers figured large in these conversations. 'Margarita says when she's alone, she can't bear the footmen staring at her. So she told them both to stand behind a screen. Then she shouted to them – What are you doing behind there? Do I hear you whispering? You must sing. So all the time she's having her lobster, they have to sing songs. Of course, they think she's wonderful.'

The grey pressed down and the squalor ground into us. Joanna, a woman of feeling, took us to Las Floras, a *pueblo joven*, a new suburb, which is to say a wretched development to house the poor, removed from the worst of the rotting shanties.

When we arrived at the Benedictine mission, Father Michael was singing vespers. We waited in the small courtyard of the cramped building. It was built, like all the surrounding houses, of dusty, unplastered brick, so as not to appear ostentatious. In the street, just outside the door, a woman sat on a low wall. She spoke to anyone who made as if to come in, though she had ignored us. She was an evangelist picket, trying to lure away the parishioners of the Benedictines.

Father Michael was English and aged seventy-four. His hair was grey, but his face, with clear blue eyes, looked young. It was his hands that revealed his age. He had just come back from the north where he had gone to say a special mass. He had been away for four days, at high altitudes. His return journey had meant travelling for four hours in the back of a pick-up and going the rest of the way by overnight bus. As soon as he got back, he had to go out to perform an emergency baptism. He showed no flicker of tiredness.

The Benedictines from Father Michael's monastery in Worth had come to Peru because his abbot had vowed that he would perform some special service if the Lord would grant him more vocations. He could not think what to do. In Rome, he met the Archbishop of Lima, who explained the particular needs of Peru.

The abbot sent several priests, including Father Michael to work for the Archbishop. So Father Michael spend many years in a lost part of the jungle in the Apurimac valley, far beyond Ayacucho. He taught the Indians modern aspects of agriculture. And he was happy. He showed me many photographs of the people he had lived among – excellent photographs, which revealed his love of the Indians and of the jungle.

Six years ago, Father Edward Cruise started the monastery at Las Floras. Michael was commanded to help him. Beside the monastery they built a parish church, its design based on one in Worth, but it was also in unplastered brick. The church could hold a thousand people and was full, the Father said, for important masses.

'Our parish has seventy thousand people, so it is spread out, and we have to say mass in ten different places. You see, the local people do not walk.' With regret, he added, 'In the jungle, everyone walked for miles.'

Next door, they had built a clinic. 'Now it is run by the state, but we do have the right of veto if anyone teaches the people unnatural forms of birth control. In the first week that it was open, somebody stole the microscope and you can see that lots of the spikes from the railings have been torn off.

'I showed a nun here a picture of a girls' school in Ascot where my sister is a nun. What interested her most were the ground-floor windows. "Don't you cover them with grilles in England?" she asked me.'

The district around the mission seemed calm. Perhaps the Benedictines do provide a focus and a core of hope in the surrounding misery. The hope is faint and the price they pay is high.

Three of the Fathers had died. Father Dominic Gaisford, the present abbot of Las Floras, was ill with hepatitis. Father Richard had had it not long before.

* * *

We drove northward out of Lima, through Callao. It was there that Cochrane, in November 1820, had stolen into the harbour and captured the 44-gun Spanish frigate *Esmeralda*, their fastest and most powerful ship. It was another of his impossible feats.

Apart from her own guns, the *Esmeralda* was lying, as an observing British naval captain wrote, 'under the guns of the castle, within a circle of fourteen gun-boats and a boom of spars chained together'. Despite two wounds, Cochrane seized her and sailed her out of Callao in an operation which lasted only fifteen minutes.

Peru does not give the same generous credit as does Chile to Cochrane's role in the winning of her independence. Not long ago, the Peruvians and Argentinians held a ceremony in honour of San Martín at Paracas – a smelly beach 160 miles south of Lima.

It was here that San Martín, who was Argentinian by birth, landed and proclaimed Peru's independence. The two modern presidents, Alfonsín and Belaunde, bathed in the reflections of liberty. The British Ambassador, Mr John Shakespeare, was not invited. He wrote, however, a letter to the newspaper congratulating everyone on the occasion. At the same time, he pointed out that San Martín's landing could not have taken place without the help of Lord Cochrane and his crew, many of them British, to transport the troops.

The effect was droll. The Argentine Ambassador wrote a furious letter in reply and the Peruvian Minister of Foreign Affairs ordered that no government official should attend Mr Shakespeare's party for the Queen's birthday, unless he or she happened to be married to a British subject.

Callao was now an industrial port and there was nothing to see. We followed the grey coast road through dirty, drab towns for a hundred miles and then turned inland to climb to Huaráz. At once the sun shone and we felt as if freed from bondage.

The people looked natural again – the women now in narrower skirts and hats of felt or grass, the men forever in their baseball caps.

The road ran between the Cordillera Blanca and the Cordillera Negra. The smooth hills were green and the valley fertile, but above them we could see Huascarán, more than 22,000 feet high, and other snowy peaks, the highest mountains of the Andes.

We took a track which led to a national park, though it was quite unmarked, which may be as well if what the park is dedicated to is to survive.

In 1850, Antonio Raimondi, an explorer and botanist, who was Italian ambassador to Peru, found a giant plant which was called after him.

The *Puya raimondii* is the largest plant in the world. It consists of a fat, tall stem that rises to a height of at least thirty feet from a spiky base, not unlike a sisal plant. Each plant lives for about a hundred years and flowers only once, in the last year of its life. The plants grow only in one valley. On average, I was told, there was one in flower in the park every four years. Mathematically, this would seem to mean that there would need to be only twenty-five of them growing. In fact, there were many more than we could count. One was flowering, the first to do so for fourteen years. The whole fat stem glowed with yellow blooms, each about the size and shape of a morning-glory. The flowers, twenty or thirty thousand of them were crammed close together, so that the stem looked, from a distance, like a gigantic yellow totem-pole.

I cannot pretend that it was particularly beautiful, but its rarity and its sheer size lent to it a strange excitement. As the sun sank lower, its colour became more intense and it appeared to be a pointer directing the eye to the pinkish snow of Huascarán.

The Huaráz valley looked so peaceful that it was hard to associate it with disaster. In 1941, the Lake Palacocha, above the town of Huaráz, split apart. The water carried away a third of the town and killed six thousand people.

At Yungay, further along the valley, the horror was greater. The great earthquake of 1970 dislodged the mountain and in a matter of seconds the town was sepulchred in mud, and twenty thousand people died.

We wandered over the broken land, bestrewn with rocks, where the town had been – a flat and useless space, where a few wild roses grew. At one point, the tops of four palm trees stuck out of the earth, forming a square. One was still alive, its leaves green. They looked absurd, until we realised with a shock of pain that, seventeen years before, they had stood proud at the corners of the Plaza de Armas.

Nearby, the only piece of masonry jutted at an angle from a mound. It had been part of an arch. Further off, there were the twisted remains of an overturned bus. Somehow, amid total devastation, its number was still legible – 9.

Most moving were the gravestones, inscribed with whole lists of families, set over the spot where their houses were judged to have been. Children played around, unconscious of tragedy. But an older woman, wandering aimlessly like us, crossed herself repeatedly.

At the edge of where the town had been, there was a hill in which those bodies that were found were buried, slotted into vaults, like pigeon-holes for hotel keys. On the top of the vaults was a large figure of Christ. I marvelled at people's faith in the face of such doom.

As we went north, I was tempted by all the strange, early civilisations of the Peruvian jungle, for instance, the Sachupoyans, said to be a white race, driven out by the Incas in the fifteenth century, leaving many buried cities. At Gran Vilaya, discovered in 1985 by Gene Savoy, there are, according to the *South American Handbook*, 'eighty inter-connected city-type layouts, comprising some 24,000 structures'.

In the end we did not even go to Chan-Chan, built by the Chimú kings, once the largest mud city in the world, surrounded by walls thirty feet high. The Incas defeated these people too, but it is a mark of the difference between the Incas and the Spaniards that they did not loot the town, let alone the burial mounds. The Spaniards, of course, despoiled both. Even as late as 1864, a Colonel la Rosa found a chamber filled with beautiful silver objects. He melted them down to make a solid cubic metre of the metal.

The immense size of South America was beginning to press on us. We could not see everything, but each neglected place of interest made me sad.

Our last night in Peru we spent in Sullana. There was a festival with dancing in the streets and it was hard to find a restaurant. Two boys of about fourteen attached themselves to us and told us that they knew a Chinese restaurant where we could get dinner.

We asked the boys to eat with us. They were intelligent and interested in so much more than I would have expected. Above all, they were fascinated by the United States.

Does the Pan-American Highway go all the way to New York? Is it true that everyone is pretty there? (They looked in admiration at Katy.) And nobody is poor in the United States, are they? But they knew that Fred Astaire had just died.

Their greatest pleasure in the dinner was that we said that they could have as much Coca-Cola as they wanted, even some to take away. They wanted to pour it on their bodies to get a tan.

Frank wanted to be a doctor, a psychiatrist. His father was an architectural draughtsman, but he also bought things in Ecuador in order to sell them in Peru. Nesto wanted to go into the petroleum business, like his father.

They asked us to go to their homes, partly from a natural spirit of hospitality, but also to reassure their parents that we had really wanted to talk to them.

'They tell us off for talking to tourists, because they think we are a nuisance. And most tourists behave as if we were.'

Frank's house was small and poky. His parents were stiffly polite, regarding us, reasonably enough I thought, with some suspicion. But the boys were reassured.

They had given me pleasure because more and more I felt that Peru, indeed all of South America, was lacking in humour. Officials always had to be melted. Children were so often unsmiling. It was a continent of music, but not of laughter. It was a comfort to find some spirited youth.

13
Ecuador
SOLDIERS AND INDIANS

In the last fifty miles before the Ecuador border, we went through six checkpoints. At the first, Katy blew bubbles for the children who played in the dust. At the second, she fed some chicks that the men kept in a hutch. At the third, it was bubbles again. After that, there were no diversions, just faceless soldiers writing, over and over again, our names in the wrong order. It was plain that the Peruvians took this border seriously, although the road was narrow, and the way was rough and little used. I had decided that it would be prettier than the coast road. And it was, despite the tedium of pointless bureaucracy.

The border itself was a bridge over a gorge. On the far side, the officials seemed more forthcoming, simpler. They even made jokes. But Katy disliked them. She said that the way in which they looked at her was degrading.

Just when it seemed that all was done, a young man came from an office marked Ministry of Agriculture and Cattle Rearing. He was fair and had blue eyes, so pale as to be almost transparent. He wore no uniform. He started to search the car, and I fretted at the sudden recollection that we still had a large bag of coca leaves. However, he looked only at books. He asked if I had any books on Peru. I showed him one, and he took it and a map.

The search went on for a long time. Finally, he said we could go. I asked for my book and my map.

'No.'

'Why not?'

'You may not pass with that.'

I explained that I needed the book for my work. His pale eyes did not flicker. I remembered that Ecuador lays claim to a large area which now belongs to Peru. I guessed that his objections had something to do with that.

'Do you want the book because of the map? If so, we can tear the map out.'

'No.'

I pressed him hard, for I could see that he did not really know what the book was as it was in English. All he could say was: 'We take these things at the border.'

'It is not a political book. It is a guide for tourists and I must keep it for information about customs and ruins and churches. What assurance can I give you?'

He was not looking for a bribe and I could see that he wanted, in the face of my quiet persistence, to give the book back to me.

'I will not be able to get the book anywhere else and I won't be coming here again.'

For some reason, the fact that I would not be coming back was important to him. There was a measure of relief in those translucent eyes, but his face did not move.

'I cannot give you the book,' he said. I saw that he was trembling. He walked with hesitant steps to the far side of the car. Then, softly he put the book on the driver's seat, without looking at me, and walked away.

At the outskirts of Macará, the border town, there was a modern hotel. It could not have been more than three years old. Nothing worked, the swimming pool was empty and the only employee said that there was no food. The town itself was dimly lit, dusty and quiet. The last quality Katy and Symon found eerie, I found it a delight. As we walked in search of dinner, we passed a hat shop. The hats for men were mostly panamas; several of those for women were cloches, suitable for 'flappers' in the 1920s. From that moment, I loved Ecuador.

After the sullen menace of Peru, I felt released. An invasion of winged crickets, which crunched under the customers' feet in the restaurant, could not dim the pleasure of finding that even the simple food of Macará was better than that of Sullana. I was puzzled to see that besides the packets of biscuits under the glass counter, they sold not only Glenfiddich whisky but track shoes. Benny Hill was on the televison.

The landscape, too, was changed. The drive to Cuenca took us, at first, through high hills, the winter scrub splashed with white trumpet-flowers and enlivened by wild bougainvillea. From the low bushes the ceibo trees stood tall, their bark strangely smooth and their bare branches looking like roots in the air, so that I wondered if they were related to baobabs.

As we neared Loja, I noticed that both the men and the women wore pigtails. The men's noses were startling for their length. A group had been gathering firewood. They loaded it on to crude go-carts and hurtled down the hill, steering with their feet, their pigtails flying from under their trilbies. After Loja, the road climbed to moorland and bare, pink rock, the colour of fake raspberry blancmange.

Cuenca kept the promise that we had from Macará. It was a town of roughly 150,000 people. The cobbled streets of colonial houses were poor but clean and, again, so much quieter than any Peruvian or Brazilian town of that size. The market simmered with incident. The fruits in geometric piles of greens and yellows and oranges competed with the reds, purples and blues of the women's skirts. Both buyers and sellers smiled throughout any transaction, their round, generous faces contrasting with the severity of their white, panama hats and shining, black pigtails. Rows of women fried thick-skinned fish over braziers and pressed us to eat. Everywhere the people seemed to be more forthcoming, even positively interested.

Of course, it was still South America. Every hundred yards there was a spray of graffito: *Fuera Yanquis*. There were, nowhere near Cuenca, some unarmed American troops who had come to help with repairing damage done by a huge earthquake in March, to roads and bridges in the east.

'That is rubbish,' said the young man in a bar. He had almost spat the word *Yanqui* when I came in.

'No, Inglés,' I had protested. And he had melted, telling me how much he hated the Americans. His hatred was as unconvincing as were his beliefs, because he was by nature friendly, reminding me of Marcelo. But he had a spray-can in his plastic carrier-bag.

'Certainly they are not building roads or bridges. They are constructing a base from which to attack Nicaragua.'

It was, I learned later, a theory put about by dotty left-wing agitators, who look to Albania for inspiration and guidance. I pointed out that Florida was possibly closer to Nicaragua than Ecuador and certainly more convenient.

'Are you sure you are not a *Yanqui?*'

I assured him I was not and we parted friends. I rather hoped it was he who had sprayed on a corner wall the lapidary sentence: 'Mickey Mouse is Russian and Superman has Aids.'

I spent several hours trying to find the collection of Indian artefacts assembled by a Padre Crespi, who died in 1982. This egregious priest had a notion that the Phoenicians reached Cuenca and his collection was formed partly in order to lend credence to this idea, which seemed to me to belong to the Albanian order of speculation. Unfortunately, I eventually discovered that the artefacts were now lodged in a bank. And the bank was closed for repairs, so I shall never know the basis of the Padre's claims.

The road to Quito was easy, going up and down in a long-humped switchback through what, I gather, are known to geographers as 'intermont basins'. In these, the land was patchworked green and brown, the fields sometimes covering a huge, rounded hill which, anywhere else, might count as a mountain. And when we came close, we could see that some of the fields were planted with tiny vegetables, in rows so neat as to look like stitching. Then we came to the chain of snow-topped volcanoes, each one that beautiful shape which speaks of disaster – Chimborazo, Cotopaxi, Antisana, Cayambe.

* * *

Quito gave the impression of being two cities, both pleasant in their distinct ways. The old city was reminiscent of the old part of Salvador, but was less colourful, less tinged with sin. The baroque of its churches was more restrained, its streets were white. Round the old city, the slums clambered up the slopes as they had done in Caracas, Rio, Santiago and Lima. But the misery of Quito was comfort compared with the wretchedness of those.

The new city was bright. There were a few prescribed high-rise towers, but nothing ostentatious; some crumbling mansions, rather French with mansard roofs; and some cheerful streets of small houses like Chelsea or Georgetown in Washington.

There was a pleasant, provincial air to the city. As with so many South

American capitals, the surrounding mountains were visible from almost any part, but here the intimacy with the country was enhanced by the fact that one could see worked fields on the volcanic slopes of Pinchincha.

Quito had even more anti-American slogans. It happened that our hotel was one used by many troops helping with the rebuilding of the roads and bridges. They told me that they did not mind all the written insults, they did not believe they represented the majority feeling. They were young and extrovert and filled with energy. Until they came back from the Oriente, that is. They used to go down for ten days at a time.

When they came back, they came straight from the jungle. They were red with the mud of the forest and their faces and arms were swollen with bites. Their eyes were dull under their puffed lids. All they said was 'Jees, man, that was something.'

In two days, they recovered. They laughed and their bites had scabs on them and they were polite. I had never seen American youth like this.

One morning at breakfast, Ed, who came from Eureka, said: 'It was a close thing last night, let me tell you. There was this Rooskie in the bar. He was bugging us. You know, calling us imperialists and shit like that.

'We didn't say a thing and that riled him. So he kept at it. We let that ride. Finally, Bill couldn't take any more. He said to the Rooskie "That's bullshit." And the Russian slugged Bill.'

Bill was sitting at another table. He had a large bruise on his cheek.

'And you hit the Russian?' I half assumed and half asked.

'Hell, no,' said Ed. 'We knew better than to get into a fight in a bar. But it was damn close.'

*   *   *

Sam Caento Padilla had the straight hair of an Indian. It fell to his shoulder, parted in the middle like a theatre curtain over his low forehead. It lacked perhaps that last iota of pure gloss; it may be that he was not well. His face was pale and serious; he frowned easily but smiled little. His movement were quick, but there was a measure of uncertainty in his gait.

My first impressions of him were contradictory. He was offhand but welcoming. When we talked, he was responsive to ideas, but at the same time, looked bored.

We met in the bar that he had recently opened. It was decorated with bits and pieces from the jungle – a long blow-pipe, framed butterflies, bottles in nets. In a tank, there were several kinds of fish including piranha, which were inclined to gobble up the others. An exquisite, blue and yellow macaw wandered in and out and a parrot took tidbits from Sam's teeth.

Sam belonged to the Huaorani tribe, who were often called Aucas, from the Quechuan word for savage. Forty years ago they were unknown, living a largely nomadic life in the far east of Ecuador, bordering on the Amazon basin. Their language, Sam maintained, had no linguistic relation with any other.

In the late 1940s, the tribe became very unsettled.

'There was so much killing,' Sam said. 'My mother, Dayuma, ran away from the tribe. Her father was speared; she left the next day. She was captured by some white people and lived on a *hacienda*.

'I was born in 1950. I had a brother too, but the man my mother had relations with and my brother both died of measles.'

When Sam was six, the Huaorani became world-famous.

'A man in the tribe had made contact with some missionaries. Five of them flew down and landed by the River Curaray. There was a troublemaker, married to Dayuma's sister. He made trouble because he wanted more wives. He told the people that the missionaries were planning to steal their women and children. So they killed the missionaries.

'After a time, they knew it was a mistake. The guy was hiding but they made Dayuma's sister bring him out. He was buried alive; he asked for one of his children to be buried alive with him.'

Burying alive was a custom among the Huaorani that was not regarded by them with any horror. Sam's grandfather, after he had been speared, had asked to be buried alive. Sam related these events in a matter-of-fact tone, as we sat in his bar drinking vodka and tonic.

Dayuma had, in fact, married another white man soon after Sam was born. 'The man my mother married died when I was two.' Dayuma was a forceful woman. She worked with Rachel Saint, the sister of one of the murdered missionaries, because she believed they could help her people.

When Sam was nine, Dayuma went with Rachel Saint and Guiquito, one of the murderers, on a fund-raising tour of the United States. From that time, Sam's life was divided between the jungle, school in Quito and America. The missionaries acquired more and more control over the affairs of the tribe. Their aim was to settle them in a village.

For four years from the age of seventeen, Sam lived in the jungle, learning how to survive, to hunt and to fish in the traditional ways of the

Huaorani. The missionaries had other plans for him. Rachel Saint employed him to do publicity for her fund-raising in America. He wearied of that after two months and took a job with an oil company. But the missionaries had not finished with him. They sent him, first, to a Baptist college in Tennessee, then to the Florida Bible College at Fort Lauderdale for three years.

'The idea was that I should go back to my people and preach the word of the Lord. I was twenty-five. I decided to become more independent. I became a tour guide on a Flotel.

'I had nothing against the Good Book, but I thought it wrong to force religion onto other people. I believed one should get on with making life bearable. I decided that the missionaries were not doing things right. Things like charging for medicine. On balance, there are more bad things than good things done by the missionaries.'

It was not surprising that Sam gave such contradictory impressions. He disliked what the missionaries did, yet he had considerable respect for Rachel Saint. He was fond of his mother, but felt that she had in some ways taken the wrong course for the tribe.

They had been settled on the land at Toñampari, where Dayuma now lived. She had married a tribesman, but she was regarded very much as a leader, although official leadership lay with Guiquito, now in his seventies. The settled members of the tribe numbered little more than a thousand. The nomadic ones were reduced to only about a hundred.

I had wanted to go to see those still free to wander. A friend of mine, who had told me about Sam, had given them an outboard motor, which had helped them to remove themselves further on the Coronaco river, from the reach of the missionaries. Sam said that it was impossible for us to go. The planes in which we might have gone had crashed. The missionaries occasionally took passengers, but would certainly not fly us to the nomadic group, of whom they disapproved.

Sam had done much for his tribe quite independently of the missionaries.

'I have made documentaries, trying to share the knowledge we had in the jungle, as I try to help them with what I have learned outside. I had a big campaign to get title to the land for the Huaorani. It is easy for the government to say "we have given them some land", but it does not mean anything without a formal title.

'The government talked a lot but it was just words, no deeds, so I had to threaten them. I went to a newspaper and explained. We own nothing, we have lived in that region for hundreds of years. If the government does not give us a proper title, I will move the whole tribe to Peru.

'I knew that would be most embarrassing. I would have asked Peru if we could come, not that there is any real border in the jungle. They would be very happy to embarrass Ecuador. Two weeks later, the government gave us 55,750 acres with full title. Afterwards, other tribes had to be given land as well. They're happy, I'm happy. I hope the government is happy too.'

The contradictions multiplied. Sam got married four years ago to Jeanne, an American girl. They had a son called Shane. Who can say why one person marries another? But, for Jeanne, Sam's being Indian must have played its part. She said she was fascinated by the jungle, which was to say much the same thing.

For no reason that anyone could establish, one of Sam's legs had begun to wither. He could not longer walk in the jungle. Instead he ran the bar. He continued to worry about his people.

'At Toñampari where my mother is, the children go to sleep hungry. The men have gone off to work in the oilfields or the mines. They get paid, but the money does not go to their families. It goes right back to the store run by the company, on a ghetto-blaster, clothes, batteries.

'The women are left alone and there is no one to hunt. Not that there is anything to hunt for. The monkeys and tapirs and peccaries and everything else have all been hunted out long ago. That is why we were accustomed to move on all the time.'

Sam wanted to dig a large pond for the settlement, four times the size of an Olympic pool and to put in tilapia, an African fish.

'Five months are all that is needed from putting in the larvae to overcrowding. I offered to do this some time ago with Peace Corps help, but the missionaries refused. Now the government is against tilapia, saying that they will infest the rivers. That's ignorance, but the Peace Corps won't go against the government.'

I offered to try to help to raise some money for this project. At home, I wrote two or three times to Sam, but he never answered. Three weeks after I left Quito, a bishop and a nun went to the hideout of the nomadic group. The Huaorani killed them.

The British Embassy residence was not far from Sam's bar. I had invited the Ambassador's daughter to lunch. When I went to pick Carina up, she came to the high, solid, wooden gates and talked to me through a grille. She explained that she could not come out. It was not that she did not want to. There was a power cut and without electricity there was no way to open the gates.

*   *   *

There was a cock crowing somewhere in Quito airport while we waited for our plane. At Macas, we walked down the runway to a hangar, where a mechanic was working on a small plane.

As I had not been able to visit the Huaorani, I had arranged to fly down to Taisha, in the hope of meeting some the Shuar people. It was hot and the damp-laden air of the jungle was heavy to breathe after the crispness of the Andes, to which we had become used.

Could someone fly us to Taisha? The mechanic looked doubtful. Juan would be back soon. He might. The planes belonged to the Salesian Fathers, the followers of San Giovanni Bosco, who dreamed the dream of Brasília. Juan came, and when I mentioned the name of the army officer who had arranged our trip, he said he would take any friend of the Major's anywhere.

It was a twenty-five-minute flight over the forest in a Cessna 152. At first, the land below was comparatively flat and from a height it looked like a knotted carpet stretching to the horizon. Soon there were hills and the forest rushed up to us, so that it was no longer a blur and we could distinguish different shades of green and an occasional splash of purple. We could see small rivers like fuse wire, twining through the trees. Sometimes there was a clearing with huts and long, thatched houses, never more than two or three together.

The army barracks lay on the left of the airstrip and we stopped by the entrance. As soon as we got down, a young soldier brought drinks of fruit juice for the pilot and ourselves. Another led us to the officers' mess. It was early afternoon and nothing was happening. A soldier brought a sandwich. I sat wondering what to do with it as it was inedible. No one came. I decided to wander round. First, I buried my sandwich in the scrappy garden just outside the officers' mess. It might nourish the paw-paw tree, I thought.

Everything was very rudimentary, though there was a football field and a tennis court and a *bodega de víveres* where the soldiers could supplement what I imagined was an indifferent diet, judging by my experience with the sandwich.

On the parade ground, the soldiers marched round and round as if playing follow-my-leader. Discipline seemed haphazard and many of the boys were out of step. As they marched, they chanted rather than sang, at one point, to the tune of 'John Brown's Body'. At the end of the parade they yelled: 'Las Amazonas para Ecuador. Viva.'

The Colonel was mystified as to what I was doing in his barracks, but was too polite to say so. My friend, the Major, had been the commander here before. He was interested in the Indians of the region – the Shuar. He had hoped that the Colonel would arrange for me to visit some of their more distant villages. The Colonel, however, had no interest in the Shuar and it did not occur to him to provide that kind of help. He spoke darkly of the possibility of rain and my getting trapped in Taisha, as the airstrip was unusable when wet.

We walked in the village on the other side of the airstrip. After so many cities, the quiet was as soothing as a balm. The only sounds that came from the bar were those of soft, Indian voices. A little further along the bumpy track was a house where a slightly deranged boy had a colony of parrots. He could not say how many he had, nor explain how he encouraged or forced them to stay.

We moved into the even greater stillness of the forest, broken only when parrots screeched and a pair of macaws flew past in full cantankerous voice, while on the ground the crickets rasped. A gossamer mist hazed the canopy trees with blue as the sun went down and the moon took over.

Back in the officers' mess, I struggled with some unchewable meat. The young officers and Symon ate merrily. The Colonel wisely ate in his quarters with his family. The young men were oddly incurious about us, although they answered my questions with good grace. After supper, they watched a soft-porn movie on the video machine. At half-past eight the troops once again protested that Las Amazonas belonged to Ecuador. And, in the morning, we woke to the same vociferous claim.

The Colonel thought that we should meet Father Thomas, who lived on the far side of the village. The track was rocky and steep, so he lent me three soldiers to help with the chair. The sun beat hard, even in the first part of the morning. The soldiers sweated, uncomplaining as they dragged me through the forest. I felt like a Victorian explorer. When we were half-way to the priest's house, we learned that he had gone, on a different path, to the airstrip, to fly to Macas.

We found him in the bar, waiting for his plane. Father Thomas was a big, shaggy man, not fat except for his stomach. His hair was grey and I guessed that he was a little short of sixty. He was American by birth and had trained as a doctor. After serving in the army as a paediatrician, he had taken holy orders and had been in Ecuador with the Salesian Fathers for seventeen years. He had that confident familiarity and superiority which comes of being accustomed to giving advice for a long time.

There was more talk of rain and being stuck in Taisha for many days. I asked the Father if we might go with him to Macas. We went back to thank the Colonel, who looked much relieved at our leaving.

While Symon packed, I talked to Father Thomas. He was peppery but without vanity.

'The military are a pernicious influence. We have had three rapes in Taisha in a week.'

I was surprised, as the soldiers had seemed kind and innocent. It must have been that they regarded the Indians, as the Latins have always regarded them, as of no importance.

'Then we have trouble with the Evangelists who come here to destroy the local culture and replace it with the culture of the southern United States – not of today but of the last century.'

Seeing, perhaps, that I was wondering how their interference differed from that of the Evangelists, Father Thomas volunteered that the Salesian Fathers now operated quite differently from the way that they had done in the past.

'After the second Vatican Council, we realised that the boarding-school system which we used with young children at primary level was useless. The children came and were obedient at school. They went home and reverted entirely, so that they had learned nothing useful.

'We tried local schools with white teachers. That was useless too, because everybody wanted to be like the white teacher. So we initiated what we call the Federation, by which every group is responsible for itself. Each centre has a committee and belongs to an association of several centres, and every association belongs to the Federation.

'We have a radio-school which broadcasts from Macas, each village having its own monitor. The Fathers do not run the radio-school themselves and the government approves the curriculum. We give our opinion if we are asked, but not otherwise. The radio is primarily funded from abroad, so a changed government would find it hard to interfere.'

The plane came and we flew back to Macas. Father Thomas offered to take us to Sevilla – a mission founded in 1945, now a technical school.

The country around Macas was at one time all forest. Now a road had been cut, making it accessible from Puyo. The village had grown rapidly and trees had been felled in ruthless swathes. We drove in a taxi over a shaking bridge, the new concrete one having been swept aside by a sudden torrent.

215

Father Alberto, an Italian, ran the technical college. There were eighty boys and seventy-two girls ranging in age from twelve to twenty-seven. The boys were taught agriculture and the girls what Father Alberto called *manualidad*, which translates as dexterity, but which I suspect meant the equivalent of housework. Certainly, they did all the cooking for the boys. Their day started at five forty-five in the morning and was minutely organised until nine fifteen when they went to bed.

The Father was immensely proud of the school, but was agreeably modest in his explanations. He took me into every room of the boys' half of the rickety wooden buildings. They were built around a large courtyard where the few pupils who were there in this holiday time were playing netball. We looked at the classrooms, the pathetically thin library and, last, the boys' dining-room. Then we moved to the girls' half of the buildings. They, too, were playing netball in their yard, separated from the boys by a high wall, the door locked on the girls' side.

Father Alberto drew on the ground the oval shape of the houses we had seen from the air. Then he drew a line from one end to the other.

'That is the traditional shape of the Shuar house with a division in the middle – men on one side, the women on the other. It is the same here.'

The boys worked in the fields. They grew fruit, vegetables, plantain. They kept bees and raised tilapia in a large pond. Father Alberto had not heard of any government disapproval of this fish. They also had some Holstein cows.

'I am not sure whether raising cattle will catch on. The hope is that they will make the Shuar more independent.'

Father Alberto was determinedly detached. He never assumed that what they were doing was right, he merely hoped so.

'Education does not change people overnight. Even the most educated in a crisis, say when someone is ill, will go to the shaman just in case.'

It was difficult to decide whether Sam's judgement that all missionaries did 'more bad things than good things' was true in this case. He would have been distressed that the pupils had to pay for their own clothes, books, and machetes. The school provided only food and lodging. The government gave fifteen cents a day for each pupil.

One could well wish that the Shuar had been left alone in the first place, but the damage was long since done. Now, as we were to see, it was probably as well that someone should be minding what happened to these attractive, skilful people.

Father Thomas was anxious to see Santa Rosa, a village he knew well when he first came to the region. A new road had been laid to it. It used to take Father Thomas eight hours to ride there on a horse. We drove for half an hour. All the way, the priest was miserable. What he had known as glorious forest had been cut in the grimmest bands of desolation.

When we reached Santa Rosa, Father Thomas sank deeper in gloom. Where there had once been a thriving Shuar village of exquisitely thatched huts, there were only some dismal houses from which Latin faces peered with hostility. There was not one Shuar.

'Santa Rosa didn't join the Federation, I'm sad to say. I was afraid that this is what might have happened. They will have lost their land in one of two ways. The Shuar don't need money, of course, but they are attracted by it, so they may just have sold their land. They will have spent the money and will have nothing. They'll be destitute. The other possibility is that the government simply took the land to resettle people from other areas.

'Often it is tenant farmers from big *haciendas* who have woken up to how they are exploited. They get together to agitate. To keep them quiet the government quickly gives them land, often land in the Amazonas which traditionally belongs to the Indians, who of course have no deeds. They send them here decked with promises and then abandon them. Either way the result is the same for the Shuar.'

We drove back to Macas in lugubrious silence.

In the morning, the rain started. I was thankful that we had left Taisha. We waited two hours for the plane to come. A man borrowed a youth's guitar and played and sang, quite unselfconscious. When, at last, we landed at Quito, there was a cock crowing somewhere in the airport.

14

Colombia

MONUMENTS AND COCA BARONS

A border should change everything. There is little fun in moving imperceptibly from one country to another. Northern Ecuador had been rolling and green, a little Irish. The Otavalo Indians had looked very peaceful people in their dark ponchos and brilliant white trousers. They achieved this dazzling effect, I was told, by washing their clothes in the Lago de San Pablo, not with soap, but with a special reed that had properties that soap manufacturers would envy.

As soon as we crossed into Colombia there was a transformation. The soft greenery woven with crystal streams was soon forgotten. The road soared to heights where we gasped at the superb views, and waterfalls threaded down the cliffs, and then plunged to the depths of valleys where brown rivers hustled among fallen boulders. It was a harsh, raw land.

The Andes were a constant meteorological and botanical mystery to me. For five thousand miles or more, we had climbed in and out of this vast range. Sometimes the valleys were fertile and lush; sometimes they were barren and brown. One might pass through both in one morning. They could even be bare below, but covered in vegetation above. Obviously, it was a question of water – but why should they ever be brown below if they were green above? The vegetation itself was puzzling. On our first day in Colombia, I saw again some yellow daisies of a kind that I had seen two months earlier, at quite a different altitude, in northern Argentina. Why had we not seen them in Chile, Peru, Bolivia or Ecuador? Even the snow seemed to obey no rules, sometimes covering mountains far lower than others that had been green with pasture. The effects, however, were ravishing, and constantly surprising in their beauty, for no combinations of geology and nature were ever repeated. It was easier simply to enjoy each new variation and to ask for no explanations.

We headed for Popayán. Twice the car was searched. The first time, the soldiers unscrewed the tailgate and left us to put it together again. The second time, just before the city, they barked at Symon to get out. 'Hands up. Up against the car.' And they frisked him. This sort of thing always made me laugh. Any European looking at Symon would know at once that he couldn't be guilty of anything, let alone terrorism.

Popayán was founded 450 years ago. In 1983, it was destroyed in eighteen seconds by an earthquake. It was a beautiful colonial town and in four years the rebuilding and restoration had been extraordinary. We walked in the streets with real pleasure, despite warnings about footpads from the *South American Handbook*. The baroque of the only two churches open was restrained and the houses were more conventionally Spanish than we had seen elsewhere. It had the feeling of a university town and there was indeed a university, called after Francisco de Caldas, a scientiest who discovered the relation of altitude to the boiling-point of water. He was born in Popayán, but executed, when only forty-five, for his writings in the cause of independence.

We had, in principle, a choice of two roads to San Agustín. The main one was shut. The guerillas had, the day before, attacked a mine near the road and stolen a large supply of dynamite, which accounted for the frisking of Symon the day before.

The charming woman at the tourist office struggled between her duty and her natural sympathy for our welfare.

'Of course you must go to San Agustín. It is so wonderful and historic. My dear, you will be careful. I mean, the road is quite safe, but please don't stop for anyone unless you are sure they are the army. The trouble is that the guerillas wear the same uniform as the army. You will be quite all right. Oh dear, I wish you could stay a little longer in Popayán.'

The military were everywhere. At the beginning of the alternative road, I thought that they were going to say that that too was closed. They were unsmiling, as they are doubtless taught to be, and hard to melt with jokes.

219

The most successful ploy was to bring up the price of the car, which never failed to evoke a lively interest.

'What do you think of the car?' I would say. They would not have seen many of this kind here in the south.

'It's big.'

'Cheap, though.'

'Never. How much?' And we were away.

As always, we found country unlike any we had seen before. Popayán lay in the Cauca valley, green with sugar-cane, palms and bamboos. We soon left this richness, rising to a marshy moorland, brown and peaty. This unimportant road was little used and foreigners were a rarity. At one village, there was a horse fair. The people looked dark and saturnine. They might have been taken for Gypsies. They responded gravely to any greeting, but would not offer more.

We would, the woman in the tourist office had said, have a grand view of two volcanoes – Paracé and Sotara. In the event, a thick mist obscured everything. We moved through a tropical forest, the heavy drips from the tall trees resounding on the metal of the car. Ferns waved from the rocky verges and occasional clusters of bright flowers shone from the grey, wet wall of trees. We were somehow conscious of huge chasms to our right, but we never saw them. Eventually, we came below the cloud again to find a gentle landscape and, sloshing over the laterite roads, we arrived at San José de Isnos, an insignificant town with the most forthcoming inhabitants.

A boy, aged about fourteen, whom I at first took to be retarded, shuffled over on awkward feet to speak to me. He shook hands and then would not let go of my hand. He spoke quite a lot of English and was the only person in the town to do so. He said he could get no textbooks. I gave him a dictionary and, at last letting go of my hand, he danced on his groggy legs from house to house showing off his book to everyone. Six or seven of his friends came to thank me.

These delightful people, many of them descendants of the Paez Indians, who fought bravely against the *conquistadores*, deny any connection with the unknown sculptors who inhabited the region in pre-Columbian and pre-Incan times.

We spent two days looking at the scattered sites with their carvings, huge sarcophagi, statues and other relics, all of which are a puzzle to archaeologists. They know that people have lived in the area known as San Agustín for certainly 2,500 years. Twice at least during that time, there were sudden and complete changes in the population. In roughly 50

AD, a new group drove out or subjugated the essentially primitive, hill-top dwellers who had been in the region for six hundred years or more.

The invaders brought new systems of farming, of building villages, of road-building and probably of religion. It is not known whether these people were the first sculptors, but the general speculation is that the finest work was done during their time. Their tenure, however, was short. It seems that, for some reason, they left in the fifth century and nobody else came to live in the region for seven or more hundred years. By 1400, a large number of people had resettled the area. Again, these people could have been the artists, but all traces of them disappeared in about 1630. After that, the Paez must have come, only to be trampled on by the invading Spaniards.

The sculptures were immensely stimulating. They stood in this grand landscape, its rolling hills slashed by precipitous gorges, as if they had been placed there by nature rather than by design. Their forms were as varied as those of the flowering trees and plants among which they stood. Some statues were squat, but others were twelve or fifteen feet high, one looking exactly like Sir Stephen Spender, with a broad friendly smile, but having in its hands a child held upside-down. Some had big, round eyes, while others had narrow slits, or curved lids or heavy bags. Many had clenched teeth, with exaggerated eye-teeth like Dracula, and just as many had open circles for mouths. There were long, pointed noses, Roman noses, snub noses and flat, broad nostrils. One repeated theme was of a man with another on his back, like a male equivalent of an incubus. It might have represented a duality of character, or merely have been a representation of a person in a mask. Nearly all the figures looked straight ahead, but I remember one of a woman with her head turned three-quarters. Traced on her trunk were the lines of her fallopian tubes.

There were many carvings of animals. A stumpy, fat eagle sat in front of one temple, a serpent in its claws. An anthropomorphic cat with huge genitals guarded the entrance to a burial chamber. Salamanders and aquatic creatures romped in a flat sculpture, carved in the bedrock of a stream.

It was impossible to find a coherent thread. It was as if a thousand imaginations were at work with no conventions to hamper them. It may have been that several separate cultures carved in different styles, but I preferred to think that these were the products of a liberated people, free to do as they pleased.

Somehow the tourism which the monuments attracted had affected the people very little. Even the police at the checkpoint between Isnos and

221

San Agustín itself were ready to laugh. On our way to the hotel on our first evening, we stopped to look at a bridge which was building. The men working on it offered us a drink from a bottle of rough spirit. We declined.

'You won't drink with Colombians, eh?'

'Tomorrow.'

'Tomorrow is another day. The time to drink is now.'

We drank looking at the waterfall of Mortiño, a shimmering braid falling six hundred feet.

At the hotel, boys with manners offered us stones carved with frogs. They did not hassle; nor did they bargain. It would have been discourteous, I thought, to offer them less than they asked.

As I waited by an empty stall near the rocks where the Río Magdalena narrowed to a torrent almost not too wide to jump, a woman came.

'Buenos días,' she said.

A moment or two later came another woman.

'Buenas tardes,' she said.

I looked at my watch. It was half a minute past noon. It was always a wonder to me how precise South Americans were about the moment at which the day became afternoon, when they were so unpunctual in all other ways.

The two women thought my speculations about this very comical. They had come to set up their stall with woven bags and hats, and with cool drinks. The same honesty shone from them as had done from the boys, as we discussed why one bag was more expensive than another, being made from a rarer, more durable reed.

Above, on the plateau, there was a lonely village – Obando. It consisted of little more than an open square surrounded by the low houses of the Paez, built with mud and straw and bamboo, and roofed with Roman tiles. In the centre of the square was a figure of Christ with two of the ancient sculptures on either side. Nearby all the houses had small gardens, with flowers blooming, and hanging pots with more flowers. One garden in particular was splendid. I asked the man who was tending it the name of one of his bushes.

'I don't know,' he said. 'I love flowers, but I don't know the names of any of them.'

San Agustín was a place of magic. The sculptures, the waterfalls, the coffee growing on the mountains, the other crops like petit-point on the steep hillsides. The horses working. Everything so clean. Above all the people, the children in frilly dresses, the laughing Paez, a people filled I felt with kindness. I would like to go back to San Agustín, more than anywhere else in South America.

*   *   *

In Bogotá they said, 'You didn't really go to San Agustín did you? You must be mad. No one goes there, it is very dangerous.'

'And Bogotá is not?' I asked.

In the hotel there was a leaflet, warning the guests not to hail taxis in the street lest they be kidnapped. The Italian ambassador's house had been robbed three times, despite guards. Everyone carried some money to give to the muggers.

Actually, I liked Bogotá. It had a rackety charm and was far more sophisticated than any other South American capital. The shops were filled with trendy clothes that it would have been impossible to find in any other country. And we fell in with Ivan and Felipe.

We had met Ivan Santos briefly months before, at the border between Venezuela and Brazil. He was nearing the end of the trip we were embarking upon, though he had made it in the opposite direction. He had given us advice and told us to find him when we reached Bogotá.

Ivan was a painter of great talent. His studio was filled with large triptychs of wind-blown forests. His paintings were full of the movements of nature and love of the countryside. He and his friend Felipe, who also painted a little but worked more on one of his family's farms, took us round Bogotá.

Their way of life hung between two worlds. Ivan was handsome, tall and bearded. His large dark eyes held an innocent wickedness. His studio was usually full of high-spirited friends and he appeared to have two concurrent girlfriends. It was the kind of life any young man might have lived in, say, Philadelphia. At the same time, his family life was far more important than it would be to a North American. He was one of eight children, but one of his three brothers had died in a motorcycle accident.

Felipe's family was smaller; he had only three brothers. As was so often the case in all of South America, his inheritance was mixed. His grandmother was French. His father, Señor Sanchez, was a most distinguished old man, whom one might have taken for an English country squire. He spoke perfect English, but was very deaf.

'Too much shooting, don't you know.' He made the gesture of raising a shotgun. 'Now tell me about the fishing in Chile, is it as good as they say?'

The young men took us to their farms, which happened to be only a couple of miles apart though, curiously, Ivan and Felipe had originally met each other not in Colombia but in New York.

Ivan's father was by chance at the farm when we arrived. His was a different kind of distinction, more Latin than Saxon. He was directing the replanting of pine trees on the hills which formed a large part of his acreage. Since acquiring the farm in exchange for one further away, he had planted three hundred thousand trees. Apart from forestry, he kept a herd of beef cattle.

The Sanchez farm was a very different affair, more a market garden. They grew carnations for export to Covent Garden in London. They had only eleven hectares here, six or seven of which were under ugly polythene. An acre of polythene cost seventy thousand dollars to put up and would last three years. A glasshouse of the same size would have cost 150 times as much.

'Usually we send 180 boxes a week to London. Each box contains forty-eight bunches of forty-eight flowers, so that is something like four hundred thousand flowers. We get six, seven or nine cents a flower f.o.b., depending on colour.'

I calculated this as being more than three tons of flowers each week. The buyers pay the air freight at $1.75 a kilo. It means that one flower arriving in Covent Garden costs little more than eight cents.

'For Mother's Day, Valentine's Day and Christmas we send six hundred boxes.'

*   *   *

Nothing about Colombia had matched my expectations. I had imagined the landscape tamer, Bogotá wilder and less sophisticated, the people far less friendly. Medellin lived up to my preconception. It was dark and we got lost in the complicated one-way system of this sombre town. Two trucks closed in on us, driving us on to the pavement. Police with guns leaped out. At least, I hoped they were police, remembering the woman in the tourist office in Popayán.

'Out,' they said.

I always rather dislike this moment when a man is holding a gun at my chest. Will he understand my explanation that I cannot get out without help? Or will he consider my immobility as disobedience; an excuse to shoot – especially in Colombia where the police have a right to shoot to kill in narcotics cases. He did not shoot, but he kept the gun pointed at me.

'You are contrabandistas.'

'No, tourists.'

'Why have you so much in your car? Is it your car?'

Nothing would change their decision that we were smugglers.

'You will come to the police station.'

With one truck in front of us, another behind and an armed man in the back of our car, we processed to the police station. We parked in a large yard. They started to unload our stuff – two wheelchairs, camping equipment, suitcases. Luckily, they got bored before they found the bag of coca leaves which I had again forgotten.

Every so often one of the police would come from the station office to look. 'Ah, si, contrabandistas,' he would say and go back to the office.

This went on for half an hour. At last, I got fed up and asked for the chief.

After a while he came and looked at the pile of our stuff on the ground.

'Contrabandistas, I see.'

'No, tourists, visitors to your country, enjoying your hospitality.'

'Why have you so much in your car?'

I explained all over again how far and for how long we had travelled.

'You say you are not contrabandistas?'

'We are not.'

'Then show me the receipts for all the goods.'

He was not a stupid man. He was, I decided, acting out the part he had to play to justify all the fuss.

'You show me a receipt for your hat and I will show you a receipt for all this.'

He laughed and asked which hotel I was staying in. He told his man to pack up the car and to escort us to the hotel. While they were loading he confessed that the men who had stopped us had seen my electric wheelchair, the batteries and their charger through the back window of the Toyota. They had decided it was equipment for a bomb.

This was, after all, Medellin, the supposed centre of the drug trade. There was a sense of menace which pervaded the whole country, but here it was particularly strong. It was engendered, if not primarily then at least in a substantial part, by the question of drugs.

The Colombians are not large growers of coca, although an illicit farm of twenty thousand hectares had been recently discovered. They are processors and the most conservative estimates suggest that Colombia's income from cocaine is equal to the one and three quarter billion dollars earned from coffee. Probably it is far higher. The problem is the same as in Bolivia. Three or four hundred thousand people earn their livelihood

225

from the drug. It is exacerbated in Colombia by the profit from processing being greater than it is from growing. The result is an even greater tendency to crime. Again, I found myself feeling that it was not the Colombians who were to blame. No one blames distillers for drunken driving. Few blame tobacco-growers for lung cancer.

The commonest cause of death among males between the ages of sixteen and forty-five in Colombia is murder. Many of those murders are connected with the drug trade. The judges in Colombia faced with trying a drugs case say that they have a simple choice – they can either be rich or dead. The Americans would be enraged if the Colombians were to legalise the trade, but it is an American problem not a Colombian one. The Americans are the consumers. If there were no demand, there would be no supply. While the demand continues, supply will find a way, as it did during Prohibition. Prohibition led to crime and bred the Mafia, but the lesson was not learned.

That is not to say that all crime in Colombia is associated with drugs, but, were this aspect removed, they might be able to see more clearly the fundamental cause of their instability. It is easy for the Colombians to blame the drug-traffickers for the lawless nature of their country. As we had already seen and were to see even more vividly, roughly a fifth of the nation was not really under the control of the government.

Colombia has a history of violence greater, perhaps, than that of any other South American country. As recently as the 1950s, three hundred thousand people died in a long civil war known as La Violencia. Colombia has too a tradition of corruption, and a disparity of wealth and poverty unequalled elsewhere on the continent. It is these things that the guerillas are fighting. And somehow violence hovered over our last few days. Yet it was in many ways the country I most enjoyed.

*   *   *

It seemed too difficult to take the car into the old city of Cartagena. I studied the map and asked the taximan to drop us at the Puente Román.

'You are not going to walk down that street?' he asked, pointing to just the street that I did plan to go down. 'It is the most dangerous street in Cartagena.'

The *South American Handbook* had said it was 'not a very safe neighbourhood'. We waited until the taximan was out of sight.

There was a different feeling to this stronghold of a port with, originally, five great forts and twenty-two bastions in its curtain walls. I had become accustomed to the spirit of the south, to the harsher frontier

226

ambience of those countries whose sea was the far Pacific. Cartagena, despite its history of sieges and battles, despite the Palace of the Holy Office of the Inquisition, with its rack still waiting for a victim, was Caribbean in flavour – gentler or, it may be, just more easily comprehensible.

We were back in the realms of familiar history. Hawkins had bombarded the city in 1568. His nephew, the pirate Drake, had captured Cartagena in 1586, behaving with his usual brutality, looting for a month, burning one by one some two hundred houses, destroying the half-finished cathedral and finally going off with 107,000 gold ducats.

I liked best the story of Admiral Sir Edward Vernon, old Grog, most notable as a rule for having introduced the naval rum ration. In about 1741, he arrived off Cartagena with fifty men-of-war and 130 transports. His troops numbered 25,600, including 2,000 North American infantry. His orders were to capture the city.

His opponent was Don Blas de Lezo, a Spanish admiral famous for his courage in twenty-one major naval engagements, in the course of which he had lost an eye, an arm and a leg.

Vernon started with a huge bombardment. He then landed his troops. Confident of victory, he sent a message to England to say that Cartagena had fallen. Don Blas, wounded in both his remaining limbs, held on behind the walls of the city. Vernon settled down for a siege. Meanwhile his friends in London, on the strength of his message, had medals cast showing Don Blas kneeling in submission to Sir Edward.

Fever struck Vernon's troops. He decided on a straightforward attack on the Fort of San Felipe. It failed. The Spanish rushed out in a surprise bayonet charge. At the end, eight hundred British troops lay dead and more than a thousand were prisoners.

Vernon sailed away in ignominy, to be mocked by both the Spanish and his own countrymen when news of the medals became known. His name, now that grog has been abolished, does not survive, as he had hoped, in the proud annals of naval history, but instead for a quite unexpected reason. One of his young American soldiers, Laurence Washington, built himself a house which he named after his commander. When Laurence died, his brother George bought Mount Vernon.

*   *   *

At Santa Marta, I felt mildly frustrated but, at the same time, pleased. I had very much wanted to fly up into the Sierra Nevada to see the Indian village, discovered only a few years ago, known as La Ciudad Perdida. I knew that the Indians had made representations to the government that tourists were disrupting their way of life. Unexpectedly, the government had agreed to ban visitors, but the prohibition was said not to take effect for a month.

Rather shamefaced, I wanted to be one of the resented visitors. In the event, I found that the last helicopter had gone three days before. The Indians' privacy was assured. It was astonishing in this country where respect for others did not seem of paramount importance.

At Santa Marta, I was also saddened by reflecting on the fate of Simón Bolívar. Towards the end of his life, he came to fear that, although he would be remembered as the *Libertador* of five countries, he had not added to the happiness or the stability of one South American nation.

Donald Worcester, his latest biographer, wrote:

At one o'clock on the afternoon of December 17, 1830 – the same month, day and hour that eleven years earlier he had signed the agreement uniting Venezuela and New Granada to create Gran Colombia – Bolívar breathed his last. When it was discovered that he had nothing in his wardrobe but shabby and worn clothing, General José Laurencio Silva came to the rescue. The Liberator of Venezuela, Colombia, Ecuador, Peru and Bolivia was buried in a borrowed shirt.

Bolívar died in Santa Marta rejected and in poverty. His story was the supreme example of the endlessly repeated pattern of South America. It was the story of Pedro II of Brazil, the story of the Reductions in Paraguay, the story of Brasília, of Cochrane in Chile and Peru, of Tiradentes, of the Welsh in Patagonia. South America is a continent of high hopes and grand beginnings, which gradually turn to bitterness and ashes. Then come the regrets. Bolívar was buried in Santa Marta. Twelve years later in pomp and grandeur his body was disinterred and transported to Caracas in a Venezuelan warship, escorted by the navies of Britain, France and Holland.

*   *   *

For our return to Venezuela we had to apply for visas in the town of Ríohacha, about two hours short of the border. It was a disgusting place. There was filth everywhere and there were people living in houses made of cardboard. Dust swirled in cinematic spirals and the sun burnt the colour from the land and the sky.

Most of the cars had Venezuelan number plates. They were all stolen.

The taxis and the buses were stolen, even one police car. Some vans still had on them the names of the firms in Caracas or Maracay.

The Consul was urbane to start with, speaking English to us with a comedy accent.

'I was in London. You know Annabels? Very top club. Here is nothing, no even tennis. How I keep fit? Is terrible here. You want visa, no problem. How you travel? Car?'

'Toyota Landcruiser.'

'Oh dear God no, has it air-conditioned?'

'Yes,' I said with a sparkle of pride.

'Oh no, please. Not electric windows.' His voice rose in wild fear.

'Yes.'

'Oh, don't go. They drag you from the car. They shoot you, kill you. In Maicao after four o'clock only murderers on the streets. The Indians, they are the worst.'

It was at this point that he lost me, but he ranted on.

'I drive that way one time. Never, never any more. Please not go.'

He then managed to keep us waiting for two hours, so there was no possibility of our getting through Maicao before the few good citizens locked their doors and the killers prowled abroad.

'Heaven help you,' said the Consul.

We drove through a dry, scrubby landscape. There were no villages, only occasional shacks lived in by Indians, whose simple appearance hardly led one to believe that they dealt in stolen cars. The women wore flowing robes which were wonderfully unsuitable for thornbush country and which gave them the air of runaway wives of Roman senators.

Maicao looked grim, but no worse than Ríohacha. It was true that everything was shut unusually early, but Symon, infected by the Consul's nervousness, raced through the town determined to stop for no one. As usual, no harm befell us, and back in Venezuela we slept easily.

*   *   *

Caracas, where we had spent so long, seemed like home.

'I don't know why you went away, boss,' said Alberto. 'Venezuela is the best country isn't it?'

'Of course,' I said.

It was what every Venezuelan, every South American, wanted to hear.

Index

Index

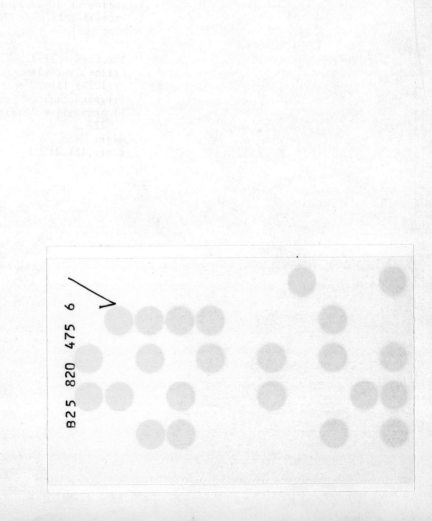